RACE AND SOCIAL EQUITY

RACE AND SOCIAL EQUITY

A Nervous Area of Government

Susan T. Gooden

Routledge
Taylor & Francis Group
LONDON AND NEW YORK

First published 2014 by M.E. Sharpe

Published 2015 by Routledge
2 Park Square, Milton Park, Abingdon, Oxon OX14 4RN
711 Third Avenue, New York, NY 10017, USA

Routledge is an imprint of the Taylor & Francis Group, an informa business

Library of Congress Cataloging-in-Publication Data
Gooden, Susan T.
  Race and social equity : a nervous area of government / by Susan T. Gooden.
    pages cm
  Includes bibliographical references and index.
  ISBN 978-0-7656-3718-5 (hardcover : alk. paper)—ISBN 978-0-7656-3719-2 (pbk. : alk. paper)
  1. Social justice—United States. 2. Equality—Government policy—United States. 3. Public
administration—Social aspects—United States. I. Title.

  HN65.G597 2014
  303.3′720973—dc23   2013038333

ISBN 13: 9780765637192 (pbk)
ISBN 13: 9780765637185 (hbk)

CONTENTS

FOREWORD

The racial and ethnic diversity of public officials and public administrators has grown dramatically over the years. In 1970, in the United States, the total number of black state and local elected officials was 1,469. The total in 2010 was 10,500 (Joint Center for Political and Economic Studies 2011). The number of black members of the U.S. Congress similarly has reached all-time highs. In 1950, the total was 2. In 1970, the total was 11. By 1990, the total had soared to 25. In 2010, the number was 42 (U.S. House of Representatives 2013).

A similar statement can be made about the dramatic growth in Latino elected officials. The number was 1,280 in 1970 (Lemus 1973). By 2011, it was 5,850 (NALEO Educational Fund 2011).

By 2013, Louisiana and South Carolina had Asian-American governors. There were Hispanic governors in Nevada and New Mexico. Massachusetts and briefly New York have boasted black governors in recent years. And, of course, for the first time in U.S. history, an African American is president.

Besides the significant representation of minorities among elected officials, there is also an impressive array of black, Hispanic, and Asian American police chiefs, welfare commissioners, prison wardens, school board presidents, school superintendents, and other top appointed officials

The diversity of public administrators—the next layer of public service—is also apparent. In 1994, 28.3 percent of all public administrators were minority group members (U.S. Office of Personnel Management 2006). By 2010, the percentage had increased to 34.1 (U.S. Office of Personnel Management 2006, 2011).

These facts belie an important reality that Susan Gooden's provocative book addresses. Although the public sector has become more racially and ethnically diverse, there remains an uncomfortable, poorly articulated, and difficult to navigate divide between racial and ethnic minority group members and white public servants. This divide mirrors the historic separation between public servants and the public they serve in America, and it is particularly prominent in the area of welfare-caseload management. As Soss, Fording, and Schram demonstrate, race and administration of welfare programs are intricately intertwined:

> Racial identities are highly salient in welfare settings and tend to frame casework relationships. In frontline interactions, interpretations and strategies depend greatly on the ways that case managers and clients' identities fit together. When it comes to sanction decisions, however, the race of the client appears to matter more than (and irrespective of) the race of the case manager. Black clients carry the greatest disadvantages, but they are not positioned as objects of unwavering discrimination. Instead they possess a precarious kind of equality that can be easily undone by a discrediting, stereotype-consistent marker. Regardless of whether they favor racial equality in principle, frontline officials tend to respond to such markers in ways that reliably contribute to institutional patterns of racial inequity. (Soss et al. 2011, 261)

This rare acknowledgment of the pervasiveness of race in public administration and the management of public programs is in stark contrast to the relative absence of discourse on race and racism within the scholarly public administration field. Thus, a principal aim of Susan Gooden's book is to correct the deficiency in our knowledge about racial disparities in the public sector.

That there are wide racial and ethnic disparities in virtually every walk of life is not in dispute. There are serious racial gaps in housing, credit, and labor markets (Darity and Mason 1998; Ladd 2002; Yinger 1995). There are also significant racial disparities in business outcomes (Bates 1999, 2002, 2006; Bates, Lofstrom, and Servon 2010; Bates and Williams 1996; Boston 1999; Fairlie and Meyer 1996, 2000; Fairlie and Robb 2007). In public procurement and contracting, for example, African-American business enterprises are far less likely than other firms to bid successfully on state and federally funded construction, professional services, and other contracts, and when they are successful, they receive contracts of smaller size than other firms do (Myers and Chan 1996; Myers, Ha, and Davila 2012).

Wide racial disparities also exist in crime, the child welfare system, education, and even swimming. African-Americans are 3 times more likely than the overall population to be found in the criminal justice system. African-American children are 1.6 times more likely than the overall population to be in child protective services and 2 times more likely to be in out-of-home placement. Moreover, in the education system there are wide disparities in important outcomes. African Americans are 3 times more likely to be suspended, 1.8

times more likely to drop out, and less likely than whites to graduate—48 vs. 65 percent. Moreover, whereas the average math SAT score for whites is 536, the average for African Americans is 429. African Americans are 1.2 times more likely to drown than are whites, and drowning is one of the leading causes of accidental death for young African Americans. In short, race continues to be a persistent marker of social and economic outcomes in American society.

The conundrum, then, is how is it possible that such substantial disparities in important economic outcomes remain when there has been so much improvement in the political and public status of minority professionals whose clients and stakeholders are arguably the very minorities who disproportionately languish at the bottom of the economic ladder? Prominent social critic and economist William Darity Jr. (1983, 1995) anticipated this question in defining what he termed the "managerial class." The managerial class plays a special role in the new industrial era, when public sector provision of services for the poorest of the poor also helped to produce an expansion of opportunities for racial and ethnic minority professionals.

Susan Gooden draws on a rich body of empirical research about managers and public administrators to uncover a heretofore underappreciated aspect of what Darity recognizes as an inherent tension between those served by public servants and the new class of public administrators and managers. Professor Gooden introduces the concept of nervousness and race. She demonstrates in her very lucid prose that race specificall , and racial equity more generally, represent significant and perplexing *nervous areas* of government. These areas are defined, examined, and explored in this important and intellectually rigorous contribution.

This pathbreaking book introduces, justifies, and solidifies an important new phrase—"a nervous area of government"—into the public administration lexicon. Michael Lipsky gave us "street-level bureaucrats"; Charles Lindblom gave us "muddling through." Susan Gooden has now given us "a nervous area of government."

This contribution could not have come at a better time. A quick and cursory check of citation data bases and search engines reveals that more and more papers and articles are being published on "diversity," whereas the terms *racism* and *racial discrimination* appear less and less in recent publications. For example, searches on Google Scholar, EconLit, and JSTOR for article titles including the words *diversity, racism,* or *racial discrimination* reveal that during the twelve-year period 2000–2011, there were seven to nearly ten times as many references to diversity as there were to racial discrimination or racism. Scholars writing on important social science and public policy topics seem reluctant even to include racism or racial discrimination in their titles.

My own profession, economics, is particularly guilty of this nervousness. Only sixty-four articles published from 2000 to 2011 and included in EconLit (the main bibliographic source for economic journal articles and books) had *racism* in their titles, while *diversity* appeared in 1,342 titles during the same time span. *Race* and *racism*, by way of contrast, are terms often avoided in public policy discourse and are starkly absent in the titles of recent articles published in the top public policy and administration journals. In the thirty-four administration and policy journals catalogued by JSTOR during the twelve years under discussion, *racism* and *racial discrimination* appeared less than a dozen times in papers' titles, while *diversity* appeared more than six dozen times. Of course, diversity can mean many things to different researchers. By and large, it has positive connotations and can be used euphemistically by both opponents and supporters of efforts to reduce and eliminate racial discrimination or racism through affirmative e forts (Myers 1997).

Imagine the impact on his popularity ratings had President Obama used the term *racism* in his 2013 commencement address at Morehouse College to describe the disproportionate arrests of blacks for marijuana possession or the higher dropout rates of blacks from high school. Instead, President Obama safely described diversity while admonishing the graduates of perhaps the most prestigious historically black college in America—the alma mater of Martin Luther King and scores of other black leaders—that there should be "no excuses" (Williams 2013). Even the president of the United States exhibits a bit of nervousness when it comes to race.

Professor Gooden does not stop with definitions and illustrations of this new concept of nervousness and government as they relate to race and racial equity. The book is pragmatic and solution-oriented. Specificall , it profiles public agencies at the federal, state, and local levels that offer specific analysis of the complexity of the topic of race and social equity and how it can be successfully advanced. It is a must read. Gooden has produced an instant classic for the field of public administration. Readers will find essential insights into how race, racial equity, and social justice create both dilemmas and opportunities for public sector agencies and their administrators/managers.

Susan Gooden has produced a pioneering contribution to the public administration literature. This book represents a major advance in understanding how and why race and social equity remain areas of nervousness and what can be done about it.

Samuel L. Myers Jr.
Roy Wilkins Professor of Human Relations and Social Justice
Hubert H. Humphrey School of Public Affairs
University of Minnesota

References

Bates, Timothy. 1999. "Available Evidence Indicates That Black-Owned Firms Are Often Denied Equal Access to Credit." In *Proceedings, Federal Reserve Bank of Chicago 1999* (March): 267–76.

———. 2002. "Minority Businesses Serving Government Clients Amidst Prolonged Chaos in Preferential Procurement Programs." *Review of Black Political Economy* 29 (3): 51–70.

———. 2006. "Discrimination in the Chicago-Area Construction Industry Handicaps Minority-Owned Firms." *Review of Black Political Economy* 3 (4): 7–26.

Bates, Timothy, Magnus Lofstrom, and Lisa Servon. 2010. "Why Have Lending Programs Targeting Disadvantaged Small-Business Borrowers Achieved So Little Success in the United States?" *IZA Discussion Papers* (5212). Institute for the Study of Labor: Schaumburg, Germany.

Bates, Timothy, and Darrell Williams. 1996. "Do Preferential Procurement Programs Benefit Minority Business?" *American Economic Review* 86 (2): 294–97.

Boston, Thomas. 1999. *Affirmative Action and Black Entrepreneurship*. New York: Routledge.

Darity, William, Jr. 1983. "The Managerial Class and Surplus Population." *Society* 21 (1): 54–62.

———. 1995. "The Undesirables, America's Underclass in the Managerial Age: Beyond the Myrdal Theory of Racial Inequality." In *"An American Dilemma Revisited." Daedalus: Journal of the American Academy of Arts and Sciences* 124 (1): 145–65.

Darity, William A., Jr., and Patrick L. Mason. 1998. "Evidence on Discrimination in Employment: Codes of Color, Codes of Gender." *Journal of Economic Perspectives* 12 (2): 63–90.

Fairlie, Robert W., and Bruce D. Meyer. 1996. "Ethnic and Racial Self-Employment Differences and Possible Explanations." *Journal of Human Resources* 31 (4): 757–93.

———. 2000. "Trends in Self-Employment Among White and Black Men During the Twentieth Century. *Journal of Human Resources* 35 (4): 643–69.

Fairlie, Robert W., and Alicia M. Robb. 2007. "Why Are Black-Owned Businesses Less Successful than White-Owned Businesses? The Role of Families, Inheritances, and Business Human Capital." *Journal of Labor Economics* 25 (2): 289–323.

Joint Center for Political and Economic Studies. 2011. "National Roster of Black Elected Officials." Fact sheet, November. www.jointcenter.org/research/national-roster-of-black-elected-officials (accessed June 14, 2013)

Ladd, Helen F. 2002. "School Voucher: A Critical View." *Journal of Economic Perspectives* 16 (4): 3–24.

Lemus, Frank. 1973. *National Roster of Spanish Surnamed Elected Officials*. Los Angeles: Aztlan.

Myers, Samuel L., Jr. 1997. "Why Diversity Is a Smokescreen for Affirmative Action." *Change* 6 (3): 14–15.

Myers, Samuel L., Jr., and Tsze Chan. 1996. "Who Benefits from Minority-Business Set-Asides? The Case of New Jersey." *Journal of Policy Analysis and Management* 15 (2): 202–25.

Myers, Samuel L., Jr., Inhyuck Ha, and Rodrigo Lovaton Davila. 2012. "Affirmative Action Retrenchment in Public Procurement and Contracting." *Applied Economics Letters* 19 (8): 1857–60.

National Association of Latino Elected and Appointed Officials (NALEO) Educational Fund. 2011. *2011 Directory of Latino Elected Officials.* www.naleo.org/directory. html (accessed June 14, 2013).

Soss, Joe, Richard C. Fording, and Sanford F. Schram. 2011. *Disciplining the Poor: Neoliberal Paternalism and the Persistent Power of Race.* Chicago: University of Chicago Press.

U.S. House of Representatives, Office of the Historian. History, Art, & Archives. 2013. "Black-American Representatives and Senators by Congress, 1870–Present." http://history.house.gov/Exhibitions-and-Publications/BAIC/Historical-Data/ Black-American-Representatives-and-Senators-by-Congress (accessed October 9, 2013).

U.S. Office of Personnel Management. 2006. *2006 Demographic Profile of the Federal Workforce Publication.* Washington, DC: OPM. www.opm.gov/policy-data-oversight/data-analysis-documentation/federal-employment-reports/demographics/ data-analysis-documentation/ (accessed June 14, 2013).

———. 2011. *Federal Equal Opportunity Recruitment Program Report FY 2011.* Washington, DC: OPM. www.opm.gov/policy-data-oversight/diversity-and-inclusion/reports/feorp2011.pdf (accessed June 14, 2013).

Williams, Vanessa. 2013. "Obama Needs to Stop Lecturing Predominant Black Audiences, Some Supporters Say." *Washington Post,* May 20. www.washingtonpost. com/lifestyle/style/to-critics-obamas-scolding-tone-with-black-audiences-is-getting-old/2013/05/20/4b267352-c191–11e2-bfdb-3886a561c1ff_story.html (accessed June 14, 2013).

Yinger, John. 1995. *Closed Doors, Opportunities Lost: The Continuing Costs of Housing Discrimination.* New York: Russell Sage Foundation.

PREFACE

Recently, France's National Assembly voted to drop the word "race" from French laws. As Erik Bleich (2001) explains, "For many Frenchmen, the very term race sends a shiver running down their spines, since it tends to recall the atrocities of Nazi Germany and the complicity of France's Vichy regime in deporting Jews to concentration camps." Leaders in France are attempting to manage or, perhaps more accurately, to avoid a nervous area of government. Like the air we breathe, nervousness about race surrounds us. Sometimes, the air gets quite thick and we notice it more than usual. At other times, it is a constant state operating under an illusion of not existing. Race and social equity is "a nervous area of government."

Ironically, around the same time as the France National Assembly activity, my father called and asked me whether I'd heard about the quilt. "What quilt?" I asked. "Get on the computer and read about it," he said. "It's been all over the news." Since the evening news isn't often filled with reports from my rural hometown of Martinsville and Henry County, Virginia, this immediately sparked my attention. A quick search on the Internet revealed a heated racial controversy involving an image on a quilt designed by a local group of school students and presented to Martinsville's City Council. After significant discussion and community attention, the City Council decided to display the quilt. As I was putting the finishing touches on this book manuscript, a nervous area of gover - ment had in fact hit home.

On the whole, public administrators and elected officials are largely un- equipped to navigate this nervous area of government. The discomfort becomes overwhelming, often paralyzing, which suggests a significant area of vulner- ability for public administrators: This vulnerability has real implications for the public they serve. This book offers a description and characterization of a nervous area of government. But, arguably more importantly, it profiles rich examples at the federal, state, and local level that are largely further along than their counterparts in navigating such nervousness.

The idea for writing this book was inspired by independent research during interviews I conducted after working on a welfare policy implementation study of Wisconsin Works for MDRC. I am greatly appreciative of the many individuals who provided support, comments, and criticisms of this manuscript. Bill Spriggs, Sam Myers, Meredith Newman, and H. George Frederickson engaged me in many discussions about this concept and provided me with excellent suggestions to strengthen my work. Also, I offer a special thanks to the City of Seattle, a place that is truly engaging in pioneering work in the area of race and social justice in the provision of local government services. I am particularly grateful to J. Paul Blake, who facilitated my data collection in the City of Seattle and helped me to track down so many of its former employees as well. I am very thankful for my supportive colleagues in the L. Douglas Wilder School of Government and Public Affairs, as well as the Grace E. Harris Leadership Institute at Virginia Commonwealth University. Additionally, I am indebted to students in my graduate Social Equity and Public Policy Analysis course over several years, who always keep me on my toes. I am also very grateful for the thoughtful comments I received from colleagues and graduate students at Florida International University and Syracuse University who listened to my early thoughts about a nervous area of government and provided insightful.

I am grateful to my editor at M.E. Sharpe, Harry Briggs, who was very patient and supportive. I am also appreciative to Susan Burke, who copyedited the manuscript, and Elizabeth Parker, who prepared the manuscript at M.E. Sharpe. Megan Bray, an undergraduate student at VCU, read through every line of the manuscript, tracked down articles, and made endless formatting and citation corrections. I cannot thank her enough. I am also thankful to my daughter, Caper Gooden, an undergraduate student at the College of William & Mary, who so patiently transformed my pitiful hand-drawn figures into excellent computer-generated ones. I lost count of how many versions of the saturation of racial inequities figure she so graciously prepared and reprepared as I continued to add additional elements.

My deepest gratitude goes to my loving and incredibly supportive family. I thank my parents, John and Shirley Tinsley, for their unconditional support and for instilling in me, at a young age, the importance of being an independent thinker. I also cherish the support of my daughter, Caper, and my "son," Donnie, of whom I am exceedingly proud, and my loving soul mate and husband, Basil, who has been incredibly supportive of all my professional endeavors for the past twenty years (and counting).

Finally, I am honored to dedicate this book to my grandmother, Kate S. Tinsley, who at 91 is still one of the smartest and strongest women I have ever known; to my sister, Gwen, who got an unfair deal in the prime of her life but never complains; and to my late father-in-law, Allen C. Gooden Jr., a true lifelong warrior in the quest for racial equity.

Reference

Bleich, Erik. 2001. *Race Policy in France*. Research article, May. www.brookings. edu/research/articles/2001/05/france-bleich.

RACE AND SOCIAL EQUITY

1 NERVOUSNESS, SOCIAL EQUITY, AND PUBLIC ADMINISTRATION

Americans must face up to their dream and
decide whether they really mean it to be a reality.
—Jennifer Hochschild (1995, xii)

What does it mean to be nervous? Nervousness has both emotional and physical characteristics. It may present itself differently from individual to individual. Some of us display outward signs of nervousness—our palms become sweaty, we start pacing or fidgeting, our hands start to tremble. Others may exhibit few outward signs, but we recognize the internal signals—we feel a knot in our stomach, our appetite changes, we find it difficult to focus—our body clearly communicates to us that we are no longer in a comfortable state. While individual markers of nervousness may vary, it is a common human characteristic. We all become nervous from time to time, and particularly in certain situations when we are afraid. Although nervousness is an emotional reaction we all experience, it becomes problematic when it begins to interfere with our ability to perform our daily tasks. Normally, we think of nervousness as an individual emotion. But what about nervousness in organizations?

In this book, I contend that social equity, specifically racial equity, is a nervous area of government. Over the course of history, this nervousness has stifled many individuals and organizations, leading to an inability to seriously advance the reduction of racial inequities in government. Until this nervousness is effectively managed, public administration efforts to reduce racial inequities cannot realize their full potential. For public administrators, nervousness or fear of addressing racial inequities within the services a public agency provides is problematic. It interferes significantly with the daily task of public agencies to provide governmental services in ways that align with our guiding democratic principles as set forth in the U.S. Constitution. As days turn into weeks, weeks years, years into decades, and decades into centuries, the consequences of failing to address this nervous area of government—racial equity in the distribution and provision of services—are compounded in significant ways, with very real societal implications

3

Issues of equity and justice are fundamental concerns of public administrators, who constantly struggle to evaluate the country's social climate and
ensure equity in governance (Akram 2004). Such evaluation is unlikely to
occur in a serious way if organizations are fundamentally too uncomfortable
to directly engage the topic. The result is an important, taken for granted but
unacknowledged, context of nervousness, which is debilitating to our public
sector organizations and thwarting our progress toward achieving racial equity
in governance.

A few years ago, I interviewed several senior administrators who were
serving on a steering committee designed to examine racial disparities in
Wisconsin's welfare program. The work of the steering committee was quite
labor intensive, and the subject matter was sensitive. Essentially, a state agency
was dissecting the presence of racial disparities in its welfare program. As I
proceeded with coding the interviews, I was struck by the number of times
respondents used the term "nervous" to express their disposition toward this
examination of racial disparities within their agency. Stated directly, one senior
administrator said, "Examining racial disparities is a nervous area of government." This book offers a direct examination of this idea and its implications.
What is a nervous area of government? How extensive are racial inequities
in American society? How is the nervous area of government manifested in
individuals and organizations? What can we learn from public sector organizations that are engaging in this nervousness work? What challenges remain
in the path ahead? These are the questions that shape the foundation of this
book and define its contribution to the field of public administratio

Race and Social Equity: A "Nervous Area of Government"

A primary contribution of this book is the introduction of the term "nervousness" into the lexicon of public administration. While the concept of nervousness has not been systematically examined in relationship to public sector
organizations, it does have important conceptual lineage. Merton (1952, 364)
discusses the "dysfunctions of bureaucracies" in which "the positive attain-
ments and functions of bureaucratic organizations are emphasized and the
internal stresses and strains of such structures are almost wholly neglected."
Similarly, Merton cautioned against "structural sources of overconformity"
where trained incapacity is clearly derived from structural sources (366). In
his seminal work discussing dynamics of bureaucracies, Blau (1963) addresses
how unofficial norms of groups within bureaucracies can serve as a powerful force toward their acceptance by all members of the group, regardless of
individual attitudinal differences; certain behaviors are concealed, particularly
if such actions are shameful; questioning provokes hostility and emotional

reactions; myths develop to explain conforming behavior; and ostracism becomes the enforcement penalty for violations of basic norms. Downs (1967) discusses the important concept of "biased" behavior affecting all public administrators. As he conceptualizes it, the four major biases that an official is subject to are (1) distorting the information he passes upward to superiors; (2) exhibiting biased attitudes toward certain policies and alternative actions normally associated with his position; (3) a varying degree of compliance with directives, depending upon which ones he personally favors; and (4) a varying willingness to seek out additional responsibilities and assume risk within his position (77–78).

The conceptualization of racial and social equity, this nervous area of government, is grounded in an extended application of organizational justice. Issues involving organizational justice involve some person or group benefit ing or harmed in a manner that is unfair. As Sheppard, Lewicki, and Minton (1992, 2) explain, "The justice phenomenon is pervasive in all organizations; however, justice is invisible until attention is focused on it by the experience or perception of injustice." Much of the literature on organizational justice adopts a human resource management perspective that is largely focused on fairness concerns of employees. Such issues include employee recruitment and selection, employee conflict, employee compensation and promotion, and employee layoffs and downsizing (see, for example, Aram and Salipante 1981; Avery and Faley 1988; Clay-Warner, Hegtvedt, and Roman 2005; Ewing 1989; Feuille and Delaney 1992; Folger and Greenberg 1985; Greenberg and McCarty 1990; Tyler and Bies 1990). While these areas are important, understanding the nervous area of government involves an approach to organizational justice that is more systemic. It prioritizes the treatment and experiences of the publics the organization serves. The dominant concern is how the organization provides public justice rather than solely internal, employee justice. Public justice is the larger organizational value within which issues of social equity reside. Although public justice is similar to social equity, the latter is more concerned with the actual delivery of public services, whereas the former is more value-oriented.

As the model in Figure 1.1 depicts, the nervous area of government is conceptualized by a structural approach that includes both internal and external dimensions. Understanding how the organization effectively or ineffectively provides public justice requires an examination of four core areas that operate within a context characterized by nervousness when racial equity is the focus. These four areas are the external environment; senior public administrators; public servants; and organizational values. All of these areas exist within an overall context of nervousness and influence its intensity within an organization.

Figure 1.1   **Conceptual Model of the Nervous Area of Government**

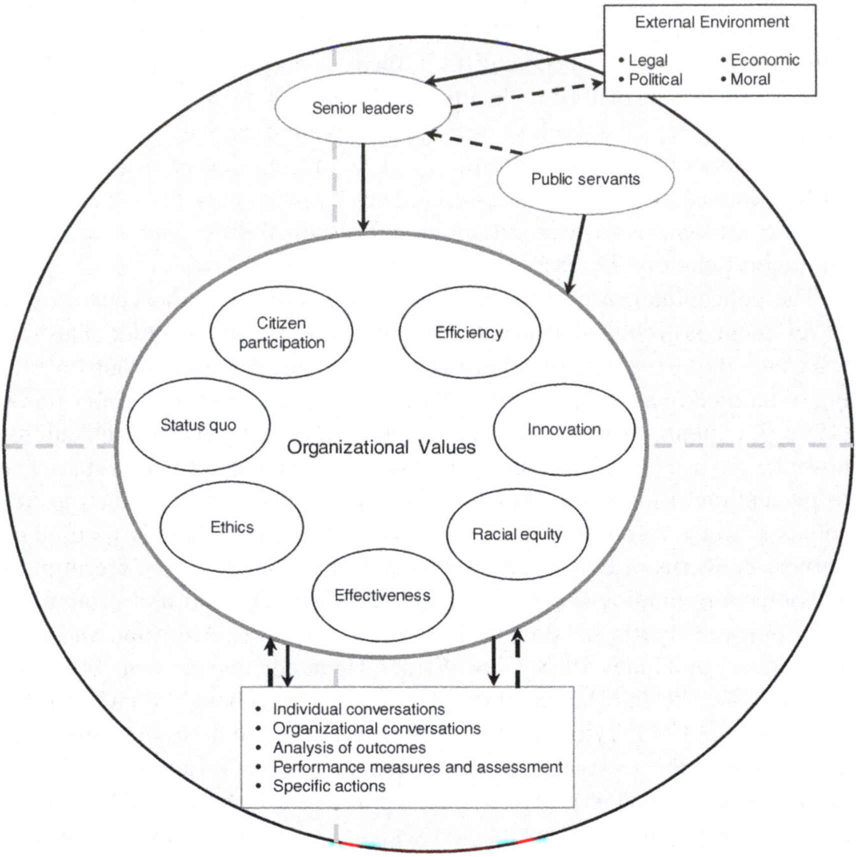

External Environment

Motivators from the external environment often operate as the catalyst for examination of racial equity. Most external motivators originate from a political, legal, economic, or moral trigger. The political area includes racial-equity motivation provided by elected officials, when political candidates are elected on a specific platform or advance a specific racial-equity concern. Seattle's Race and Social Justice Initiative, discussed in detail in chapter 7, was largely motivated in the political arena by former mayor Greg Nickels.

The legal area includes laws, regulations, court decisions, and/or litigation concerns advanced by advocacy groups. The examination of racial disparities in the sanctioning of welfare clients in Wisconsin (chapter 5) provides such an example, as it was prompted by a complaint filed by the American Civil Liberties Union (ACLU) and the Milwaukee Branch of the National Association for the Advancement of Colored People (NAACP).

Economic triggers advance racial-equity issues on an agency's agenda in monetary terms, such as a cost-benefit analysis, return on investment, behavioral incentives based on large funding sources, or improved overall organizational efficiency. As Norman-Major and Wooldridge assert, "A common focal point of research on the economic costs of social equity is the cost of poverty to society" (2011, 213). A Denver study on homelessness, for example, found that "The cost of services comes to about ten thousand dollars per homeless client per year. An efficiency apartment in Denver averages $376 a month, or just over forty-five hundred a year, which means that you can house and care for a chronically homeless person for at most fifteen thousand dollars, or about a third of what he or she would cost on the street" (Gladwell 2006, 103).

Moral triggers that land racial-equity items on an agency's agenda include grassroots concerns, civic participation, media attention, or larger shifts in societal perspectives that wield organizational pressure. Legislation that was a direct result of the civil rights movement is an example of a moral trigger of racial equity. Within the model, these external triggers gain the attention of senior public administrators within the agency.

Senior Public Administrators

Senior public administrators largely operate as the concentrated source of tangible power within an agency. "Every organization has an individual or set of individuals at the top decision-making level who can exercise power simply by giving orders and making decisions" (Hall 1991, 137). They also control personnel and budgetary assets and their subsequent allocation within the agency. Although related, leadership and power are distinct. Leadership involves "the persuasion of individuals and innovativeness in ideas and decision making that differentiates leadership from the sheer possession of power" (137). As Selznick (1957) noted, the critical tasks of leadership involve four important tasks: definition of the institutional mission and role; institutional embodiment of purpose (e.g., deciding how the organization will use the means to achieve the desired ends); defense of the organization's integrity (which involves a mixture of organizational values and public relations); and provision of order to internal conflict (among individual employees or subgroups of employees)

Specific to racial equity, senior public administrators communicate important messages and allocate resources that influence the overall value of public justice and the administration of social equity. They operate as important translators of the external racial-equity triggers. Their actions influence nervousness intensity and largely determine the acceptable "racial analysis" boundaries within the agency.

Public Servants

Public servants include the bulk of the agency's employees—frontline staff, managers, and midlevel supervisors. In particular, actions of public servants involve daily implementation decisions that affect life-chances of the clients they serve and establish patterns of routine and service with important racial-equity consequences. As Lipsky explains, "They socialize clients to expectations of government services and a place in the political community. They determine the eligibility of citizens for government benefits and sanctions. They oversee the treatment (the service) clients receive in those programs. Thus, in a sense street-level bureaucrats implicitly mediate aspects of the constitutional relationship of citizens to the state. In short, they hold the keys to a dimension of citizenship" (1980, 4).

> Policemen decide who to arrest and whose behavior to overlook. Judges decide who shall receive a suspended sentence and who shall receive maximum punishment. Teachers decide who will be suspended and who will remain in school, and they make subtle determinations about who is teachable. Perhaps the most highly refined example of street-level bureaucratic discretion comes from the field of corrections. Prison guards conventionally file injurious reports on inmates whom they judge to be guilty of "silent insolence." Clearly what does or does not constitute a dirty look is a matter of some subjectivity. This is not to say that street-level workers are unrestrained by rules, regulations, and directives from above, or by the norms and practices of their occupational group . . . [however] professionals are expected to exercise discretionary judgment in their field. They are regularly deferred to in their specialized areas of work and are relatively free from supervision by superiors or scrutiny by clients. (Lipsky 1980, 13–14)

Racial-equity analysis of patterns of service within an agency is an important dimension of the nervous area of government. It is largely affected by socialization processes within the agency about acceptable and unacceptable behavior. It is both fueled by and provides fuel for core organizational values.

Organizational Values

While the other three identifi d areas are important factors in understanding the nervous area of government, organizational values are the single most important factor. All organizations have cultures that largely establish and maintain their hierarchy of values, such as efficienc , effectiveness, quality, citizen participation, and innovation. These values are directly and indirectly communicated within the agency. They define organizational tolerance for racial-equity analysis and its associated acceptable boundaries. These values also affect the elevation and decline of overall nervousness intensity within the organization. The value of public equity largely defines the extent to which racial equity is discussed, administered, advanced, ignored, or evaluated. While racial-equity work can occur through multiple strategies—including, for example, audit studies, statistical analysis, Geographical Information System (GIS) mapping, qualitative assessments of program implementation, and other performance measures—the clear marker of this work is the occurrence of racial-equity conversations within the agency. If racial equity is a clear value of the organization, it is evidenced by related written and verbal communication. (Chapters 3 and 4 examine the nervousness of race talk at individual and organizational levels, respectively.)

The nervous area of government is how an organization considers, examines, promotes, distributes, and evaluates the provision of public justice in areas such as race, ethnicity, gender, religion, sexual orientation, class, and ability status. This area is "nervous" because examination of such areas has an emotional historical or societal context. It is "of government" because public administrators are responsible for providing services to the public at large, which includes minority groups in each of these areas. It is also "of government" because agencies have both a historical and present-day record in how equitably their services have been provided to these groups. The degree to which this record is open for internal as well as public examination and discussion is also influenced by nervousness

Additionally, the nervous area of government operates largely on a continuum. When the nervousness intensity is low, this typically signals that the organization is very minimally engaged in these topics as it delivers public services. When the nervousness intensity is high, this usually is a sign that the organization is in the early stages of engaging in these types of analysis. It is a new area of focus for the organization or one that has not recently been seriously considered. While high intensity is expected, especially in the initial stages as the culture of the organization is changing, it cannot be sustained for years. Either it will be ineffectively managed, and the organization will largely return to a low-intensity state; or it will be effectively managed, and the organization will operate in a moderate-intensity state. Moderate intensity is desirable over the long term, because racial-equity analysis remains a vital component of the organization's core values, but it is also a level that facilitates productive and effective delivery of equity in the provision of public services.

Why Focus on Race?

Issues of social equity are not exclusive to race. Gender, class, sexual orientation, religion, and disability embody important social-equity dimensions as well. The premise of this book is not to engage in oppression olympics by ranking group inequities relative to one other. Rather, it conceptualizes the idea of a nervous area of government by focusing on the specific area of race. Race and social equity is best understood as *a* nervous area of government, not *the* nervous area of government.

However, the racial-equity component within social equity produces considerable nervousness, which is why this book focuses exclusively on race. Examining issues of race is fundamental to understanding important shortcomings in America's philosophical commitment to justice. In delivering his famous speech, "To the Nations of the World," W. E. B. Du Bois poignantly stated, "The problem of the twentieth century is the problem of the color line, the question as to how far differences of race—which show themselves chiefly in the color of the skin and the texture of the hair—will hereafter be made the basis of denying to over half the world the right of sharing to their utmost ability the opportunities and privileges of modern civilization" (1900, 85).

Racial inequality remains a fundamental concern today.

> Nearly a century and a half after the destruction of the institution of slavery, and a half-century past the dawn of the civil rights movement, social life in the United States continues to be characterized by significant racial stratification. Numerous indices of wellbeing—wages, unemployment rates, income and wealth levels, ability test scores, prison enrollment and crime victimization rates, health and mortality statistics—all reveal substantial racial disparities. (Loury 2002, 4)

All of these areas are shaped or influenced by public administration

Throughout this book, I employ Loury's definition of race: "a cluster of inheritable bodily markings carried by a largely endogamous group of individuals, markings that can be observed by others with ease, that can be changed or misrepresented only with great difficult , and that have come to be invested in a particular society as a given historical movement with social meaning" (2002, 20–21). As he further explains, "What is 'essential' here is that these physical traits are taken to signify something of import within a historical context" (21).

> It is important to attend to racial stigma in American political culture because, in general, people do not freely give the presumption of equal

humanity. Only philosophers do that, and may God love them! But the rest of us tend to ration the extent to which we will presume an equal humanity of our fellows. One cannot necessarily count on getting the benefit of that presumption. So in an industrial society of nearly three hundred million people with a history going back centuries, what happens when tens of millions of those people cannot in every situation of moral reflection and significant public deliberation rely upon being extended the presumption of equal humanity? (Loury 2002, 87)

Historical and contemporary racial disparities are grounded in structural racism. The concept of structural racism was largely developed by john a. powell and researchers from the Kirwan Institute, the Applied Research Center, the Harvard Civil Rights Project, the Aspen Institute Roundtable on Community Change, the Institute for Race and Poverty, and the Philanthropic Initiative for Racial Equity. Structural racism

refers to the many factors that work to produce and maintain racial inequities in America today. It identifies aspects of our history and culture that have allowed the privileges associated with "whiteness" and the disadvantages associated with "color" to endure and adapt within the political economy over time. It also points out the ways in which public policies, institutional practices, and cultural representations reproduce racially inequitable outcomes. (Aspen Institute, 1)

Structural racism research involves "a cross section of academics, advocates, practitioners, civil rights leaders and social policy analysts to highlight current racial disparities, explain why race continues to be such a potent predictor of socioeconomic well-being, and identify the implications for policy and practice" (Kubisch 2006, 1).

Structural racism is largely concerned with "discrimination in contract" as opposed to "discrimination in contact." Discrimination is contact refers to "the unequal treatment of otherwise like persons on the basis of race in the execution of formal transactions—the buying and selling of goods and services, for instance, or interactions with organized bureaucracies, public and private" (Loury 2002, 95). Discrimination in contract is the standardization of racial bias through public and private structures. Comparatively, discrimination in contact refers to "the unequal treatment of persons on the basis of race in the associations and relationships that are formed among individuals in social life, including the choice of social intimates, neighbors, friends, heroes, and villains. It involves discrimination in the informal, private spheres of life" (Loury 2002, 96).

Analyzing discrimination in contact involves understanding five dominant contexts that embody structural racism As explained by Kubisch (2006, 3):

1. The values context that allows Americans to operate with the mind-set that we live in an equal opportunity nation, where everyone has a chance for self-improvement and where lack of success is due to flaws in individual ability and e fort.
2. The knowledge context that normalizes racial inequities and allows Americans to accept statistics about disproportionality in, for example, the educational or criminal justice systems as "just the way things are."
3. The cultural context that permits racialized images and stereotypes to persist in the media.
4. The psychological context that reinforces a sense of entitlement on the part of the white population and a sense of "non-entitlement" and low societal expectations on the part of people of color.
5. The political context in which power is exercised in ways that sustain white privilege.

Structural racism expands upon institutional racism by recognizing the cumulative effects of social inequity across organizations that compound and reinforce one another in particularly real ways. By comparison, "Institutional racism can be prescribed by formal rules but depends, minimally, on organizational cultures that tolerate such behaviors. Racist institutional decisions neither require nor preclude the participation of racist individuals" (Grant-Thomas and powell 2006, 4). While structural racism is similar to institutional racism in that individual racial attitudes are not the target, it offers a more expansive framework. As Grant-Thomas and powell (2006) explain,

> The [institutional racism] framework fails to account for the ways in which the joint operations of social institutions produce important outcomes. This is a crucial gap, for it is often the interaction between institutions, rather than the operation of each in isolation, that generates racial group disparities. ... Structural racism emphasizes the powerful impact of inter-institutional dynamics, institutional resource inequities, and historical legacies on racial inequalities today. (2006, 4)

A fundamental approach within structural racism is that any systematic, intentional promotion of racial equity must include race-conscious action. In particular, color-blind approaches to issues of race are ineffective.

It implies, for example, than an end to formal discrimination against blacks in this post–civil rights era should in no way foreclose a vigorous public discussion about racial justice. More subtly, elevating racial equality above race-blindness as a normative concern inclines us to think critically, and with greater nuance, about the value of race-blindness. . . . It obscures from view the most vital matter at stake in the contemporary debate on race and social equity—whether public purposes formulated explicitly in racial terms (that is, violating race-indifference) are morally legitimate, or even morally required. (Loury 2002, 139–40)

Lani Guinier and Gerald Torres offer a similar assessment: "We concluded that the colorblind paradigm has led to paralysis rather than action" (2002, 37). They further write, "[W]e argue, as a practical matter, that it is impossible to be colorblind in a world as color-conscious as ours. Moreover, efforts to be colorblind are undesirable because they inhibit racialized minorities from struggling against their marginalized status" (2002, 42). As Bonilla-Silva explains,

Much as Jim Crow racism served as the glue for defending a brutal and overt system of racial oppression in the pre–Civil Rights era, color-blind racism serves today as the ideological armor for a covert and institutionalized system in the post–Civil Rights era. And the beauty of this new ideology is that it aids in the maintenance of white privilege without fanfare, without naming those who it subjects and those who it rewards. (2003, 3–4)

In essence, "ideological colorblindness inhibits the kind of democratic engagement necessary for confronting some of the most deeply entrenched problems facing our society" (Guinier and Torres 2002, 37). Addressing these entrenched inequities requires public administrators to directly confront the nervous area of government.

Social Equity, Public Administration, and Notions of American Democracy

Social equity is directly related to the democratic principle of justice. It is the concept of fairness applied to all, not just select groups. In some instances, achieving justice requires treating everyone the same; in other cases it means treating groups differently based upon current and/or past inequities. The implementation of justice is context-based—determining what is fair is dependent upon understanding a complex array of historical, political, and social factors. "The 'social' aspect of equity means that public administrators are particularly attentive to differences in fairness and justice based on important social characteristics" (Johnson and Svara 2011, 17).

It is important for public administrators to deliver public services in fair and just ways. This idea is rarely opposed in principle; however, implementation has often fallen short. "Despite the long-standing commitment to fairness as an administrative principle, administrators must be humbled by the realizations that they contributed to the discrepancy and in many places helped to institute inequality in the past by enforcing discriminatory laws and using their broad discretion to advance exclusionary social mores" (Smith 2002).

Although specific definitions of social equity vary somewhat, they all share a common core of justice and fairness. H. George Frederickson (1974) identifies several specific considerations of social equity a

1. The basis for a just democratic society,
2. Influencing the behavior of o ganizational man,
3. The legal basis for distributing public services,
4. The practical basis for distributing public services,
5. Understood in compound federalism, and
6. A challenge for research and analysis.

Shafritz and Russell define social equity as: "Fairness in the delivery of public services; it is egalitarianism in action—the principle that each citizen, regardless of economic resources or personal traits, deserves and has a right to be given equal treatment by the political system" (2002, 395).

In 2000, the National Academy of Public Administration's Board of Trustees authorized a Standing Panel on Social Equity. This panel defined social equity as "[t]he fair, just, and equitable management of all institutions serving the public directly or by contract, and the fair and equitable distribution of public services, and implementation of public policy, and the commitment to promote fairness, justice, and equity in the formation of public policy" (National Academy of Public Administration 2000).

This same panel developed four criteria for measuring equity: procedural fairness, access, quality, and outcomes.

> Procedural fairness involves the examination of problems or issues of procedural rights (due process), treatment in a procedural sense (equal protection), and the application of eligibility criteria (equal rights) for existing policies and programs. . . . Practices such as failure to provide due process before relocating low-income families as part of an urban renewal project, using racial profiling to identify suspects, or unfairly denying benefits to a person who meets eligibility criteria all raise obvious equity issues.

Access—distributional equity—involves a review of current policies, services, and practices to determine the level of access to services/benefits and analysis of reasons for unequal access. . . . Equity can be examined empirically—do all persons receive the same service and the same quality of service (as opposed to the procedural question of whether all are treated the same according to distributional standards in an existing program or service)—or normatively—should there be a policy commitment to providing the same level of service to all?

q uality—process equity—involves a review of the level of consistency in the quality of existing services delivered to groups and individuals. . . . For example, is garbage pickup the same in quality, extent of spillage or missed cans, in all neighborhoods? Do children in inner-city schools have teachers with the same qualifications as those in suburban schools

Outcomes involve an examination of whether policies and programs have the same impact for all groups and individuals served. Regardless of the approach to distribution and the consistency of quality, there is not necessarily a commitment to an equal level of accomplishment or outcomes. . . . Equal results equity might conceivably require that resources be allocated until the same results are achieved . . . a critical issue in consideration of equity at this level is how much inequality is acceptable and to what extent government can and should intervene to reduce the inequality in results. (Johnson and Svara 2011, 20–22)

Although the concept of equity can be traced back centuries to Aristotle and Plato, Rutledge (2002) points out that a specific focus on social equity within public administration began in earnest in the 1960s.

My scholarly friends in the profession can trace our current thoughts and dilemmas around social equity back to Aristotle and Plato. Others would stop at Woodrow Wilson's seminal writings on the study of public administration. But in my own mind, I trace the "invention" of social equity as a practical tool in public administration to the Minnowbrook conferences convened by Dwight Waldo, George Frederickson, and a group of young Turks in the 1960s. (Rutledge 2002)

Against the national 1960s context focused on civil rights, racial inequality, and injustice, the young Minnows noted: "A government built on a Constitution claiming the equal protection of the laws had failed in that promise. Public administrators, who daily operate the government, were not without responsibility" (Frederickson 1990, 228). Reflecting in 2005, Frederickson recalled, "It was during the 1960s that it became increasingly evident that the results of governmental policy and the work of public administrators implementing those policies were much better for some citizens than for others" (2005, 31).

As Wooldridge and Gooden (2009) contend, the Minnowbrook I conference served as the foundational basis of the New Public Administration. Three major works are generally identified with the New Public Administration: Frank Marini's *Toward a New Public Administration* (1971), Dwight Waldo's *Public Administration in a Time of Turbulence* (1971), and a 1971 article titled "Creating Tomorrow's Public Administration" (Frederickson 1980). The New Public Administration rejected the idea that administrators are value neutral and recognized a constellation of five normative core values that, although legitimate, can often be conflictual. These values are responsiveness, worker and citizen participation in decision making, social equity, citizen choice, and administrative responsibility (Frederickson 1980). "A primary managerial means to achieve social equity includes a managerial commitment to the principle that majority rule does not overturn minority *rights* to equal public services" (Frederickson 1980, 47, emphasis in original). The link between the New Public Administration and social equity is so strong that Shafritz and Russell define the New Public Administration as: "An academic advocacy movement for social equity in the performance and delivery of public service; it called for a proactive administrator with a burning desire for social equity to replace the traditional impersonal and neutral gun-for-hire bureaucrat" (2002, 466).

Frederickson (1990) wrote that he developed the theory of social equity in the late 1960s to remedy a glaring inadequacy in both thought and practice. He suggested that this concept should be a "third pillar" for public administrators, a concept that holds the same status as economy and efficiency values to which public administrators should adhere. As Frederickson explained, "It is time for public administrators of all kinds to ask the so called second question. The first question is whether an existing public program or proposed program is effective or good. The second question is more important. For whom is this program effective or good?" (2005, 36).

The answer to Frederickson's second question requires consideration of how opportunity is structured in the United States. Social structures, including public bureaucracies, are important transmitters of opportunity. "[They] promote racially inequitable distributions of social, political and economic goods and services even in the absence of avowed 'racists,' even absent self-sabotaging behavior by racial minorities, and notwithstanding the play of macroeconomic, cultural and other large-scale factors. Any promising attempt to dismantle the underpinning of durable racial inequality must account for structural dynamics" (Grant-Thomas and powell 2006, 4).

There is a troubling disconnect between how terms like "opportunity" and "success" are conceptualized and how they operate in practice. Consider, for example, the American Dream. As Hochschild (1995) explains, the American Dream consists of fundamental tenets about achieving success (general defined as the attainment of a high income, a prestigious job, economic security). Success can be absolute, meaning a threshold of well-being is reached; success can be relative, meaning being better off than a comparison point; or success can be competitive, meaning achieving victory over someone else.

The premise of the American Dream rests on several tenets, including: (1) there is an equal opportunity to participate and the ability to start over; (2) there is a reasonable anticipation of success; and (3) success is under one's individual control. "The first tenet, that everyone can participate equally and can always start over, is troubling to the degree that it is not true. . . . For most of American history, women of any race and men who were Native American, Asian, black or poor were barred from all but a narrow range of 'electable futures'" (Hochschild 1995, 26). Fulfillment of the second tenet requires "enough resources and opportunities that everyone has a reasonable chance of having some expectations met" (27). The third tenet directly stipulates success as controlled by individual actions and behaviors. "Americans who do everything they can and still fail may come to understand that effort and talent alone do not guarantee success. But they have a hard time persuading others. After all, they are losers—why listen to them? Will we not benefit more by listening to winners (who seldom challenge the premise that effort and talent breed success)?" (30). Certainly, in the research realm, there have been studies ad nauseam on individual deficits and ineffective behaviors. By comparison, the larger structures in which these policies operate are far less frequently analyzed. The individual approach leads "one to focus on people's behaviors rather than on economic processes, environmental constraints, or political structures, as the causal explanation for social orderings" (36). Employing a structural approach requires us to first acknowledge and understand the nervous area of government, which is the focus of this book.

Conclusion

This book is presented by first examining the intersection of race and social equity in public administration, as well as the saturation of racial inequities in the United States. It then applies the concept of nervousness in an individual and organizational basis. I contend that social equity is a nervous area of government, especially where issues of race are concerned. Further, I argue that organizational nervousness needs to be effectively managed in order for governmental agencies to proactively address social inequities.

Through an examination of contemporary examples at the federal, state, and local level, the book profiles organizations that are directly operating in the nervous area of government. Their approaches provide useful insight for how organizations may begin to effectively undertake this work. Akin to nervousness in individuals, nervousness in organizations cannot be completely eliminated, but it can be significantly reduced. It also considers the role of (and the increased need for) accountability and performance measures in assessing organizational progress.

Finally, the book examines other important contexts for understanding the nervous area of government, including public administration programs as well as comparative, global challenges. It concludes by presenting core principles to equip public administrators to better navigate the nervous area of government.

References

Akram, R. 2004. *Social Equity and the American Dream. Standing Panel on Social Equity in Governance*. Washington, DC: National Academy of Public Administration.

Aram, John D., and Paul F. Salipante Jr. 1981. "An Evaluation of Organizational Due Process in the Resolution of Employee/Employer Conflict." *Academy of Management Review* 6 (2): 197–204.

Aspen Institute. n.d. "Dismantling Structural Racism: A Racial Equity Theory of Change." Roundtable Community Change Project on Racial Equity and Community Building. www.aspeninstitute.org/sites/default/files/content/docs/rcc/RE OC_06. PDF.

Avery, Richard D., and Robert H. Faley. 1988. *Fairness in Selecting Employees*. 2nd ed. Reading, MA: Addison-Wesley.

Blau, Peter M. 1963. *The Dynamics of Bureaucracy*. Chicago: University of Chicago Press.

Bonilla-Silva, Eduardo. 2003. *Racism Without Racists: Color-Blind Racism and the Persistence of Racial Inequality in the United States*. Lanham, MD: Rowman & Littlefield

Clay-Warner, Jody, Karen Hegtvedt, and Paul Roman. 2005. "Procedural Justice, Distributive Justice: How Experiences with Downsizing Condition Their Organizational Commitment." *Social Psychology Quarterly* 68 (1): 89–102.

Downs, Anthony. 1967. *Inside Bureaucracy*. Boston: Little, Brown.

Du Bois, W. E. B. 1900. "To the Nations of the World." In *Great Speeches by African Americans*, ed. James Daley, 85–87, 2006. Mineola, NY: Dover.

Ewing, David W. 1989. *Justice on the Job*. Boston: Harvard Business School Press.

Feuille, Peter, and John Thomas Delaney. 1992. "The Individual Pursuit of Organizational Justice: Grievance Procedures in Nonunion Workplaces." In *Research in Personnel and Human Resource Management,* ed. Gerald R. Ferris and Kendrith Rowland, 10, 187–232. Greenwich, CT: JAI Press.

Folger, Robert, and Jerald Greenberg. 1985. "Procedural Justice: An Interpretative Analysis of Personnel Systems." In *Research in Personnel and Human Resources Management,* ed. Kendrith Rowland and Gerald R. Ferris, 141–83. Greenwich, CT: JAI Press.

Frederickson, H. George. 1974. "A Symposium on Social Equality and Public Administration." *Public Administration Review* 34 (1): 1–15.

———. 1980. *New Public Administration.* Tuscaloosa: University of Alabama Press.

———. 1990. "Public Administration and Social Equity." *Public Administration Review* 50 (2): 228–37.

———. 2005. "The State of Social Equity in American Public Administration." *National Civic Review* 94 (4): 31–38.

———. 2010. *Social Equity and Public Administration: Origins, Development, and Applications.* Armonk, NY: M.E. Sharpe.

Gladwell, Malcolm. 2006. "Million-Dollar Murray: Why Problems Like Homelessness May Be Easier to Solve Than to Manage." *New Yorker* 20 (February 13): 96–107.

Grant-Thomas, Andrew, and john a. powell. 2006. "Toward a Structural Racism Framework." *Poverty and Race Research Action Council* 15 (6): 3–7.

Greenberg, Jerald, and C.L. McCarty. 1990. "Comparable Worth: A Matter of Justice." In *Research in Personnel and Human Resources Management,* ed. Gerald Ferris and Kendrith Rowland, 8, 265–301. Greenwich, CT: JAI Press.

Guinier, Lani, and Gerald Torres. 2002. *The Miner's Canary: Enlisting Race, Resisting Power, Transforming Democracy.* Cambridge, MA: Harvard University Press.

Hall, Richard H. 1991. *Organizations: Structures, Processes, and Outcomes.* Englewood Cliffs, NJ: Prentice Hall.

Hochschild, Jennifer L. 1995. *Facing Up to the American Dream: Race, Class, and the Soul of the Nation.* Princeton, NJ: Princeton University Press.

Johnson, Norman J., and James H. Svara. 2011. "Social Equity in American Society and Public Administration." In *Justice for All: Promoting Social Equity in Public Administration,* ed. Norman J. Johnson and James H. Svara, 3–25. Armonk, NY: M.E. Sharpe.

Kubisch, Anne C. 2006. "Why Structural Racism? Why a Structural Racism Caucus?" *Poverty and Race Research Action Council* 15 (6): 1–3.

Lipsky, Michael. 1980. *Street-Level Bureaucracy: Dilemmas of the Individual in Public Services.* New York: Russell Sage Foundation.

Loury, Glenn C. 2002. *The Anatomy of Racial Inequality.* Cambridge: Harvard University Press.

Marini, Frank. 1971. *Toward a New Public Administration: The Minnowbrook Perspective.* Scranton, PA: Chandler.

Merton, Robert K. 1952. "Bureaucratic Structure and Personality." In *Reader in Bureaucracy,* ed. Robert K. Merton, Ailsa P. Gray, Barbara Hockey, and Hanan C. Selvin, 361–71. New York: Free Press.

National Academy of Public Administration. 2000. *Standing Panel on Social Equity in Governance Issue Paper and Work Plan.* Washington, DC: National Academy of Public Administration. (October).

Norman-Major, Kristen, and Blue Wooldridge. 2011. "Using Framing Theory to Make the Economic Case for Social Equity: The Role of Policy Entrepreneurs in Reframing the Debate." In *Justice for All: Promoting Social Equity in Public*

Administration, ed. Norman J. Johnson and James H. Svara, 209–27. Armonk, NY: M.E. Sharpe.

Rutledge, Philip. 2002. "Some Unfinished Business in Public Administration." Paper presented at the National Conference of the American Society for Public Administration, Phoenix, AZ, March 26.

Selznick, Philip. 1957. *Leadership in Administration.* New York: Harper & Row.

Shafritz, Jay M., and E. W. Russell. 2002. *Introducing Public Administration.* 3rd ed. New York: Longman.

Sheppard, Blair H., Roy J. Lewicki, and John W. Minton. 1992. *Organizational Justice: The Search for Fairness in the Workplace.* New York: Lexington Books.

Smith, J. Douglas. 2002. *Managing White Supremacy: Race, Politics, and Citizenship in Jim Crow Virginia.* Chapel Hill: University of North Carolina Press.

Tyler, Tom R., and Robert J. Bies. 1990. "Beyond Formal Procedures: The Interpersonal Context of Procedural Justice." In *Applied Psychology and Organizational Settings,* ed. John S. Carroll, 77–98. Hillsdale, NJ: Erlbaum.

Waldo, Dwight. 1971. *Public Administration in a Time of Turbulence.* Scranton, PA: Chandler.

Wooldridge, Blue, and Susan Gooden. 2009. "The Epic of Social Equity: Evolution, Essence, and Emergence." *Administrative Theory and Praxis* 31 (2): 225–37.

2 THE SATURATION OF RACIAL INEQUITIES IN THE UNITED STATES

> *. . . the path to a more perfect union means acknowledging that what ails the African-American community does not just exist in the minds of black people; that the legacy of discrimination— and current incidents of discrimination, while less overt than in the past—are real and must be addressed.*

—Barack Obama (2008)

Racial inequities are an enduring characteristic of the United States. These inequities are profound, systemic, segregated, and cumulative. Public administrators and public agencies are at least partially responsible for the development and maintenance of these inequities. The historical and present-day impact of racial inequities is indirectly affected by actions of the public sector. All public policies involve the distribution of resources. The details of how these resources are distributed, and to whom, are significant and critical to understanding the legacy of social inequity in the United States. Public policies affect nearly every aspect of our lives—tax, education, transportation, criminal justice, housing, agriculture, economic policies—all involve distribution of resources for some and the lack of their distribution to others. Likewise, the administration of these policies also involves the distribution of penalties and sanctions to some, but not to others.

As Stone reminds us, "Every policy involves the distribution of something. There wouldn't be a policy conflict if there were not some advantage to protect or some loss to prevent. Sometimes the things being distributed are material and countable, such as money, taxes, or houses. Sometimes they are a bit less tangible, such as the chances of serving in the army, getting sick, being a victim of crime, or being selected for public office. But always, policy issues involve distribution" (1997, 55). Delivery of policies involves answering three fundamental questions: "First, who are the recipients and what are the many ways of defining them? Second, what is being distributed and what are the many ways of defining it? And, third, what are the social processes by which distribution is determined?" (1997, 55). The answers to these questions are shaped, at least in part, by public administrators. As Stone also notes, "distributions do not happen by magic. They are carried out by real people taking real actions, not by invisible hands" (1997, 54). In terms of governmental policies, these real people are public administrators or their authorized private sector contractors.

As Figure 2.1 depicts, racial inequities in the United States are saturated. This means the pattern of racial distribution is mutually compounding and permeates multiple aspects of public policies that significantly affect one's life chances. Environmental inequities affect health inequities, which affect educational inequities, and so forth. These inequities compound in predictable patterns and are maintained from generation to generation. Although their severity may decrease over time, as overall societal conditions improve, significant racial disparities are maintained. For example, although Jim Crow laws have ended, they are replaced by covert laws and practices that maintain racial disparities. Importantly, while pockets of a racial group, such as the very wealthy, may be minimally affected by these racial inequities, the general pattern holds for the racial group at large.

This chapter highlights three of the public policy areas depicted in Figure 2.1: housing, education, and the environment. The intent is not to provide a detailed history or analysis of each of these policy areas and their racial inequities, but rather to briefly highlight examples of the structural inequities that undergird present-day development and delivery of U.S. policy in each of these contexts. While these policy areas are often considered in isolation, there are important cumulative racial-inequity effects, resulting in a saturation of racial inequities across a myriad of public policies. This saturation permeates both within and across various policy contexts, resulting in a conditional structure of racial inequities. A conditional structure is particularly disconcerting because problems are solved; conditions are tolerated. Many of the racial inequities are so widespread that their existence is paradoxically viewed as normal. Because these trends constitute conditions, rather than problems, they often blend into the fabric of everyday life. These saturation conditions become accepted by elected officials, public administrators, researchers, and the public at large as a descriptive characteristic of American life, as opposed to a legitimate societal crisis.

Housing

For most Americans, housing is an important asset. It is a key factor in the determination of wealth and overall family well-being. In addition to the benefits to housing in terms of individual assets and wealth, access to safe neighborhoods, social capital, health care, employment, public safety

Figure 2.1   **Saturation of Racial Inequities**

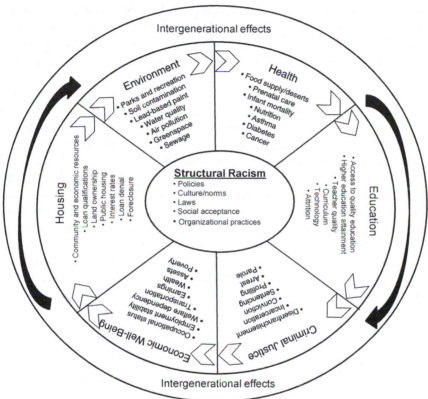

services, quality public schools, healthy foods, and transportation are all affected by the community in which one resides. Oliver and Shapiro (1995) argue that federal policies, including housing subsidy and finance programs, have promoted home ownership, land acquisition, and asset accumulation for whites but not for blacks. Other researchers have discussed racial inequities in the effects of public housing site selection and tenant selection (Bratt 1986; Keating 1994; Massey and Kanaiaupuni 1993), and government home mortgage programs of the Federal Housing Administration (FHA) and the Veterans Administration (Feagin 1994; Massey and Denton 1993). There is clear evidence, historically and in the research literature, that whites have been the overwhelming beneficiaries of federal housing programs compared to minorities, especially African Americans (Bonilla-Silva 1996; Galster 1999; Gotham 2000; Omi and Winant 1986; q uadagno 1994; Squires 2003; Winant 1994; Yinger 1995).

Government action in housing dates back to at least the early 1900s. With the goal of investigating and assisting in housing opportunities for the poor, by 1910 most large cities in the United States had implemented some sort of housing reform legislation (Axinn and Stern 2005). After the Great Depression, President Franklin Roosevelt's New Deal moved to preserve the concept of private property. "The one thousand homeowners threatened with foreclosure each month in 1933 were helped to refinance their mortgages through the Home Owners Loan Corporation, established in June 1933. The home construction industry, almost at a standstill in 1933, was revived through the Federal Housing Administration, which insured loans for home repairs and mortgages for new houses" (Axinn and Stern 2005, 178). The National Housing Act of 1934 authorized low down payments, set up extended loan maturities (with a maximum of 40 years), and regulated interest rates designed to ensure that working-class families could afford mortgage payments. This Act also established the Federal Housing Administration, designed to insure lending institutions against loan defaults. "The FHA was to behave like a conservative bank, only insuring mortgages that were 'economically sound.' In practice, economic soundness was translated into 'redlining': a red line was literally drawn around areas of cities considered risky for economic *or* racial reasons" (q uadagno 1994, 23, emphasis in original). FHA administrators were instructed per the agency's *Underwriting Manual* not to insure mortgages unless they were located in racially homogenous white neighborhoods (U.S. Federal Housing Administration 1936, 1938, 1946, 1952). "As late as 1977, private appraising manuals still contained listing of ethnic groups ranked in descending order from those who are most desirable to those who have the most adverse effect on property values. Whites were ranked at the top of the list while African Americans and Mexican Americans were ranked at the very bottom" (Missouri Housing Development Commission, August 1977, as cited in Gotham 2000, 19).

"Until 1949 the FHA also encouraged the use of restrictive covenants banning African Americans from given neighborhoods and refused to insure mortgages in integrated neighborhoods" (q uadagno 1994, 23–24). "Insurance is critical, or in the industry's term 'essential.' If a potential homebuyer cannot obtain a property insurance policy, no lender can provide a mortgage" (Squires 2003, 392). On the rental side, from the outset, public housing authorities located housing projects in racially segregated neighborhoods and selected tenants by race (Peel, Pickett, and Buehl 1970, 63–64). The governmentally supported housing patterns in the United States were intentionally designed to promote racial inequality. "From the New Deal to the 1960s, federal housing policy encouraged private home ownership for white families but not black families. Instead, federal policy reinforced barriers to residential choice erected by builders, money lenders, and realtors. Housing barriers not only relegated minorities to racially segregated housing but also virtually ensured that the quality of housing open to them was inferior" (q uadagno 1994, 89).

As part of civil rights legislation, beginning with the Fair Housing Act of 1968, there has been significant and important federal legislation related to fair housing. Table 2.1 provides an overview of such policies. As Galster summarized, the core fair housing goals include "the elimination of differential treatment, which discriminates on the basis of race; the creation of stable, racially diverse neighborhoods, and the reduction of ghettos occupied by poor minority households" (1999, 123).

Yet, discrimination in housing still actively persists. This includes differential treatment, where housing agents apply a different set of rules or practices when dealing with a minority, as well as adverse impacts, where a public policy or practice is applied evenhandedly to all races but results in disproportionately unjustifiable negative consequences for minorities (Schwemm 1992; Yinger 1995, 1998). This is particularly true in the area of Section 8 housing, mortgage loans, and racial profiling in insurance or insurance redlining.

As detailed by the U.S. Department of Housing and Urban Development's website, "The housing choice voucher program [Section 8] is the federal government's major program for assisting very low-income families, the elderly, and the disabled to afford decent, safe, and sanitary housing in the private market. Since housing assistance is provided on behalf of the family or individual, participants are able to find their own housing, including single-family homes, townhouses and apartments. The participant is free to choose any housing that meets the requirements of the program and is not limited to units located in subsidized housing projects." Beck's analysis of Section 8 housing found blatant, open discrimination revealed by landlords. "Landlords blatantly discriminate against Section 8. They told me plain and simple they don't take Section 8; that's their policy" (1996, 3). Beck concludes, "As experience with the FHA demonstrates, the reality of enforcement is often far from ideal. The source of the well-documented ineffectiveness of the FHA in alleviating housing discrimination lies in its enforcement provisions and the lack of vigilance with which those provisions have been employed, not in the classes it protects or the types of discrimination it prohibits . . . even though an estimated two million incidents of housing discrimination occur each year, only about 400 fair housing cases were decided between 1986 and 1993" (13). Ultimately, Beck concludes, "A statute that affects only selected actors cannot accomplish the 'shaping [of] collected behavior' essential to eliminating discrimination" (13). In essence, landlords continue to discriminate because they recognize there is little risk associated with doing so.

Table 2.1

Fair Housing Laws and Presidential Executive Orders

The Fair Housing Laws	
Fair Housing Act	Title VIII of the Civil Rights Act of 1968 (Fair Housing Act), as amended, prohibits discrimination in the sale, rental, and financing of dwellings, and in other housing-related transactions, based on race, color, national origin, religion, sex, familial status (including children under the age of 18 living with parents or legal custodians, pregnant women, and people securing custody of children under the age of 18), and handicap (disability).
Title VI of the Civil Rights Act of 1964	Title VI prohibits discrimination on the basis of race, color, or national origin in programs and activities receiving federal financial assistance.
Section 504 of the Rehabilitation Act of 1973	Section 504 prohibits discrimination based on disability in any program or activity receiving federal financial assistance.
Section 109 of Title I of the Housing and Community Development Act of 1974	Section 109 prohibits discrimination on the basis of race, color, national origin, sex, or religion in programs and activities receiving financial assistance from HUD's Community Development and Block Grant Program.
Title II of the Americans with Disabilities Act of 1990	Title II prohibits discrimination based on disability in programs, services, and activities provided or made available by public entities. HUD enforces Title II when it relates to state and local public housing, housing assistance, and housing referrals.
Architectural Barriers Act of 1968	The Architectural Barriers Act requires that buildings and facilities designed, constructed, altered, or leased with certain federal funds after September 1969 must be accessible to and usable by handicapped persons.
Age Discrimination Act of 1975	The Age Discrimination Act prohibits discrimination on the basis of age in programs or activities receiving federal financial assistance.
Title IX of the Education Amendments Act of 1972	Title IX prohibits discrimination on the basis of sex in education programs or activities that receive federal financial assistance.

Fair Housing–Related Presidential Executive Orders

Executive Order 11063	Executive Order 11063 prohibits discrimination in the sale, leasing, rental, or other disposition of properties and facilities owned or operated by the federal government or provided with federal funds.
Executive Order 11246	Executive Order 11246, as amended, bars discrimination in federal employment because of race, color, religion, sex, or national origin.
Executive Order 12892	Executive Order 12892, as amended, requires federal agencies to affirmatively further fair housing in their programs and activities, and provides that the secretary of HUD will be responsible for coordinating the effort. The order also establishes the President's Fair Housing Council, which will be chaired by the secretary of HUD.
Executive Order 12898	Executive Order 12898 requires that each federal agency conduct its program, policies, and activities that substantially affect human health or the environment in a manner that does not exclude persons based on race, color, or national origin.
Executive Order 13166	Executive Order 13166 eliminates, to the extent possible, limited English proficiency as a barrier to full and meaningful participation by beneficiaries in all federally assisted and federally conducted programs and activities.
Executive Order 13217	Executive Order 13217 requires federal agencies to evaluate their policies and programs to determine if any can be revised or modified to improve the availability of community-based living arrangements for persons with disabilities.

Source: U.S. Department of Housing and Urban Development 2012.

In regard to mortgage loans for the middle class, statistical research found that high minority denial rates across the United States persist, even when legitimate financial factors were controlled (Schafer and Ladd 1981). These findings were reaffirmed by the Federal Reserve Bank of Boston's analysis of more than 3,000 mortgage loan underwriting decisions by 131 Boston-area banks, savings and loans, mortgage companies, and credit unions in 1991. Their analysis found that African Americans and Hispanics were 60 percent more likely to be denied, even after controlling for differences in down payments and credit histories (Munnell et al. 1996).

Gotham concludes, "the various economic and political dimensions of housing-related activities have been conducted through an organized and interconnected system of racial discrimination." He further explains, "As decades of research on housing and real estate have revealed, racial discrimination has been, and continues to be, an institutionalized and persistent feature of the housing industry that cuts across a variety of public agencies, private firms, and includes landlords, homeowners, bankers, real estate agents and government officials . . . informal patterns and institutional mechanisms of housing discrimination remain a persistent and undeniable characteristic of American society" (Gotham 2000, 17).

As Figure 2.2 reports, there are significant and enduring differences in home ownership rates by race and ethnicity. In 1996, 69.1 percent of whites owned a home; compared with 44.1 percent of blacks, 51.6 percent of American Indians, 50.8 percent of Asians, and 42.8 percent of Hispanics. In 2010, a similar pattern remains with 71 percent of whites owning a home, compared with 45.4 percent of blacks, 52.3 percent of American Indians, 58.9 percent of Asians, and 47.5 percent of Hispanics.

Education

Education is a very important factor in understanding social inequities. There is a consistently positive association between education and economic well-being. As Frederickson notes, "American public education has always been about educational achievement on the one hand, and educational opportunity, on the other. Educational achievement has to do with student and teacher merit, quality, grades, advancement, capability, performance, and work. Educational opportunity has to do with justice, fairness, and an equal chance for students and their families" (2010, 113).

In many ways, higher educational achievement is viewed as the most promising investment to counter racial discrimination. Much has been written about racial inequities, segregation, and resegregation in the United States. Access to education is deeply rooted in structural racial disparities created

Figure 2.2   **Home Ownership Rates by Race and Ethnicity of Householder**

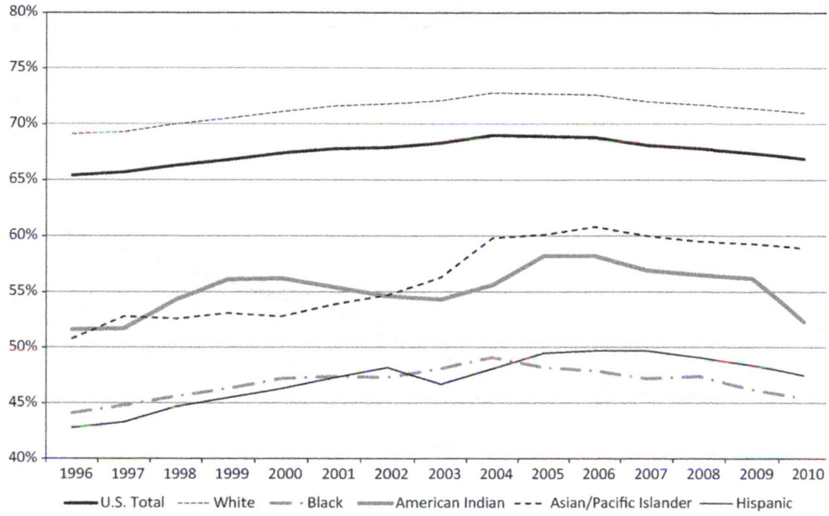

Source: U.S. Census Bureau 2012.

by government. For example, the Morrill Land Grant Act of 1892 was based on a government-funded system of higher education with stark differences in the allocations awarded to white colleges versus black colleges. The federal government entrusted these funding-allocation decisions to state governments, resulting in white colleges' receiving much more than half of the land-grant funding when it was divided, in addition to the state funding that already favored white colleges (Preer 1990). These allocation formulas remain important in understanding the context of performance differences in historically black and historically white land-grant colleges today.

The landmark 1954 Supreme Court decision, *Brown v. Board of Education*, was squarely focused on equality, ruling that the doctrine of separate but equal was both unequal and unconstitutional. Despite the *Brown* decision, racial inequities in American public education are indisputable (see, for example, Jencks and Phillips 1998; Kozol 1991). Nearly sixty years after *Brown*, the educational achievement gap between white and minority students remains large, and differences in access to quality public education are astounding.

Figure 2.3 provides data from the National Center for Educational Statistics on educational attainment by race. It shows that racial inequities in educational attainment persist over time. In 2010, 34 percent of whites and 50.8 percent of Asians ages twenty-five and above had a college degree, compared to 20.2 percent for blacks and 14.1 percent for Hispanics.

Figure 2.3   **Educational Attainment by Race, 1940–2010** (ages 25 and over)

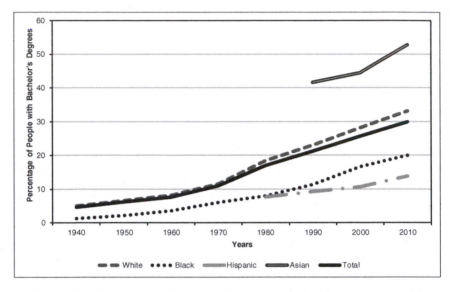

Source: U.S. Department of Education 2011.

While explanations abound that blame minority children and their families for educational inequality, such explanations are not contextualized against important realities. As Darling-Hammond articulates, "Educational outcomes for students of color are much more a function of their unequal access to key educational resources, including skilled teachers, and quality curriculum, than they are a function of race" (2007, 320). For example, a study of California high schools found many high-minority schools so severely overcrowded that they operate using a multitrack schedule offering a shortened school day and school year, lack basic textbooks and materials, do not offer the courses students need for college admission, and are routinely staffed by untrained, inexperienced, and temporary teachers (Oakes and Saunders 2004). In a study of Texas schools, Ferguson (1991) found that the single highest predictor of student achievement gaps was teacher expertise (measured by teacher performance on a state certification exam, along with teacher experience and master's degrees). When controlling for socioeconomic status, black students' achievement was comparable to that of whites if they had been assigned equally qualified teachers

Even more disturbing, however, are the racial disparities in educational payoffs in the labor market. As Lang and Manove (2006) discuss, even when blacks have higher levels of educational attainment and cognitive scores than whites do, they still earn noticeably less. Importantly, some of the black-white wage differential is not explained by pre–labor market differentials in educational quality, but by different racial treatment in the labor market (Gooden 2000).

However, much of this literature devotes very little attention to the educational experiences of American Indians. Ironically, the first Americans are often researched and discussed last (if at all) in social equity analysis. A similar pattern holds for the public administration literature more generally, with only a few public administrators articulating the need to include tribal governance in public administration studies (Aufrecht 1999; Luton 1999; Ronquillo 2011). As Lomawaima and McCarty assert, "How the U.S. government and its nontribal citizens wrestle with their relationship with tribes lies at the core of the question of whether social justice and democracy can coexist" (2002, 281).

> American Indians and Alaska Natives (AI/AN) are generally designated as Native Americans. An estimated 4.7 million people in the United States— or about 1.5 percent of the U.S. population—self-identify under official Census categories as American Indian or Alaska Native. Of these, 3.3 million people identify as being of single-race Native American ethnicity. Approximately 1.2 million Native Americans reside on Indian reservations (known collectively as "Indian Country") or in Alaska Native Villages. This leaves approximately 2.1 million of those who identify themselves as single-race American Indian or Alaska Native living outside Indian Country and Alaska Native villages. (Cornell and Kalt 2010, 1)

The enduring racial inequities in the education of American Indians is staggering. American Indian and Alaska Native dropout rates are the lowest among all racial and ethnic groups. Faircloth and Tippeconnic report average graduation rates for American Indians and Alaska Natives of 46.6 percent, compared to 69.8 percent for whites, 54.7 percent for blacks, 77.9 percent for Asians, and 50.8 percent for Hispanics (2010, 12). Although the majority (approximately 92 percent) of Native students attend regular public schools, a significant number (approximately 8 percent) attend schools operated or funded by the Bureau of Indian Education (BIE) or by individual tribes (DeVoe and Darling-Churchill 2008).

Much of the history of American Indian policy, including education, involves an important battleground between federal powers and tribal sovereignty. As Lomawaima and McCarty (2002) explain,

> Tribes have a singular legal status that both predates and is recognized by the U.S. Constitution. The Commerce Clause delegates the power to Con-

gress "to regulate Commerce with foreign nations, and among the several States, and with the Indian tribes" (quoted in Pommersheim 1995, 214, note 40). The Constitution empowers the President to negotiate treaties with foreign nations (ratification requires a two-thirds vote by the Senate); and the formative United States used the treaty process—as did earlier colonial powers—to conduct diplomatic relations with Indian nations (Wilkins and Lomawaima 2001). The statements of the Constitution—coupled with subsequent federal legislation, the bureaucratic rules of the federal agencies charged with supervising Indian affairs, and judicial decisions—have shaped the contours of life in Indian country today. (Lomawaima and McCarty 2002, 284)

Specificall , a 1928 report commissioned by the U.S. secretary of the Interior, *The Problem of Indian Administration* (commonly referenced as the Meriam Report), set the stage for enduring federal government action and behavior in regard to Indian education by advocating a "civilizing" campaign designed to assimilate American Indians into white society and ameliorate American Indian language and culture or afford them with *the unprecedented possibility of maintaining a distinctively Indian life* (Lomawaima and McCarty 2002, 206 emphasis added). "What was unprecedented in their proposal was the idea that Indian people should have the power to make choices and that the federal government should support them in their choices" (Lomawaima and McCarty 2002, 287).

The level of federal government support and investment in Indian communities has been, and continues to be, woefully low. According to data from the U.S. Commission on Civil Rights (2003), per capita federal spending on Indians and Indian Affairs averages $3,000 per capita, compared to $4,500 per capital for the United States at large (based on 2000 dollars).

In fact, federal U.S. budget spending on Indian affairs peaked in real dollars in the mid-1970s—approximately coincident with the advent of the major legislation in Congress that made tribal self-determination the core principle of U.S. Indian policy. By the early 2000s, the U.S. Commission on Civil Rights labeled the spending levels in Indian Country a "quiet crisis." The Commission reported that while American Indians were marked by the most severe poverty in America and had suffered treaty violations and other forms of deprivation over the centuries at the hand of the federal government, governmental spending in Indian America was dramatically and disproportionately below levels of funding provided to other groups in the United States and the general U.S. population. (Cornell and Kalt 2010, 9)

As Lomawaima and McCarty explain, "Unlike public school districts funded chiefly by property taxes, reservation schools must rely on congressional appropriations for the majority of their funding. . . . Also, unlike nonreservation public schools, community-controlled schools are independent units that must provide all the services necessary for their operation. The costs of these largely rural schools are significantly higher, yet their financial resources are more limited and volatile than those available to nonreservation public schools" (2002, 293).

Similarly, the educational standards and accountability focus of the twenty-firs century is administered in a context that further promotes inequity, with standardized tests containing English-only content and depreciation of Indian culture. "A more basic injustice is a system that bestows educational resources on the privileged, rewards their cultural capital, then consecrates their ensuing advantage with standardized tests. There is nothing democratic about this process. It standardizes inequality and ensures that existing race- and class-based hierarchies are legitimized and reproduced" (Lomawaima and McCarty 2002, 298).

Equity issues in U.S. public education are important and complex. Educational opportunity raises fundamental questions about the equity of financial investments in racial groups, fairness in the allocation of resources, and access to opportunity. Within the American Indian community, the policy of self-determination "has proven to be the only policy that has worked to make significant progress in reversing otherwise distressed social, cultural, and economic conditions in Native communities" (Cornell and Kalt 2010, 5). However, self-determination policies that are embedded in larger inequities defined by inadequate federal funding and white cultural privilege operate from an important structural disadvantage.

Environment

There is a long history of environmental risks and hazards disproportionately affecting racial minorities and the poor (see, for example, Anderson et al. 1994a, 1994b; Been 1993, 1994; Been and Gupta 1997; Bullard 1993; Bullard 1994; Daniels and Friedman 1999; Downey 1998; Faber and Krieg 2001; Krieg 1995; Logan and Molotch 1987; Mohai and Bryant 1992; United Church of Christ 1987; U.S. GAO 1983). During the 1980s, protests from grassroots communities led by people of color and the poor over these blatant environmental racial disparities, coupled with inattention from the mainstream environmental groups in addressing such concerns, resulted in the emergence of an environmental justice movement (Bullard 1994; Cable, Hastings, and Mix 2002). It was founded directly on democratic principles, noting environmental quality as a basic right of all individuals (Bullard 1994).

As Exhibit 2.1 summarizes, there has been significant federal legislation designed to address environmental racism. Despite the passage of significant federal legislation, racial minorities continue to be denied this right due to racism, discrimination, and prejudice, as well as differences in political and influential power among white communities and communities of color. As Krieg explains,

> The struggle for control over environmental regulations stems from capital's need to shift costs, negative externalities (resource depletions, pollution) onto third parties. Maximizing cost externalization enables producers of waste to minimize "unproductive" expenses such as waste handling, purchasing environmentally "friendly" technologies, and cleaning up waste sites. In this way, capital's treatment of nature as "tap and sink" is dependent upon social conditions that minimize the monetary risks associated with environmental destruction (the dumping of toxic wastes). It is likely that poor communities and communities of color lacking control capacity provide the social conditions that are conducive to cost externalization. Capital's exploitation of these conditions is made possible by the imbalance of power between communities, a condition that opens the door to social and environmental injustices. (Krieg 1998, 5)

The end result is environmental racism, defined by Fisher as "any policy, practice, or directive that intentionally or unintentionally, differentially impacts or disadvantages individuals, groups, or communities based on race or color; as well as the exclusionary and restrictive practices that limit participation by people of color in decision-making boards, commissions, and staffs" (1995, 290).

Governmental agencies have also contributed to these racial inequities through the location of public facilities, such as sewage facilities and hazardous waste facilities (Greenberg and Cidon 1997; Norton et al. 2007). Also, government agencies have been criticized for their slow response to contaminated communities of color and levying lower fines on businesses that pollute in black communities (Head 1995; Lavelle and Coyle 1992). For example, Lavelle and Coyle (1992) found that penalties issued pursuant to hazardous waste laws at sites having the greatest white population were about 500 percent higher than penalties at sites with the greatest minority population.

Environmental justice scholars call attention to the broad structures that enable racial disparities to persist. Such factors include, for example, the relatively low level of political and economic power among minorities and the poor; the focus on race-blind processes that create and sustain environmental inequities and fail to differentiate real differences confronting minority communities relative to whites; and the employment, housing, and

Exhibit 2.1
Environmental Justice Legislation

Nondiscrimination
Title VI of the Civil Rights Act of 1964 and Environmental Justice

It has been the longstanding policy of the Federal Highway Administrations (FHWA) and the Federal Transit Administration (FTA) to actively ensure nondiscrimination under Title VI of the 1964 Civil Rights Act in federally funded activities. Under Title VI and related statutes, each federal agency is required to ensure that no person is excluded from participation in, denied the benefit of, or subjected to discrimination under any program or activity receiving federal financial assistance on the basis of race, color, national origin, age, sex, disability, or religion. The Civil Rights Restoration Act of 1987 clarified the intent of Title VI to include all program and activities of federal-aid recipients, subrecipients, and contractors whether those programs and activities are federally funded or not.

The National Environmental Policy Act of 1969 (NEPA) stressed the importance of providing for "all Americans safe, healthful, productive, and esthetically pleasing surroundings" and provided a requirement for taking a "systematic, interdisciplinary approach" to aid in considering environmental and community factors in decision making.

This approach was further emphasized in the Federal-Aid Highway Act of 1970: 23 United States Code 109(h) established further basis for equitable treatment of communities being affected by transportation projects. It requires consideration of the anticipated effects of proposed transportation projects upon residences, businesses, farms, accessibility of public facilities, tax base, and other community resources.

On February 11, 1994, President Clinton signed Executive Order 12898: Federal Actions to Address Environmental Justice in Minority Populations and Low-Income Populations (PDF, 20KB). The executive order requires that each federal agency shall, to the greatest extent allowed by law, administer and implement its programs, policies, and activities that affect human health or the environment so as to identify and avoid "disproportionately high and adverse" effects on minority and low-income populations.

In April 1997, the U.S. Department of Transportation (DOT) issued the DOT Order on Environmental Justice to Address Environmental Justice in Minority Populations and Low-Income Populations (DOT Order 5610.2) to summarize and expand upon the requirements of Executive Order 12898 on Environmental Justice. The order generally describes the process for incorporating environmental justice principles into all DOT existing programs, policies, and activities.

In December 1998, the FHWA issued FHWA Actions to Address Environmental Justice in Minority Populations and Low-Income Populations (DOT Order 6640.23) that requires the FHWA to implement the principles of the DOT Order 5610.2 and E.O. 12898 by incorporating environmental justice principles in all FHWA programs, policies and activities.

Source: U.S. Department of Transportation 2013.

community segregation that enables environmental burdens to be inequitably distributed in the first place (Higgins 1993, 287). Mohai and Bryant (1992) identify twelve studies that document both race and income as significan factors in the inequitable distribution of pollution. Ten of the twelve studies assessed the relative importance of race and income, and seven found race to be more important. As Krieg explains, "Associations of minority populations with environmental hazards are not spurious; structural forces bring environmental hazards into contact with working-class and people of color" (1998, 4).

As Exhibit 2.2 conveys environmental racial disparities are well documented. A series of studies by Bullard (1983, 1990; Bullard and Wright 1986) found a pattern of locating urban landfills, incinerators, and polluting industries in minority and low-income neighborhoods. A nationwide study by the United Church of Christ Commission for Racial Justice (1987) found race to be the most significant variable associated with the location of hazardous waste facilities. The U.S. South, which has the highest percentage of African Americans, also has nine of the twelve states with the worst environmental records (Hall and Kerr 1991). Similarly, American Indian communities have been impacted significantly by ongoing poorly regulated uranium mining (Angel 1991). Lopez found that "in every large U.S. metropolitan area of over one million people, Blacks are more likely than Whites to be living in census tracks with higher estimated total air toxic levels" (2002, 289). He further concludes that three factors explain more than half of the variation in the net difference for exposure to air toxics. These factors are black/white poverty levels, percentage employed in manufacturing, and degree of segregation (Lopez 2002, 293).

Minority workers are disproportionately represented in industries with high levels of occupational health risks (Davis and Rowland 1983; Wright 1992). Such industries involve increased exposure to pesticides, cleaning chemicals, exposure to carcinogens, and hepatitis risk in hospital environments, and high exposure to agrichemicals as farm workers. Exposure to environmental risks is particularly strong among Hispanics. "Ambient air pollution, worker exposure to chemicals, indoor air pollution, and drinking water quality are among the top four threats to human health and are all areas in which indicators point to elevated risk in Hispanic populations" (Metzger, Delgado, and Herrell 1995, 25). Wernette and Nieves (1992) found that 80 percent of Hispanics live in an area failing to meet Environmental Protection Agency (EPA) air quality standards, compared to 65 percent of blacks and 57 percent of whites. The proportion of Hispanics who are migrant workers is 95 percent (U.S. Department of Labor 1994). Agricultural workers are particularly at risk for exposure to pesticides, especially workers who mix,

Exhibit 2.2
Environmental Racial Disparities

Facts on Environmental Racism Handout

I. Excerpts from Robert Bullard, "Environmental Justice for All," *Unequal Protection: Environmental Justice & Communities of Color* (Sierra Club Books, 1994).

A. The Commission for Racial Justice's landmark study, *Toxic Waste and Race in the United States*, found race to be the single most important factor (i.e., more important than income, home ownership rate, and property values) in the location of abandoned toxic waste sites. The study also found that:
    1. three out of five African Americans live in communities with abandoned toxic waste sites;
    2. three of the five largest commercial hazardous waste landfills are located in predominantly African American or Latino American communities and account for 40 percent of the nation's total estimated landfill capacity; and
    3. African Americans are heavily overrepresented in the populations of cities with the largest number of abandoned toxic waste sites (pp. 17–18).

B. Millions of Americans live in housing and physical environments that are overburdened with environmental problems, including older housing with lead-based paint, congested freeways that crisscross neighborhoods, industries that emit dangerous pollutants into the area, and abandoned toxic waste sites.
    Virtually all of the studies of exposure to outdoor air pollution have found significant differences in exposure by income and race. African Americans and Latino Americans are more likely than whites to live in areas with reduced air quality (p. 12).

C. A 1992 study by staff writers from the *National Law Journal* uncovered glaring inequities in the way the federal EPA enforces its laws. The authors write:

    There is a racial divide in the way the U.S. government cleans up toxic waste sites and punishes polluters. White communities see faster action, better results and stiffer penalties than communities where blacks, Hispanics and other minorities live. This unequal protection often occurs whether the community is wealthy or poor (p. 9).

D. After examining census data, civil court dockets, and the EPA's own record of performance at 1,177 Superfund toxic waste sites, the *National Law Journal* report revealed the following:

1. Penalties under hazardous waste laws at sites having the greatest white population were 500 percent higher than penalties with the greatest minority population, averaging $335,566 for white areas compared to $55,318 for minority areas.
2. The disparity under the toxic waste law occurs by race alone, not income. The average penalty in areas with lowest income is $113,491, which is 3 percent more than the average penalty in areas with the highest median incomes.
3. For all the federal environmental laws aimed at protecting citizens from air, water, and wasted pollution, penalties in white communities were 46 percent higher than in minority communities.
4. Under the giant Superfund cleanup program, abandoned hazardous waste sites in minority areas take 20 percent longer to be placed on the national priority list than those in white areas.

II.   Vital Statistics from the Congressional Black Caucus Foundation

1. African American children are five times more likely to suffer from lead poisoning than white children, and 22 percent of African American children living in older housing are lead poisoned.
2. An estimated 50 percent of African Americans and 60 percent of Hispanics live in a county in which levels of two or more air pollutants exceed governmental standards.
3. Communities with the greatest number of commercial hazardous waste facilities have some of the highest proportions of minority residents.
4. Half of all Asian/Pacific Islanders and American Indians live in communities with uncontrolled toxic waste sites.
5. Communities with existing incinerators have 89 percent more minorities than the national average.
6. African Americans are heavily overrepresented in cities with the largest number of abandoned toxic waste sites, such as Memphis, St. Louis, Houston, Cleveland, Chicago, and Atlanta.

Source: Race: The Power of Illusion. www.pbs.org/race/000_About/002_04-teachers-02.htm.
©2003 California Newsreel, www.newsreel.org.

load, and apply such chemicals (Moses 1993). Exposure to lead, linked to a host of health concerns in children including learning disabilities, central nervous system damage, and functioning of blood cells, is more pronounced in Hispanic communities that are more likely to rent older homes or apartments that may contain antiquated lead plumbing (Olson 1993).

Higgins (1993) summarizes the cumulative institutional effect of environmental exposures on racial minorities:

In sum, the total environmental impact on the life chances of a low income person of color might be expressed thusly; as a child, one faces elevated risks of lead poisoning and chemical or radiation exposure in the home, risks that reflect in part the working environments of one's parents; at home and in the community, this growing child faces a disproportionate risk of exposure to pollutants from solid and toxic waste generators, landfills, incinerators, and illegal dumps. Having located work in a situation of high minority unemployment, the young adult may spend a lifetime segregated into jobs and industries with high levels of occupational health risks. The health impacts of these conditions in turn are magnified by lower likelihood of adequate health care throughout one's life and by other stresses of limited income security. (Higgins 1993, 284–85)

Conclusion

Racial inequities in the United States are largely saturated because they are cumulative and reinforcing. Racial outcomes in health, education, employment, environmental risk, occupational status, and crime are not randomly assigned. They are embedded in a historical structure where racial minorities chronically experience pervasive negative differences. These differences compound exponentially to generate a cycle of racial saturation that continues generation after generation. While there are definite pockets of exceptions within and among racial groups, the general trends are still dominant.

Although laws are vital in promoting racial equity, the persistence of racial inequities is not solely a legal question. Full implementation of both the intention and the spirit of these laws requires robust policies, norms, and cultures at the agency level. The successful implementation of racial equity in American society requires attentive public administrators who determinedly monitor, assess, and eradicate the permeation of racial inequities that are advanced through structural racism. Given the saturation of racial inequities in the United States, eliminating these inequities requires direct discussions about race. As public administrators, we cannot have discussions about fiscal resources without discussing budgets. Neither can we have a discussion about personnel without discussing positions, units, and people. Similarly, we cannot have a discussion about inequities in the provision of public services without talking about race. Nor, as public administrators, can we turn a blind eye to our contributions to and responsibilities for reversing these inequities. Like it or not, comfortably or not, race and social equity—a nervous area of government—is a clear reality in the windshield of public administration that compels our attention.

References

Anderson, Douglas L., Andy B. Anderson, John Michael Oakes, and Michael R. Fraser. 1994a. "Environmental Equity: The Demographics of Dumping." *Demography* 31 (2): 229–48.

Anderson, Douglas L., Andy B. Anderson, John Michael Oakes, Michael R. Fraser, Eleanor W. Weber, and Edward J. Calabrese. 1994b. "Environmental Equity: Issues of Metropolitan Areas." *Evaluation Review* 18 (2): 123–40.

Angel, Bradley. 1991. *The Toxic Threat to Indian Lands: A Greenpeace Report.* Durango, CO: Indigenous Environmental Network.

Aufrecht, Steven E. 1999. "Missing: Native American Governance in American Public Administration Literature." *American Review of Public Administration* 29 (4): 370–90.

Axinn, June, and Mark J. Stern. 2005. *Social Welfare: A History of the American Response to Need.* 6th ed. Boston: Allyn & Bacon.

Beck, Paula J. 1996. "Fighting Section 8 Discrimination: The Fair Housing Act's New Frontier." *Harvard Civil Rights–Civil Liberties Law Review* 31 (155): 1–32.

Been, Vicky L. 1993. "What's Fairness Got to Do with It? Environmental Justice and the Siting of the Locally Undesirable Land Uses." *Cornell Law Review* 78 (6): 1001–85.

———. 1994. "Locally Undesirable Land Uses in Minority Neighborhoods: Disproportionate Siting or Market Dynamics." *Yale Law Review* 103 (6): 1383–1422.

Been, Vicky L., and Francis Gupta. 1997. "Coming to the Nuisance or Going to the Barrios? A Longitudinal Analysis of Environmental Justice." *Ecological Law Quarterly* 24 (1): 1–56.

Bonilla-Silva, Eduardo. 1996. "Rethinking Racism: Toward a Structural Explanation." *American Sociological Review* 62 (3): 465–80.

Bratt, Rachel G. 1986. "Public Housing: The Controversy and Contribution." In *Critical Perspectives on Housing,* ed. Rachel G. Bratt, Chester Hartman, and Ann Meyerson, 335–61. Philadelphia: Temple University Press.

Bullard, Robert D. 1983. "Solid Waste Sites and the Black Houston Community." *Sociological Inquiry* 53 (2–3, April): 273–88.

———. 1990. *Dumping in Dixie: Race, Class, and Environmental Quality.* Boulder, CO: Westview Press.

———. 1993. *Confronting Environmental Racism.* Boston: South End Press.

———., ed. 1994. *Unequal Protection: Environmental Justice and Communities of Color.* San Francisco: Sierra Club Books.

Bullard, Robert D., and Beverly Hendrix Wright. 1986. "The Politics of Pollution: Implications for the Black Community." *Phylon* 47 (1): 71–78.

Cable, Sherry, Donald W. Hastings, and Tamara L. Mix. 2002. "Different Voices, Different Venues: Environmental Racism Claims by Activists, Researchers, and Lawyers." *Human Ecology Review* 9 (1): 26–42.

Cornell, Stephen, and Joseph P. Kalt. 2010. "American Indian Self-Determination: The Political Economy of a Successful Policy." *Joint Occasional Papers on Native Affairs,* 1. Cambridge, MA: The Harvard Project on American Indian Development.

Daniels, Glynis, and Samantha Friedman. 1999. "Spatial Inequality and the Distribution of Industrial Toxic Releases: Evidence from 1990 TRI." *Social Science Quarterly* 80 (2): 244–62.

Darling-Hammond, Linda. 2007. Third Annual Brown Lecture in Education Research: "The Flat Earth and Education: How America's Commitment to Equity Will Determine Our Future." *Educational Researcher* 36 (6): 318–34.

Davis, Morris E., and Andrew S. Rowland. 1983. "Problems Faced by Minority Workers." In *Occupational Health: Recognizing and Preventing Work-Related Disease*, ed. Barry S. Levy and David H. Wegman, 417–30. Boston: Little, Brown.

DeVoe, Jill Fleury, and Kristen E. Darling-Churchill. 2008. *Status and Trends in the Education of American Indians and Alaska Natives: 2008.* Report NCES 2008–084. Washington, DC: National Center for Education Statistics, Institute of Education Sciences, U.S. Department of Education.

Downey, Liam. 1998. "Environmental Injustice: Is Race or Income a Better Predictor?" *Social Science Quarterly* 79 (4): 766–78.

Faber, Daniel, and Eric J. Krieg. 2001. *Unequal Exposure to Ecological Hazards: Environmental Justice in the Commonwealth of Massachusetts.* A Report by the Philanthropy and Environmental Justice Research Project. Boston: Northeastern University.

Faircloth, Susan C., and John W. Tippeconnic, III. 2010. *The Dropout/Graduation Rate Crisis Among American Indian and Alaska Native Students: Failure to Respond Places the Future of Native Peoples at Risk.* Los Angeles, CA: The Civil Rights Project/Proyecto Derechos Civiles at UCLA. www.civilrightsproject.ucla.edu.

Feagin, Joe R. 1994. "A House Is Not a Home: White Racism and U.S. Housing Practices." In *Residential Apartheid: The American Legacy*, ed. Robert D. Bullard, J. Eugene Grigsby III, and Charles Lee, 17–48. Los Angeles: CASS Urban Policy Series.

Ferguson, Ronald F. 1991. "Paying for Public Education: New Evidence on How and Why Money Matters." *Harvard Journal on Legislation* 28 (2): 465–98.

Fisher, Michael. 1995. "Environmental Racism Claims Brought Under Title VI of the Civil Rights Act." *Environmental Law Review* 25 (2): 285–334.

Frederickson, H. George. 2010. *Social Equity and Public Administration: Origins, Developments, and Applications.* Armonk, NY: M.E. Sharpe.

Galster, George. 1999. "The Evolving Challenges of Fair Housing Since 1968: Open Housing, Integration, and the Reduction of Ghettoization." *Cityscape: The Journal of Policy Development and Research* 4 (3): 123–38.

Gooden, Susan T. 2000. "Race and Welfare: Examining Employment Outcomes of White and Black Welfare Recipients." *Journal of Poverty* 4 (3): 21–41.

Gotham, Kevin Fox. 2000. "Separate and Unequal: The Housing Act of 1968 and the Section 235 Program." *Sociological Forum* 15 (1): 13–37.

Greenberg, Michael, and Michal Cidon. 1997. "Broadening the Definition of Environmental Equity: A Framework for States and Local Governments." *Population Research and Policy Review* 16 (4): 397–413.

Hall, Bob, and Mary Lee Kerr. 1991. *1991–1992 Green Index: A State-by-State Guide to the Nation's Environmental Health.* Washington, DC: Island Press.

Head, Rebecca A. 1995. "Health-Based Standards: What Role in Environmental Justice?" In *Environmental Justice: Issues, Policies, and Solutions*, ed. Bunyan Bryant, 45–56. Washington, DC: Island Press.

Higgins, Robert R. 1993. "Race and Environmental Equity: An Overview of the Environmental Justice in the Policy Process." *Polity* 26 (2): 281–300.

Jencks, Christopher, and Meredith Phillips. 1998. *The Black-White Test Score Gap.* Washington, DC: Brookings Institution Press.

Keating, W. Dennis. 1994. *Suburban Racial Dilemma: Housing and Neighborhoods.* Philadelphia: Temple University Press.

Kozol, Jonathan. 1991. *Savage Inequalities: Children in America's Schools.* New York: Harper Perennial.

Krieg, Eric J. 1995. "A Socio-Historical Interpretation of Toxic Waste Sites: The Case of Greater Boston." *American Journal of Economic Sociology* 54 (1): 1–14.

———. 1998. "The Two Faces of Toxic Waste: Trends in the Spread of Environmental Hazards." *Sociological Forum* 13 (1): 3–20.

Lang, Kevin, and Michael Manove. 2006. *Education and Labor Market Discrimination.* NBER Working Paper 12257. National Bureau of Economic Research, Cambridge, MA.

Lavelle, Rita M., and Jean M. Coyle. 1992. "Unequal Protection: The Racial Divide in Environmental Law—A Special Investigation." *National Law Journal* 15 (3): S1-S2.

Logan, John R., and Harvey L. Molotch. 1987. *Urban Fortunes: The Political Economy of Place.* Berkeley: University of California Press.

Lomawaima, K. Tsianina, and Teresa L. McCarty. 2002. "When Tribal Sovereignty Challenges Democracy: American Indian Education and the Democratic Ideal." *American Educational Research Journal* 39 (2): 279–305.

Lopez, Russ. 2002. "Segregation and Black/White Differences in Exposure to Air Toxics in 1990." *Environmental Health Perspectives* 110 (2): 289–95.

Luton, Larry S. 1999. "History and American Public Administration." *Administration & Society* 31 (2): 205–21.

Massey, Douglas S., and Nancy A. Denton. 1993. *American Apartheid: Segregation and the Making of the Underclass.* Cambridge, MA: Harvard University Press.

Massey, Douglas S., and Shawn N. Kanaiaupuni. 1993. "Public Housing and the Concentration of Poverty." *Social Science Quarterly* 71 (1): 109–22.

Metzger, Raphael, Jane L. Delgado, and Robert Herrell. 1995. "Environmental Health and Hispanic Children." *Environmental Health Perspectives* 103 (6): 25–32.

Missouri Housing Development Commission. 1977. *Housing and Neighborhood Investment.* Part VI. "An Analysis of Underwriting and Appraisal Practices and Their Impact on Credit Availability." Prepared by Ochsncer and Associates. X1458, Box 206. Arthur A. Benson. Legal Papers. KC250. Western Historical Manuscript Collection—Kansas City.

Mohai, Paul, and Bunyan Bryant. 1992. "Environmental Racism: Reviewing the Evidence in Race and the Incidence of Environmental Hazards." In *Race and the Incidence of Environmental Hazards,* ed. Bunyan Bryant and Paul Mohai, 162–77. Boulder, CO: Westview Press.

Moses, Allan M. 1993. *Pesticides in Occupational and Environmental Reproductive Hazards: A Guide for Clinicians.* Baltimore: Williams and Wilkins.

Munnell, Alicia H., Geoffrey M. B. Tootell, Lynn E. Browne, and James McEneaney. 1996. "Mortgage Lending in Boston: Interpreting HMDA Data." *American Economic Review* 86 (1): 25–53.

Nam, Hyung Kyu. 2003. "Just an Environment or a Just Environment? Racial Segregation and Its Impacts." *Race—The Power of an Illusion: Lesson Plans.* www.pbs.org/race/000_About/002_04-teachers-02.htm.

Norton, Jennifer M., Steve Wing, Hester Lipscomb, Jay Kaufman, Stephen Marshall, and Altha Cravey. 2007. "Race, Wealth, and Solid Waste Facilities in North Carolina." *Environmental Health Perspectives* 115 (9): 1344–50.

Oakes, Jeannie. 1985. *Keeping Track*. New Haven, CT: Yale University Press.
Oakes, Jeannie, and Marisa Saunders. 2004. "Education's Most Basic Tools: Access to Textbooks and Instructional Materials in California's Public Schools." *Teachers College Record* 106 (10): 1967–88.
Obama, Barack. 2008. "A More Perfect Union." Speech prepared for campaign at Philadelphia, March 18. www.cnn.com/2008/POLITICS/03/18/obama.transcript/.
Oliver, Melvin, and Thomas Shapiro. 1995. *Black Wealth/White Wealth: A New Perspective on Racial Inequality*. New York: Routledge.
Olson, Erik D. 1993. *Think Before You Drink: The Failure of the Nation's Drinking Water System to Protect Public Health*. New York: National Resources Defense Council.
Omi, Michael, and Howard Winant. 1986. *Racial Formation in the United States: From the 1960s to the 1980s*. New York: Routledge and Kegan Paul.
Peel, Norman, Garth Pickett, and Stephen Buehl. 1970. "Racial Discrimination in Public Housing Site Selection." *Stanford Law Review* 23 (1): 63–147.
Pommersheim, Frank. 1995. *Braid of Feathers: American Indian Law and Contemporary Tribal Life*. Berkeley: University of California Press.
Preer, Jean. 1990. "'Just and Equitable Division': Jim Crow and the 1890 Land-Grant College Act." *Prologue* 22 (Winter): 322–36.
q uadagno, Jill. 1994. *The Color of Welfare: How Racism Undermined the War on Poverty*. New York: Oxford University Press.
Ronquillo, John C. 2011. "American Indian Tribal Governance and Management: Public Administration Promise or Pretense." *Public Administration Review* 71 (2): 285–92.
Schafer, Robert, and Helen F. Ladd. 1981. *Discrimination in Mortgage Lending*. Cambridge: Massachusetts Institute of Technology Press.
Schwemm, Robert G. 1992. *Housing Discrimination Law and Litigation*. Deerfield, IL: Boardman, Callaghan.
Squires, Gregory D. 2003. "Racial Profiling, Insurance Style: Insurance Redlining and the Uneven Development of Metropolitan Areas." *Journal of Urban Affairs* 25 (4): 391–410.
Stone, Deborah. 1997. *Policy Paradox: The Art of Political Decision Making*. New York: W.W. Norton.
United Church of Christ Commission for Racial Justice. 1987. *Toxic Wastes and Race in the United States: A National Report on the Racial and Socio-economic Characteristics of Communities with Hazardous Waste Sites*. New York: United Church of Christ Commission for Racial Justice.
U.S. Census Bureau. 2012. "Homeownership Rates by Race and Ethnicity of Householder." Table, *Information Please* database.
U.S. Commission on Civil Rights. 2003. *A Quiet Crisis: Federal Funding and Unmet Needs in Indian Country*. July. Washington, DC: U.S. Commission on Civil Rights.
U.S. Department of Education. 2011. Table 8: "Percentage of Persons Age 25 and Over and of Persons 25 to 29 Years Old with High School Completion or Higher and a Bachelor's or Higher Degree, by Race/Ethnicity and Sex: Selected Years, 1910 Through 2011." *Digest of Education Statistics: 2011*. http://nces.ed.gov/programs/digest/d11/tables/dt11_008.asp.
U.S. Department of Housing and Urban Development. 2012. Fair Housing Laws

and Presidential Executive Orders. http://portal.hud.gov/hudportal/HUD?src=/ program_offices/fair_housing_equal_opp/FHLaws (accessed Sept. 16, 2012)

U.S. Department of Labor. 1994. *Findings from the NAWS Survey 1990: A Demographic and Employment Profile of Perishable Crop Workers*. Research Report No. 1.

U.S. Department of Transportation. 2013. "The Facts: Nondiscrimination: Title VI and Environmental Justice." Federal Highway Administrations, Office of Planning, Environment, and Realty. www.fhwa.dot.gov/environment/environmental_justice/ facts/index.cfm.

U.S. Federal Housing Administration (FHA). 1936. *Underwriting Manual*. Washington, DC: Government Printing Office

———. 1938. *Underwriting Manual*. Washington, DC: Government Printing Office

———. 1946. *Underwriting Manual*. Washington, DC: Government Printing Office

———. 1952. *Underwriting Manual*. Washington, DC: Government Printing Office

———. 1958. *This Is the FHA*. Washington, DC: Government Printing Office

U.S. Government Accountability Office (GAO). 1983. *Siting on Hazardous Waste Landfills and Their Correlation with Racial and Economic Status of Surrounding Communities*. Report No. RCED-83-168, June 1. Washington, DC: U.S. GAO.

Wernette, Dee Richard, and Leslie A. Nieves. 1992. "Breathing Polluted Air: Minorities Are Disproportionately Exposed." *EPA Journal* 18 (1): 16–17.

Wilkins, David E., and Lomawaima, K. Tsianina. 2001. *Uneven Ground: American Indian Sovereignty and Federal Law*. Norman: University of Oklahoma Press.

Winant, Howard. 1994. *Racial Conditions: Policies, Theory, Comparison*. Minneapolis: University of Minnesota Press.

Wright, Beverly Hendrix. 1992. "The Effects of Occupational Injury, Illness, and Disease on the Health Status of Black Americans: A Review." *Race and the Incidence of Environmental Hazards*, 114–25.

Yinger, John. 1995. *Closed Doors, Opportunities Lost: The Continuing Challenge of Housing Discrimination*. New York: Basic Books.

———. 1998. "Evidence on Discrimination in Consumer Markets." *Journal of Economic Perspectives* 12 (2): 23–40.

3 NERVOUSNESS WITHIN INDIVIDUAL PUBLIC ADMINISTRATORS

Race is arguably the most difficult issue for people to discuss.
—The American Assembly (2001)

At the individual level, race and social equity, a "nervous area of government," shares certain attributes with emotional labor. It often necessitates an intentional management of one's professional self, even if it is artificial. It can involve pretending to feel a particular way or hiding emotions or feelings that may be viewed as inappropriate, especially in a professional or group setting. Puligesi and Shook (1997) examined how a group of employees managed their emotions at work. They considered the extent to which people had to mask their feelings to appear pleasant, were required to convey a friendly demeanor, and were able to express their true feelings to their colleagues. Building upon this work, Gibson (1997) examined the type and intensity of emotional experiences, and whether the emotions were displayed to others. The likelihood that an emotion would be expressed depended largely upon the specific type

Emotions are central states of the brain (LeDoux 1996). The array of emotions includes joy, happiness, love, anger, fear, and grief. Generally researchers agree that emotions have the following parts: subjective feelings, body responses, and expressive behavior. Subjective feelings include the way individuals experience feelings, and this component is the most difficult to describe or measure. Subjective feelings cannot be observed; instead the person experiencing the emotion must describe it to others (Advameg 2012). "Each person's description and interpretation of a feeling may be different. For example, two people falling in love will not experience or describe their feeling in exactly the same ways" (Advameg 2012).

Nervousness is commonly associated with fear. Although the experience of nervousness can be conscious, the brain mechanics generating fear and the appraisal of stimuli as fearful are unconscious and automatic, similar to any other body organ (LeDoux 1996). As explained by Bindra (1978) and Bolles and Fanselow (1980), fear is a perceptual, behavioral, and motivational state. The perception of danger motivates defensive behavior. Environmental stimuli that are perceived as potentially dangerous cause the body to initiate defensive behaviors (Rosen and Schulkin 1998).

While nervousness is an individual emotion, it is shaped by interpersonal relationships and environmental context. Nervousness can act as a language of performance or a dramatized commentary on collectively shared hardships or oppression (Davis and Whitten 1988; Low 1989; Sluka 1989), or what Finkler (1994) has called life's lesions. As Davis and Joakimsen remark, nervousness can operate as "lived experience as it affects and is affected by interpersonal relations and social action" (1997, 372).

Within the workplace, Hochschild defines emotional labor as "the management of feeling to create a publicly observable facial and bodily display" (1983, 7). Many researchers have examined the conditions under which individuals perform emotional labor and the extent to which such performance influence psychological well-being (see, for example, Bulan, Erickson, and Wharton 1997; Erickson and Wharton 1997; Leidner 1993; Pierce 1995; Pugliesi and Shook 1997; Wharton and Erickson 1995).

Specific to public administration, in their seminal book, *Emotional Labor: Putting the Service in Public Service,* Guy, Newman, and Mastracci (2008) describe emotional labor as "the component of the dynamic relationship between two people: worker and citizen or worker and worker" (5). As they further explain, emotional labor is not explicitly stated in job descriptions but rather understood and implied for many public service positions, such as social workers, 911 call operators, and police officers. "Emotional work exists on a continuum . . . with the range being from superficial expressions of friendliness to true expression or suppression of deeply felt emotions. Jobs that are most like retail sales encounters involve the left side of the continuum while jobs that involve protective services, human tragedy, and emergencies involve the right side" (Guy, Newman, and Mastracci 2008, 66). The costs and benefits of emotional labor are complex. Some of the common costs include worker fatigue, burnout, cynicism, and emotional exhaustion. Benefits include increased job satisfaction, empowerment, psychological well-being, and an increased sense of community and inclusion (Guy, Newman, and Mastracci 2008).

However, race and social equity is also quite distinct at both the individual and organizational levels (see chapter 4 for a discussion of the latter). Generally speaking, emotional labor is more occupation specific. Gender is also an important factor, with more women than men engaged in emotional labor (Erickson and Ritter 2001). By comparison, within the nervous area of government, the extent to which individual public administrators engage the issue of race at work is more directly linked to organizational leadership and culture and, outside the agency, to external events forcing the issue onto the public agency's agenda. The common link across individuals within public agencies is individual levels of fear—fear of saying the wrong thing about race, fear of being misunderstood, fear of what will be said next, fear of speaking up, fear of not participating in the discussion, fear of interacting with colleagues after the discussion, fear of being labeled a racist, fear of being labeled a race-baiter, fear of being isolated at work.

Race Talk at Work

A core defining characteristic of individual nervousness and race is fear regarding *oral communication about race at work.* Table 3.1 offers a useful list of indicators related to individual nervousness and race. These indicators can be used to self-assess oral and written communication apprehension related to engaging race at work. While specific organizational culture and context influence individual responses, Table 3.1 is designed to provide indicators of individual predisposition toward engaging in oral and written communication about race at work.

Apprehension affects skills attainment and performance (Bennett and Rhodes 1988; Bourhis and Allen 1992; Daly 1978). Individual public administrators enter their respective public agency every day with a baseline level of comfort or discomfort in engaging in communication about race. Shaped by a complex array of factors—including, for example, individual preferences, family background and attitudes, historical influences, cultural and societal influences, geographical norms, workplace culture, previous work experiences in communicating about race, security in communication expression, and general topical interest—individual public administrators daily bring to public service a level of comfort or apprehension in communicating about race, which forms the basis of their individual nervousness at work.

This individual baseline level of nervousness has very practical implications. It influences the degree to which a public administrator is likely to raise, promote, engage, and assess or evaluate racial equity in the administration of public services within their agency. Absent other motivators, such as compliance-related reporting, legal activity or queries, political or grassroots influences, the individual baseline level of nervousness provides an indicator of how likely or unlikely a public administrator is to independently promote racial equity in the provision of government services at work. It also provides some indication of an individual's predisposition to ignore or actively address racial inequities in the provision of public services. One of the most common ways for individuals to manage nervousness is to avoid situations that make them nervous. For example, those who get nervous engaging in public speaking try to minimize or avoid doing so. Similarly, individuals who get nervous communicating about

Table 3.1

Individual Oral and Written Communication Race-at-Work Nervousness Indicators

	Response Scale (Strongly Disagree (SD) = 1, Strongly Agree (SA) = 5)				
Oral Communication					
1. I am calm and relaxed while participating in group discussions about race at work.	SD	D	N	A	SA
2. I am afraid to express myself about race in meetings at work. (R)	SD	D	N	A	SA
3. Communicating about race in meetings at work usually makes me feel uncomfortable. (R)	SD	D	N	A	SA
4. In presenting data about race at work, I forget facts I really know. (R)	SD	D	N	A	SA
5. I like to get involved in group discussions about race at work.	SD	D	N	A	SA
6. I am very calm when called upon to express an opinion about race at a meeting at work.	SD	D	N	A	SA
7. I am very relaxed when answering questions about race at work.	SD	D	N	A	SA
8. Certain parts of my body feel very tense and rigid while talking about race at work.	SD	D	N	A	SA
9. My thoughts become confused and jumbled when I talk about race at work. (R)	SD	D	N	A	SA
10. I have no fear of engaging in conversations about race at work.	SD	D	N	A	SA
Written Communication					
11. It makes me nervous to write about race in a work-related report. (R)	SD	D	N	A	SA
12. It's easy for me to write about race in a work-related report.	SD	D	N	A	SA
13. I look forward to working on projects about race at work.	SD	D	N	A	SA
14. I avoid writing about race in reports for work. (R)	SD	D	N	A	SA
15. I am afraid of writing reports about race at work. (R)	SD	D	N	A	SA

Source: Adapted from Bline et al. (2003).

Note: (R) indicates reverse coding. In administering this questionnaire, higher scores (ex., SA=5) denote less nervousness. For the items with an (R), the coding is reversed meaning lower scores (ex., SD= 1) denote less nervousness.

race at work will minimize or avoid raising race-related topics, such as service inequities by race, agency fina cial and resource allocation differentials by race, or differences in public agency personnel support by race.

Consider a scenario in which a public agency is making decisions about where to invest economic development resources. The historical pattern of the agency is to disproportionally invest agency resources in white communities.

An individual public administrator who is nervous communicating about race at work is less likely to call attention to these agency-based racial inequities, even if he or she recognizes them. The thought may remain in the back of his or her mind, rather than actively communicated within the public agency. The individual level of nervousness also affects the strength and the magnitude of this type of communication. Will the individual express the concern at all? Raise the issue once in an agency meeting? Request a racial equity analysis of the provision of previous resources before proceeding with the current allocation? Or work to institutionalize racial equity analysis as standard for all agency allocations? The level of individual public administrators' nervousness has a direct influence on the degree to which racial equity analysis becomes part of the status quo in the delivery of public services.

For many individuals, talking about race in groups is not easy. Individuals who find it difficult to talk about race cite the risk of being misunderstood or experiencing social sanction. While engaging in race talk at work can be challenging for individuals of all racial and ethnic groups, it is particularly true for whites. "Whites, while socialized in a racially constructed world, are taught not to be aware of themselves in racial terms" (Carter 1997, 199). Research shows that many whites are anxious during interracial contact and are hesitant to engage in it, even when it is relevant and reasonable to do so (see, for example, Blascovich et al. 2001; Ickes 1984; Norton et al. 2006; Pollock 2004; Shelton and Richeson 2006; Stephan and Stephan 2001).

Individual engagement in race talk facilitates intergroup dialogue that can promote racial equity in the administration of public services. Such conversational engagement challenges misconceptions and stereotypes (Geranios 1997; Zúñiga and Sevig 1997); develops increased personal awareness and understanding of social group membership (Nagda et al. 1999; Zúñiga et al. 1996); develops more complex ways of thinking (Gurin et al. 1999; Lopez, Gurin, and Nagda 1998); builds skills for communicating and working through differences; and identifie ways of taking actions to promote social equity (Gooden 2011).

> Vocabulary is not just a list, but is a system of words and expressions that indicate differences of kind and degree among the emotions. Discursively articulated emotions such as irritation . . . are not only acts in themselves, but often they may initiate further acts in the form of verbal or physical signs. Even mild displays appear to signal that if one does not take note of this now there may be trouble ahead. (Mangham 1998, 57)

When faced with the opportunity to talk about race at work, nervousness may ensue and individuals may rely upon an array of common strategies to assist them in navigating the conversation. Table 3.2 provides a continuum of some of the more common strategies individuals use when discussing race.

Table 3.2

Race Talk Strategies

Ineffective

Strategy	Description	Example
Conversation avoidance	Race is not discussed; race is viewed as a divisive subject that is best not discussed	"Let's not focus on race. Rather, let's focus on . . ."
Strategic colorblindness	Individual does not "see" or acknowledge race differences	"Race is not a factor here. I do not even see race." "People are people, I don't see color."
Assimilation	Individual seeks to identify a homogenous culture; typically often based upon dominant or majority culture	"We have to keep in mind that most of our clients . . ."
Conversational variability	Individual strategically shifts comments to align with perceived social acceptability	"I'm not prejudiced but . . ." "Well, yes and no . . ."
Personal experience	Experiences reported by individual public administrator become representative of general client experiences of particular group; anecdotes operate as reliable data	"In my neighborhood . . ." "The experience of my children is . . ."
Cultural pluralism	Racial and ethnic differences recognized and appreciated; practical approaches to serving multiple publics is minimized or ignored	"Cost and time are not a factor. We must . . ."
Multicultural mosaic	Racial and ethnic differences understood within a broad institutional, structural, and societal context; need to effectively work across differences is recognized and valued	"The racial differences we see in our program outcomes today are the result of many important historical and institutional factors. . . ."

Effective

Conversational Avoidance

Conversations about race can be uncomfortable. Rather than run the risk of offending another person or saying the wrong thing, some individual public administrators may avoid talking about race and ethnicity altogether. In difficult conversations, individuals can feel alienated, misunderstood, attacked, and even victimized (Stone, Patton, and Heen 1999).

> When a conversation that involves an aspect of a person's social identity and group allegiance is between people with varied social identities, the potential for misunderstanding increases. Differences in social identity do not involve "difference," but also represent societal inequities of power, privilege and oppression. (Miller, Donner, and Fraser 2004, 377)

So, if talking about race is difficult for public administrators, why should we do it? Discomfort, nervousness, and even pain are elements of racial dialogues. However, there are important individual and public sector consequences for avoiding race talk. Individuals who continuously avoid such conversations remain developmentally immature. Similar to the individual who avoids technology, society continues to move forward. The social knowledge gap continues to increase, and individuals who avoid race talk will not miraculously one day find themselves able to comfortably engage in conversations about race. As others become more comfortable, those who avoid such conversations fall even further behind.

As public administrators in a democracy, avoiding race talk conversations specific to the administration of public services contravenes our professional values. "People who serve the public in government and nonprofit organizations have a special responsibility to make certain that there is 'justice for all'" (Johnson and Svara 2011, 4). Promoting justice for all requires active engagement in conversations about race by public administrators in their respective agencies. This strategy is most ineffective because it eliminates race as a discussion topic.

Strategic Colorblindness

One approach many whites adopt is strategic colorblindness—lack of acknowledgment of any racial difference—in an effort to avoid the appearance of bias (Apfelbaum, Sommers, and Norton 2008). While race is among the first, quickest, and most automatic dimensions people use to categorize others (Ito and Urland 2003; Montepare and Opeyo 2002), whites, in particular, frequently claim an inability to do so (Norton et al. 2006). Individuals who utilize strategic colorblindness are especially concerned with how others would react to the appearance of prejudice (Apfelbaum, Sommers, and Norton 2008). Interestingly, their findings also suggest that whites' intention of using colorblind behavior to prevent the appearance of prejudice—and, more generally, to promote positive interracial interaction—often backfires. In fact, it leads to negative interpersonal perceptions on the part of blacks and is generally indicative of greater racial prejudice (929). "One practical implication of these findings for intergroup relations is straightforward: in situations where race is potentially relevant, Whites who think that avoiding race altogether will shield them from being perceived as biased should think again" (93). This behavior yields an important discrepancy between the perception of race and the acknowledgment of racial differences in a social or professional context.

Use of strategic colorblindness by public administrators facilitates the unspoken implication that because individuals do not "see" race, it is not a viable factor to consider in the administration of public services. Within this strategy, the larger context of racism and discrimination is external and largely irrelevant to providing specific public services. It permits engagement of others in abstract, general discussions about public services to all rather than to explore the effects of power, privilege, and racism in the current provision of public services. Strategic colorblindness denies that the construction of race has any meaning in people's lives and the public services they receive.

Public administrators who employ this strategy use the "anything but race" explanation in their conversations. For example, employees within a state department of education are discussing local school systems that are virtually all white, all Latino, or all black. These discussions occur in a colorblind context with differences attributed only to differences in economic context, without any acknowledgement of race or ethnicity.

Assimilation

Individuals who engage in race talk by using an assimilationist or melting pot strategy approach the discussion by seeking to identify a single ideal, homogenous culture. For example, they may utilize this assimilationist language to focus the discussion on "societal expectations" regarding individual performance and merit. They fail to assess the personal, institutional, or cultural impact of assimilation for those who are "different" (Young 1990). By failing to recognize their own distinctiveness, majority group members regard their values as the universal reality (Nagda and Zúñiga 2003).

Public administrators who are guided by melting pot strategies approach their conversations, analysis, and recommendations through the lens of one public rather than multiple publics. For example, when discussing Web-based services offered to public agency clients, individuals engaging the discussion using an assimilation strategy may remark, "The vast majority of the people we serve have Internet access." While this statement may be factually true, it casually minimizes the agency's public service obligations to clients who do not have such access and the racial patterns within this minority group of clients. When these same patterns occur over time, with similar patterns, there is a cumulative racial bias in the public services provided.

Conversational Variability

Conversational variability permits individuals to strategically shift their verbal expressions based on context. "Interaction in conversation is fluid, variable, and uncertain because once dialogue is initiated, each interlocutor speaks into spaces created by the other and the final outcome of the conversation can never be known in advance" (Barnes, Palmary, and Durrheim 2001, 324). This means an individual can shift his or her opinion to maintain the impression of being antiracist, resulting in variability in the expression of opinions (Potter and Wetherell 1987). Conversational variability permits the speaker to negotiate conversational space about race, based on perceived receptivity of the group. Van Dijk (1984) further claims that when individuals talk about sensitive topics such as race, the use of rhetorical devices is unavoidable because a core challenge is to manage potentially racist comments while distancing the speaker from inferences of racism.

Conversational variability facilitates individual public administrator elusiveness. It permits individuals to act as a chameleon, expressing shifting messages regarding racial equity in their agency depending upon the setting and audience. An individual public administrator may verbally express one set of statements to senior management, another set to colleagues or line staff, and yet a third to citizens and residents.

Personal Experience

Individuals may share personal experiences about race, racism, or racial groups that cannot be externally verified. By drawing upon personal experience, the speaker positions himself or herself as an observer and subsequent reporter of facts and events. Such facts are based on justifiable anecdotes that may or may not reinforce stereotypes. Utilizing this strategy, the role of the audience is to accept these facts' value as true. In practice, however, these personal anecdotes operate as generalizations. The behavior of some individuals is directed toward and becomes representative of the larger group to which those individuals belong (van Dijk 1987).

Individual public administrator use of personal experience can inappropriately influence the direction of the organization. This is particularly true when personal experience operates as an acceptable substitute for decision-making based upon agency data. Consider a situation in which a local governmental agency is examining its record in providing prompt snow removal services. One colleague raises this as a potential issue for the agency to examine, expressing concerns that minority neighborhoods may receive snow removal services inferior to those of white neighborhoods. As the conversation ensues, both white and minority public administrators who work in the agency exchange personal experiences about their snow removal. At the end of their exchange, they conclude that, based on their experiences (based largely on the location of their individual homes), there is no discernible racial pattern in the snow removal services provided by their agency. By the end of the meeting, the agency director concludes there is no need to explore agency performance in this area any further. The personal experience data shifts this item off the agency work list. The problem in this scenario is that rather than provide a racial analysis of the agency's snow removal performance using empirical data, reported personal experiences operate, in effect, as factual truths.

Cultural Pluralism

Within cultural pluralism, diverse groups maintain their distinctiveness while living in a multicultural/ethnic society. Individuals who employ cultural pluralism in their race talk acknowledge that increased knowledge about other racial groups, cultures, and traditions can reduce prejudice and stereotype. Cultural pluralism is beneficial in that those who take this approach to race talk value racial and ethnic differences, rather than seeing them as a distraction, threatening, or divisive. An important concern with cultural pluralism, however, is that it does not offer a practical approach for engaging racial/ethnic groups in mutual coexistence (Nagda and Zúñiga 2003).

Additionally, cultural pluralism can lose its effectiveness when the discussion replaces important discussions of racial disparities with a more comfortable discussion on class, urban, or inner city factors. This shift in language avoids a discussion of race and replaces it with a less nervous area of discussion, such as class.

Ultimately, public administrators are responsible for providing equitable services to the clients they serve. At any given time, multiple publics are being served, and these publics coexist. The delivery of public services is made with consideration of staffing capacity, fiscal constraints, and political realities. Approaches designed to promote social equity will have to consider the complexities of these factors while continuously making significant progress

Multicultural Mosaic

With an explicit recognition that oppression exists and is carried out through structural, institutional, and social arrangements, the multicultural mosaic strategy "emphasizes the interweaving nature of human relationships where both cultural distinctiveness and the need to work across differences" is important (Nagda and Zúñiga 2003, 112). Public administrators who utilize this strategy explicitly research and acknowledge the institutional factors that influence current-day public service patterns that di fer by race.

Conclusion

This chapter examines the concept of nervousness in individual public adminis-trators. Many aspects of public service have an important emotional context. A key component of examining issues relative to race within public administration is the need to have effective race talk at the individual level within public sector organizations. Too often, these conversations do not occur because there is an overarching context of discomfort, apprehension, and fear—all attributes of nervousness. This context of fear is ineffective in that it thwarts essential discus-sions needed to advance social equity in the administration of public services. Rather than discussing race, individuals develop and employ multiple strate-gies to explicitly avoid discussing race, in an attempt to shift the conversation to more comfortable ground. However, if race is not discussed by individual public administrators within an agency, analyzing and improving racial equity in the delivery of public services is unlikely to occur.

Conversations operate as connectors. At the individual level, conversations among public administrators connect them with each other and to the diverse public they serve. "Individuals expect their verbal interactions to accomplish conversational goals, and pursue linguistic strategies which vary as a function of the situation, the other participants, and social relations among participants" (Woodilla 1998, 36). Engaging in conversations about race at work can be uncomfortable and challenging. Such conversations are a core challenge for a nervous area of government. With the aforementioned difficulties in engaging in discussions about race, "productive interracial communication is rendered difficult, if not impossible, at times" (Rich 1974). In particular, the first three strategies in Table 3.2 are particularly problematic because they allow individu-als to avoid discussion of the inequitable distribution of power and privilege that undergirds the administration and distribution of public services. Instead, it keeps the conversation on "nonracial" ground that may be more comfortable for individual conversation participants. So, why should public administrators even engage in conversations about race, given this difficulty

Conversations, dialogues, and meetings about race, racism, and the administration of public services offer individuals an opportunity to have an increased understanding of the role social identity and group membership plays in the provision, administration, and delivery of public services. "Emotions are crucial in making us aware of the 'peculiarly *human* reality' of a specific situation" (Vetlesen 1994, 190). Such conversations form the basis of "democratic conversations"—interactions that invite multiple perspectives while acknowledging the institutional and structural context in which they are based (Schultz, Buck, and Niesz 2000). From such conversations and meetings, learning can occur that results in a better understanding of and appreciation for the differing historical and social circumstances that directly impact (both positively and negatively) present-day public services. Ultimately, the aggregate effect of improved individual-level understanding of the role of race in the administration of public services should lead to intentional, specific organizational actions that will eliminate racial inequities in the administration of public services.

References

Advameg. 2012. "Emotions." *Human Diseases and Conditions.* www.humanillnesses. com/Behavioral-Health-Br-Fe/Emotions.html (accessed August 6, 2012).

The American Assembly. 2001. *Racial Equality: Public Policies for the Twenty-first Century.* Report, Ninety-eighth American Assembly, April 19–22, Harriman, New York. http://americanassembly.org/publication/racial-equality-public-policies-twenty-first-centur .

Apfelbaum, Evan P., Samuel R. Sommers, and Michael I. Norton. 2008. "Seeing Race and Seeming Racist? Evaluating Strategic Colorblindness in Social Interaction." *Journal of Personality and Social Psychology* 95 (4): 918–32.

Barnes, Brendon, Ingrid Palmary, and Kevin Durrheim. 2001. "The Denial of Racism: The Role of Humor, Personal Experience, and Self-Censorship." *Journal of Language and Social Psychology* 20 (3): 321–38.

Bennett, Kaye, and Steven C. Rhodes. 1988. "Writing Apprehension and Writing Intensity in Business and Industry." *Journal of Business Communication* 25 (1): 25–39.

Bindra, Dalbir. 1978. "How Adaptive Behavior Is Produced: A Perceptual-Motivational Alternative to Response-Reinforcement." *Behavioral and Brain Sciences* 1 (1): 41–91.

Blascovich, Jim, Wendy Berry Mendes, Sarah B. Hunter, Brian Lickel, and Neneh Kowai-Bell. 2001. "Perceiver Threat in Social Interactions with Stigmatized Others." *Journal of Personality and Social Psychology* 80 (2): 253–67.

Bline, Dennis, Dana Lowe, Wilda Meixner, and Hossein Nouri. 2003. "Measurement Data on Commonly Used Scales to Measure Oral Communication and Writing Apprehensions." *Journal of Business Communication* 40 (4): 266–88.

Bolles, Robert C., and Michael S. Fanselow. 1980. "A Perceptual-Defensive Recuperative Model of Fear and Pain." *Behavioral and Brain Sciences* 3 (2): 291–323.

Bourhis, John, and Mike Allen. 1992. "Meta-analysis of the Relationship Between Communication Apprehension and Cognitive Performance." *Communication Education* 41 (1): 68–76.

Bulan, Heather F., Rebecca J. Erickson, and Amy S. Wharton. 1997. "Doing for Others on the Job: The Affective Requirements of Service Work, Gender, and Emotional Well-Being." *Social Problems* 44 (2): 701–23.

Carter, Robert T. 1997. "Is White a Race? Expressions of White Racial Identity." In *Off White: Readings on Race, Power, and Society,* ed. Michelle Fine, Lois Weis, Linda C. Powell, and L. Mun Wong, 198–209. New York: Routledge.

Daly, John A. 1978. "Writing Apprehension and Writing Competency." *Journal of Educational Research* 72 (1): 10–14.

Davis, Dona Lee, and Lisa Moe Joakimsen. 1997. "Nerves as Status and Nerves as Stigma: Idioms of Distress and Social Action in Newfoundland and Northern Norway." *Qualitative Health Research* 7 (3): 370–90.

Davis, Dona Lee, and Richard Whitten. 1988. "Medical and Popular Traditions of Nerves." *Social Science and Medicine* 26 (12): 1209–22.

Erickson, Rebecca J., and Christian Ritter. 2001. "Emotional Labor, Burnout, and Inauthenticity: Does Gender Matter?" *Social Psychology Quarterly* 64 (2): 146-63.

Erickson, Rebecca J., and Amy S. Wharton. 1997. "Inauthenticity and Depression: Assessing the Consequences of Interactive Service Work." *Work and Occupations* 24 (2): 188–213.

Finkler, Kaja. 1994. *Women in Pain: Gender and Morbidity in Mexico.* Philadelphia: University of Pennsylvania.

Geranios, Christine. 1997. "Cognitive, Affective and Behavioral Outcomes of Multicultural Courses and Intergroup Dialogues in Higher Education." Unpublished doctoral dissertation, Arizona State University.

Gibson, Donald A. 1997. "The Struggle for Reason: The Sociology of Emotions in Organizations." In *Social Perspectives on Emotion,* ed. Rebecca J. Erickson and Beverley Cuthbertson-Johnson, 211–56. Greenwich, CT: Emerald Group.

Gooden, Susan T. 2011. "Assessing Agency Performance: The Wisconsin Experience." In *Justice for All: Promoting Social Equity in Public Administration,* ed. Norman Johnson and James Svara, 228–46. Armonk, NY: M.E. Sharpe.

Gurin, Patricia, Timothy Peng, Gretchen E. Lopez, and Biren A. Nagda. 1999. "Context, Identity, and Intergroup Relations." In *Cultural Divides: Understanding and Overcoming Group Conflict,* ed. Deborah Prentice and Dale Miller, 133–70. New York: Russell Sage Foundation.

Guy, Mary E., Meredith A. Newman, and Sharon H. Mastracci. 2008. *Emotional Labor: Putting the Service in Public Service.* Armonk, NY: M.E. Sharpe.

Hochschild, Arlie Russell. 1983. *The Managed Heart.* Berkeley: University of California Press.

Ickes, William 1984. "Compositions in Black and White: Determinants of Interaction in Interracial Dyads." *Journal of Personality and Social Psychology* 47 (2): 330–41.

Ito, Tiffany A., and Geoffrey R. Urland. 2003. "Race and Gender on the Brain: Electrocortical Measures of Attention to the Race and Gender of Multiply Categorizable Individuals." *Journal of Personality and Social Psychology* 85 (4): 616–26.

Johnson, Norman J., and James H. Svara. 2011. "Social Equity in American Society and Public Administration." In *Justice for All: Promoting Social Equity in Public Administration,* ed. Norman J. Johnson and James H. Svara. Armonk, NY: M.E. Sharpe.

LeDoux, Joseph E. 1996. *The Emotional Brain*. New York: Simon & Schuster.

Leidner, Robin. 1993. *Fast Food, Fast Talk: Service Work and the Routinization of Everyday Life*. Berkeley: University of California Press.

Lopez, Gretchen E., Patricia Gurin, and Biren A. Nagda. 1998. "Education and Understanding Structural Causes for Group Inequalities." *Journal of Political Psychology* 19 (2): 305–29.

Low, Setha M. 1989. "Gender, Emotion and *Nervios* in Urban Guatemala." In *Gender, Health, and Illness: The Case of Nerves*, ed. Dona L. Davis and Setha M. Low, 23–48. New York: Hemisphere.

Mangham, Iain L. 1998. "Emotional Discourse in Organizations." In *Discourse and Organization*, ed. David Grant, Tom Keenoy, and Cliff Oswick, 51–64. London: Sage.

Miller, Joshua, Susan Donner, and Edith Fraser. 2004. "Talking When Talking Is Tough: Taking on Conversations About Race, Sexual Orientation, Gender, Class, and Other Aspects of Identity." *Smith College Studies in Social Work* 74 (2): 377–92.

Montepare, Joann M., and Almanzia Opeyo. 2002. "The Relative Salience of Physiognomic Cues in Differentiating Faces: A Methodological Tool." *Journal of Nonverbal Behavior* 26 (1): 43–59.

Nagda, Biren (Ratnesh) A., and Ximena Zúñiga. 2003. "Fostering Meaningful Racial Engagement Through Intergroup Dialogues." *Group Processes & Intergroup Relations* 6 (1): 111–28.

Nagda, Biren A., Margaret Spearmon, Lynn C. Holly, Scott Harding, Mary Lou Balassone, Dominique Mosie-Swanson, and Stan De Mello. 1999. "Intergroup Dialogues: An Innovative Approach to Teaching About Diversity and Justice in Social Work Programs." *Journal of Social Work Education* 35 (3): 433–49.

Norton, Michael I., Samuel R. Sommers, Evan P. Apfelbaum, Natassia Pura, and Dan Ariely. 2006. "Color Blindness and Interracial Interaction: Playing the Political Correctness Game." *Psychological Science* 17 (11): 949–53.

Peri, Josep Maria, and Xavier Torres. 1999. "Modelos cognitivos y trastornos de ansiedad." [Cognitive Models and Anxiety Disorders]. *Ansiedad y Estrés* 5 (2, 3): 285–98.

Pierce, Jennifer L. 1995. *Gender Trials: Emotional Lives in Contemporary Law Firms*. Berkeley: University of California Press.

Pollock, Mica. 2004. *Colormute*. Princeton, NJ: Princeton University Press.

Potter, Jonathan, and Margaret Wetherell. 1987. *Discourse and Social Psychology: Beyond Attitudes and Behavior*. London: Sage.

Pugliesi, Karen, and Scott L. Shook. 1997. "Gender, Jobs, and Emotional Labor in a Complex Organization." In *Social Perspectives on Emotion*, 4th ed., ed. Rebecca J. Erickson and Beverley Cuthbertson-Johnson, 283–316. Greenwich, CT: JAI.

Rich, Andrea L. 1974. *Interracial Communication*. New York: Harper & Row.

Rosen, Jeffrey B., and Jay Schulkin. 1998. "From Normal Fear to Pathological Anxiety." *Psychological Review* 105 (2): 325–50.

Schultz, Katherine, Patricia Buck, and Tricia Niesz. 2000. "Democratizing Conversations: Racialized Talk in a Post-Desegregated Middle School." *American Educational Research Journal* 37 (1): 33–69.

Shelton, J. Nicole, and Jennifer A. Richeson. 2006. "Interracial Interactions: A Relational Approach." In *Advances in Experimental Social Psychology*, ed. Mark P. Zanna, 121–81. New York: Academic Press.

Sluka, Jeffrey 1989. "Living on Their Nerves: Nervous Debility in Northern Ireland."

In *Gender, Health, and Illness: The Case of Nerves,* ed. Dona L. Davis and Setha M. Low, 127–52. New York: Hemisphere.

Stephan, Walter G., and Cookie White Stephan. 2001. *Improving Intergroup Relations.* Thousand Oaks, CA: Sage.

Stone, Douglas, Bruce Patton, and Sheila Heen. 1999. *Difficult Conversations: How to Discuss What Matters Most.* New York: Viking.

van Dijk, Teun A. 1984. *Prejudice in Discourse.* Amsterdam: John Benjamins.

———. 1987. *Communicating Racism.* Newbury Park, CA: Sage.

Vetlesen, A.J. 1994. *Perception, Empathy, and Judgment: An Inquiry into the Preconditions of Moral Performance.* University Park: Pennsylvania State University Press.

Wharton, Amy S., and Rebecca J. Erickson. 1995. "The Consequences of Caring: Exploring the Links Between Women's Job and Family Emotion Work." *Sociological Quarterly* 36 (2): 273–96.

Woodilla, Jill. 1998. "Workplace Conversations: The Text of Organizing." In *Discourse and Organization,* ed. David Grant, Tom Keenoy, and Cliff Oswick, 31–50. London: Sage.

Young, Iris Marion. 1990. *Justice and the Politics of Difference.* Princeton, NJ: Princeton University Press.

Zúñiga, Ximena, and Todd D. Sevig. 1997. "Bridging the 'Us/Them' Divide Through Intergroup Dialogues and Peer Leadership." *Diversity Factor* 6 (2): 23–28.

Zúñiga, Ximena, Carolyn M. Vasques, Todd D. Sevig, and Biren A. Nagda. 1996. "Dismantling the Walls: Peer-Facilitated Inter-Race/Ethnic Dialogue Processes and Experiences." Program on Conflict Management Alternatives Working Paper Series no. 49, University of Michigan.

4 NERVOUSNESS IN PUBLIC SECTOR ORGANIZATIONS

Race is the great taboo in our society. We are afraid to talk about it. White folks fear their unspoken views will be deemed racist. People of color are filled with sorrow and rage at unrighted wrongs. Drowning in silence, we are brothers and sisters drowning each other. Once we decide to transform ourselves from fearful caterpillars into courageous butterflies, we will be able to bridge the racial gulf and move forward together towards a bright and colorful future.

—Eva Paterson, president and founder of the
Equal Justice Society

Engaging in conversations about race at an individual level is a necessary, but not sufficient, condition to addressing racial inequities in the services provided by public sector organizations. Nervousness at the organizational level must be understood and addressed as well. This chapter expands the concept of individual nervousness to public sector organizations. Organizations have powerful cultures that define, shape, steer, and direct the work they perform. Organizational culture particularly influences the agency's willingness to perform racial-equity analysis of the services it provides. Within that culture, nervousness in public sector organizations exists throughout five key areas: organizational values and goals; organizational socialization; organizational leadership and change; organizational discourse; and organizational learning and performance. After a brief discussion of organizational culture, this chapter considers each of these areas in turn.

Organizational Culture

There are several definitions of organizational culture. Goffman (1959, 1967) and Van Maanen (1979) define it as observed behavioral regularities when people interact, such as the language used and the rituals around deference and demeanor. Deal and Kennedy (1982) conceptualize it as the dominant values espoused by an organization. Schein (1968, 1978), Van Maanen (1976, 1979), and Ritti and Funkhouser (1982) define culture as the rules of the game for getting along in an organization; and Tagiuri and Litwin (1968) define it as the feeling or climate that is conveyed in an organization by the physical layout and the way in which members of the organization interact with outsiders. According to Schein (1985), culture is a body of solutions to problems that have worked consistently and are transmitted to new members as the correct way to perceive, think about, and feel in relation to those problems. These shared assumptions and norms bind an organization together. Marcoulides and Heck contend that "an organization's collective culture influences both the attitudes and subsequent behaviors of its employees, as well as the level of performance the organization achieves" (1993, 211).

Schein (1985) distinguishes various levels of culture. Artifacts are the most visible level. Included in this level are written and spoken language, constructed physical and social environment, and art. The next level, values, includes a sense of what ought to be in an organization. They reflect social consensus. The final level includes underlying assumptions—the taken-for-granted, invisible norms of behavior. "In fact, if a basic assumption is strongly held in a group, members would find behavior based on any other premise inconceivable" (Schein 1985, 17).

An organization's culture is a force that strongly influences organizational behavior, but it also provides an important cultural framework for individuals (Chao and Moon 2005).

> From the organizational culture perspective, the personal preferences of organizational members are not restrained by systems of formal rules, authority, and by norms of rational behavior. Instead they are controlled by cultural norms, values, beliefs, and assumptions. In order to understand or predict how an organization will behave under varying circumstances, one must know and understand the organization's patterns of basic assumptions—its organizational culture. (Shafritz and Ott 1992, 482)

Public sector organizations transmit messages regarding appropriate or inappropriate norms and behaviors related to race and social equity. Cultural norms within the agency affect discussions about and analysis of racial equity. They determine, for example, the extent to which race is examined directly or indirectly. Indirect examinations include broader categorical analysis that provides racial substitutes, such as use of the terms "urban," "disadvantaged populations," or "underserved populations." Cultural norms that promote direct examination of race support an atmosphere of more specificity—examining, for example, experiences by specific racial or ethnic groups, offering a more complex and nuanced examination of public sector outcomes.

In order to understand the nervous area of government within a particular agency, it is important to develop a baseline of the organization's orientation regarding race and social equity by performing a cultural audit. A cultural audit can offer an important assessment of the agency's core assumptions and current cultural state. The agency director is in the best position to make the cultural audit a clear priority. Claver et al. (1999) include the following eight factors in providing this diagnosis: (1) making a diagnosis of the present culture; (2) explaining the need for modifications; (3) defining the values desired; (4) involving management; (5) making collaborators aware of this new need; (6) changing the symbols; (7) changing training programs to incorporate the new values; and (8) periodically revising the values. The primary goals of a cultural audit are to examine cultural artifacts and determine their consistency with espoused values and assumptions; to identify conflicts in espoused and actual beliefs and values; to re-examine deeply held assumptions and identify their validity; and to develop an action plan for addressing inconsistencies in any of the cultural levels (Testa and Sipe 2011, 6).

Performing a cultural audit requires an organization to identify its vision, mission, values, and strategic goals; provide a description of the desired culture; select an audit team; collect data; interpret and report the findings. A cultural audit is most appropriately viewed as a tool to provide a gap analysis between the desired organizational culture and the actual organizational culture. Table 4.1 provides an example of a cultural audit summary sheet. The results of a cultural audit should lead to specific modifications in standards, principles or values, and observable behaviors that promote racial equity.

Organizational Values and Goals

Nearly all conceptualizations of culture embody a values component. While organizational values can differ, certain values are central to public administration, such as efficiency and effectiveness. Similarly, all public sector organizations share a value commitment to justice. "Justice matters when actions or decisions by people within organizations potentially benefit or harm the interests of some individuals or groups in a differential manner (Sheppard, Lewicki, and Minton, 1992, ix). This is particularly important for public organizations that are entrusted to serve "the people" in totality.

Justice is guided by two core principles: balance and correctness. The principle of balance requires a judgment that compares a given action against similar actions in similar situations. Correctness is the quality that makes the decision seem "right." This determination includes consistency, accuracy, clarity, and procedural thoroughness (Sheppard, Lewicki, and Minton 1992). Decisions that unduly benefit or harm some individuals or groups at the expense of others

Table 4.1

Race and Social Equity Cultural Audit Summary Sheet Example

Culture Category	What to Look for	Example Gaps
1. Physical characteristics and general environment What do the physical components of the department say about its racial equity?	• Wall hangings • Symbols and logos • Program website • Brochures • Agency reports	• Website contains racially diverse photos, but very limited mention of racial equity goals or outcomes in agency reports.
Specific actions to be taken (specify time frame; e.g., next month, six months, year)		
2. Policies, procedures, and structures What do the agency's policies, procedures, and structures say about the importance of racial equity?	• Mission statement • Units within the agency where racial equity work occurs • Linkage of these units to agency at large • Routinization of racial impact analysis of agency procedures and policies	• Units within the agency where racial equity work occurs are marginalized within the agency. The same units receive limited financial resources. • Racial impact analysis of agency procedures does not formally occur.
Specific actions to be taken (specify time frame)		
3. Socialization • What regular behaviors and expectations are in place that affect the culture relative to racial equity? • What impact do these have on the clients the agency serves? • Is consideration of racial equity a norm or priority within the agency? • How are employees socialized to think (or not think) about the racial impact of public services provided? *Specific actions to be taken (specify time frame)*	• Presentation of racial equity data by program area • Presentation of racial equity client data through statistics, audit studies, mapping, and interviews/focus groups • Clear relationship between racial equity data and agency action • Formal and informal agency rules and norms that foster racial equity analysis	• Limited presentation of racial equity data. • Racial equity analysis not required by agency. • Results from racial equity analysis do not impact actions and practices of agency—data is informational only.

(continued)

Table 4.1 *(continued)*

Culture Category	What to Look for	Example Gaps
4. Leadership Behavior • What level of priority do agency leaders give to racial equity? • How does this impact culture? • Are senior leaders who value racial equity respected? *Actions to be taken (specify time frame)*	• Articulation of organizational justice values • Allocation of personnel and budgetary resources to racial equity work	• Priority of racial equity work within agency is sporadic and varies by leader. • No sustained racial equity initiatives over time. • No positions or units expressly dedicated to equity/justice work.
5. Rewards and Recognition • How are reductions in racial inequities acknowledged and rewarded? • How does this impact culture? • Are racial equity champions recognized and respected? • What are the typical circumstances under which racial equity champions exit the organization, and how are they treated when they leave? *Actions to be taken (specify time frame)*	• Administrator and employee performance reviews • Types and quantity of rewards offered • Types of formal and informal recognition within the agency	• No formal or informal recognition of racial equity–related work. • Employees engaging in racial equity work typically become "casualties." • Such employees are either forced out or burn out. • Limited or no mention/recognition by organization of racial equity work when racial equity champions leave the organization.

6. Discourse		
- How are messages regarding racial equity formally and informally communicated? - How is the agency's history relative to racial equity understood and communicated? - Do employees speak up on the importance of racial equity?	- Conversations about racial equity in the provision of public services commonly occur within the organization - Organization's history and commitment to racial equity are displayed prominently on the agency website - Racial equity analysis is a routine component of program evaluation and assessment - Conversations about racial equity are progressive in nature; employees can articulate racial equity work with analytical depth	- Conversations about racial equity in the provision of public services are sporadic. - Employees are reluctant to discuss areas of racial inequity. - Employees who do discuss areas of racial inequity are not generally respected or are viewed as "troublemakers." - Agency's historical and current record in terms of racial equity is largely unknown and not discussed.

Actions to be taken (specify time frame)

7. Learning and performance		
- What is the agency's reputation regarding racial equity? - Does the organization demonstrate innovation in racial equity approach? - How does the organization's performance of racial equity work compare to leading governmental organizations that are engaged in this work?	- Organization supports and encourages racial equity analysis - Employees are encouraged to seek out and adopt "best practices" in racial equity work - Organization routinely receives requests from other agencies about its racial equity work - Organization's racial equity work receives external recognition from peers.	- Agency not viewed as a leader in racial equity work among peers. - Agency's racial equity performance is not routinely assessed, evaluated, or reported.

Actions to be taken (specify time frame)

Source: Inspired by Testa and Sipe 2011.

are unfair. For fairness to exist, public agency practice must pass tests at three levels: "the level of the outcome itself, the procedure that generated and implemented the outcome, and the system within which the outcome and procedure was embedded" (Sheppard, Lewicki, and Minton 1992, 14).

Consider an example in which a workforce development agency is responsible for providing skills training to individuals through Workforce Investment Agencies (WIAs) located throughout the state. However, there are important structural inequities across specific WIAs. WIAs located in disproportionately white populations have higher-performing staff, more financial resources, and stronger public-private partnerships with potential employers. Their classes offer lower teacher-student ratios, and they offer strong skill-building training. In comparison, WIAs located among disproportionately African American populations have lower-performing staff, fewer financial resources, and weaker public-private partnerships with potential employers. Their classes have higher teacher-student ratios, and they offer very limited skill-building training that translates well in the labor market. The public sector value of organizational justice is clearly violated in terms of both balance and correctness. From a balance perspective, similar clients are not receiving similar treatments from their public sector WIA, yet all clients are being assessed on similar programmatic outcomes (e.g., receipt of employment, earnings, and job tenure). Clients are receiving varying levels of public sector investment but are expected to achieve similar levels of outcomes. From a correctness perspective, the reality of servicing similarly situated clients is not "right."

Similarly, public sector organizations seek to claim "objectivity" by shifting the problem beyond the parameters of a particular agency. For example, agency officials want to hire more people of color, but there are not enough qualified minority applicants, which they claim is a problem of colleges and universities. Colleges and universities shift the blame downward to K–12, which likewise shifts the blame to early childhood education, lack of quality prenatal health care, and so forth. The public organization simultaneously acknowledges the disparity problem while absolving itself of any specifi responsibility to treat it.

The extent to which an agency is willing to acknowledge, examine, and address structural inequities along these dimensions falls within the nervous area of government. Overcoming this nervousness is dependent upon the organization's willingness to name, blame, and claim the injustice (Sheppard, Lewicki, and Minton 1992). As Figure 4.1 displays, the naming process occurs through the initial identification of a public agency practice that is harmful. "Naming" entails recognizing that a public sector policy or practice is racially unjust. "The naming of an event is critical, because how we define the nature of harm affects or 'transforms' the evolution of all subsequent beliefs, feelings,

Figure 4.1   **Naming, Blaming, and Claiming**

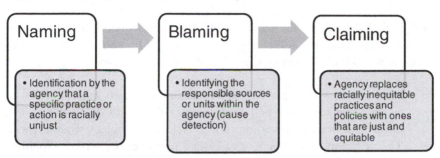

and actions (Sheppard, Lewicki, and Minton 1992, 47). The next step, blaming, involves finding out the cause of the injustice. It identifies who or what is responsible. In the Workforce Investment Agency above example, blaming involves identifying who determines agency budgets or assigns agency personnel. Blaming is important because until the source(s) of the injustice can be identified, solutions may be inappropriately targeted. Nervousness becomes particularly high around issues of blaming because being labeled as an agent of racial injustice is not desirable and evokes strong emotional reactions. Individuals or units who are blamed may not hear that they are responsible for promoting racial injustice. Rather, they may inappropriately translate this into "I am being called a racist." It is important to distinguish individual motives and prejudices (being a racist, which includes intentionality) from actions that result in important racial equity consequences. Such consequences may not have been previously known or analyzed. While systems can be blamed, it is important to distill where the responsibility within a system lies for the implementation of specific agency policy or practice. "Claiming" involves the agency's changing its racially inequitable practices and policies to ones that are just and equitable. It also involves continued monitoring of agency practices using a racial-equity lens.

Put simply, justice matters, especially in public sector organizations. Public administrators have a responsibility for ensuring that clients are treated fairly and for accounting for, acting upon, and remedying situations in which clients served by their agencies are systematically treated unfairly (Sheppard, Lewicki, and Minton 1992). Organizational justice is a core value of public administration. Organizational value systems have a direct impact on individual behavior (Beyer 1981; Hochschild 1983; Sutton 1991). Thus, organizational values perform two important functions in providing direction for organization members (James, James, and Ashe 1990) and as a social tool that informally approves, constrains, or prohibits behaviors (O'Reilly 1989).

Organizational Socialization

As Schein (1970) discusses, the psychological contract between an organization and an individual is informally negotiated over time through the organizational socialization process. Carroll and Tosi (1977) agree:

> New members learn performance expectations of their superiors, as well
> as the organizationally-preferred values and ways of doing things. . . .
> Most behaviors, however, are probably learned through reinforcement.
> Of course, the consequences of certain responses are mixed—approval
> for some, disapproval for others—but the individual's future behavior is
> going to be influenced importantly by reinforcements from his dominant
> reference group. (Carroll and Tosi 1977, 96)

The process of organizational socialization begins when an employee
first joins an organization, and if she or he terminates employment with this
organization, she or he is resocialized when joining a different organization.
Leaders, peers, and subordinates all play a vital role in the organization socialization process. They communicate messages, both directly and indirectly,
about "how things are done here."

The culture of public sector organizations transmits important messages
about the socialization contract as it relates to expectations regarding racial
equity. The socialization contract contains two dimensions: public boundaries
and real boundaries. As Carroll and Tosi (1977) explain, the public boundaries are generally agreed-upon work activities, but they do not represent an
employee's real boundaries, which are much broader. Although an employee
will do more than is represented in the public zone, "the real boundaries do,
however, define the limits beyond which he will not go" (213) if he wants to
remain in compliance with the organizational socialization contract.

Figure 4.2 provides a hypothetical race and social equity socialization
contract in a public agency. The public boundaries encompass the employee's
normal call of duty. She is clearly expected to avoid using racist or discriminatory language when interacting with clients or other agency employees.
This may be explicitly stated in agency policy that governs the work of all
employees. Similarly, she may be required to seek out minority contractors
for agency work.

Agency culture may communicate a limited approach, such as a requirement
for open and competitive bidding during procurement, or a more aggressive
approach of developing effective relationships with minority contractors.
By comparison, items in the real boundaries are actions an employee will
engage in that communicate she has gone "above and beyond" specifi

Figure 4.2   **Hypothetical Race and Social Equity Socialization Contract**

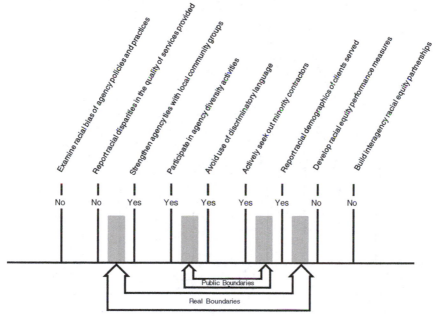

Source: Adapted from Carroll and Tosi 1977, 213.

agency expectations in promoting racial equity. For example, the employee
has distinguished herself in the area of racial equity by strengthening ties
with community organizations or adding racial demographic data when
reporting on the clients served in his particular unit. While these activities
are not required, they are *permissible* within the real race and social-equity
boundaries of the agency. The items on the far ends (e.g., examining racial
biases of agency policies and practices) are activities that fall outside of the
real boundaries of the agency. Engaging in such practices will produce clear
responses of disapproval, either formally or informally, from superiors and/or
peers. When an employee engages in these activities, she is operating within
the agency's nervous area of government.

The organizational challenge here is to expand the socialized boundaries
as captured in Figure 4.3. Specificall , the externalities of the "real" boundaries need to be expanded to include activities that currently reside in the
"nervous" area. For example, "examining racial biases of agency policies and
practices" and "developing racial equity performance measures" should be
included within the real boundaries of permissible activities. This culturally
redefincs these behaviors as acceptable. Current and future employees can
then engage in racial equity work with less fear, and the expanded socializa-

Figure 4.3   **Hypothetical Expanded Race and Social Equity Socialization Contract**

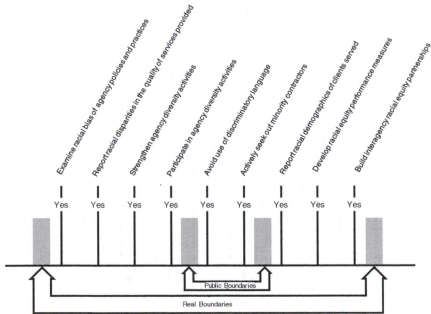

Source: Carroll and Tosi 1977, 213.

tion boundaries of the organization now recognize such work as legitimate activities. The boundary expansion work is most effective when promoted by organizational leaders.

Organizational Leadership and Change

Organizational leadership is a critically important factor in the nervous area of government. It is the process of influencing others to act in a particular manner. Leaders within organizations, by virtue of their position, formal authority, perceived and real power, and influence, routinely articulate strong messages to organizational members about what is important, what is unimportant, and what resides in the zone of indifference. Larger values of an agency, such as a commitment to organizational justice, are largely affirmed or moderated by leadership action and behavior. The assessment of these values at a leadership level includes an examination of how leaders spend their time (and steer the time of others) and how they allocate their resources, especially discretionary resources.

According to Schein (1970), individuals in any situation, including work, will do many things because they feel they should. How *should* an employee feel about analyzing and promoting racial equity within an organization? The answer to this question is largely influenced by the employee's perception of how others in the organization, especially leaders, feel about the value of organizational justice in general and racial equity in particular. Agency leaders personify the organization and its motives (Avery, et al. 2007). As discussed in chapter 5, the success of Seattle's Race and Social Justice Initiative was largely influenced by actions among public sector leaders and their unwavering commitment to social justice. Leaders can affect individual behavior in at least three important ways. They can affect expectations; they can set organizational goals; and they can clarify how to achieve goals (Carroll and Tosi 1977).

Organizational goals are "desired and intended ends to be achieved" (Etzioni 1964, 6). All activities performed by a public sector organization have as their ultimate purpose some end state of client benefit (Neugeboren 1991). Organizational goals have three primary functions: they guide activity by determining the tasks that need to be performed and the associated division of labor; they provide a standard for evaluating organizational performance; and they legitimize the functions of the agency. This legitimization clearly connects public sector organizations as a larger part of the society in which they operate (Neugeboren 1991).

The role of leaders in overcoming the nervous area of government is particularly significant. Promoting racial equity within many public sector agencies will involve cultural change, which begins with an overall strategy aligned with the desired future. This future needs to be clear and compelling but also adaptable, so that the organization can allow space to learn and make necessary adjustments along the way. Organizational change of any nature is subject to resistance. This is particularly true for promoting racial equity because it involves deeper changes. "Old habits and automatic responses are hard to recognize and change. The deeper the changes, the more likely they will enter realms of life invisible to employees" (Deetz, Tracy, and Simpson 2000, 40).

As Carroll and Tosi (1977) discuss, certain conditions must be present before change can occur.

> First, the causes of the present unsatisfactory state of knowledge, behavior, or attitudes must be understood. . . . Second, the obstacles standing in the way of change must not be insurmountable. . . . A third prerequisite of change is motivation to change. An individual—or group—must be motivated to change an existing level of knowledge, behavior patterns, or attitudes, or the influence programs will fail. Fourth, defensiveness must be minimized. Since most individuals have a favorable self-image, they are not inclined to accept information about themselves which is at variance with this favorable self-image. (486)

As discussed in chapter 2, racial inequity in public sector organizations is often viewed as a condition rather than a problem. The role of leadership in redefining racial inequity as a problem is an important step. It moves racial inequity in the distribution of government services from a status quo condition to a solvable problem. In understanding the current unsatisfactory state, data on the causes of current racial inequities must be examined. All public policies in the United States exist within a historical context—one that was shaped by and influence by racism that was once legal. For example, understanding the determination of present-day local property assessment values begins with an understanding of the once-legal discriminatory practice of redlining. Undertaking such an analysis often illuminates the clear influences of historical racism that still impacts the allocation, structure, and implementation of current public sector services.

The perception of insurmountability is an important factor. Even those who are most motivated toward racial equity work do not want to participate in a losing cause. Once the nature of the current racial inequity problem is understood, a road to realizing necessary changes needs to be articulated and shared. Performing a process analysis to determine what specific procedures and practices within the agency work to maintain existing racial inequities is important. This procedure identifies core areas of current public administration that need to change in order to realize racial equity in the provision of public services. Leaders set the tone for committing the agency to do this important work.

Public sector leaders can perform a vitally important role in motivating change among employees throughout the agency. Amount of buy-in among managers and supervisors will consist of a mixture of early adopters, those who are indifferent, and active resisters. Linking racial equity analysis to performance evaluations, internal reward and incentive systems, and internal communication venues can motivate and influence behavior that is more aligned with realizing organizational justice.

Leaders can minimize defensiveness by focusing on the institutional and structural inequities within the agency that need to change. Earlier in this chapter, the concept of "blame" was discussed as a particularly emotional aspect of organizational justice work. Assuming that there are only a very few public administrators who are intentionally racist, leaders need to strongly communicate that unintentional behaviors and status quo norms and practices can maintain the existence of racial inequity. In order to promote racial equity within public organizations, public administrators have an obligation to examine systematic behaviors, practices, and norms within all agency units. In many cases, this simply involves adding a racial analysis lens to functions that are already routinely examined. So, the current agency question "How user friendly is our agency website for the public we serve?" employs an expanding operational definition of public by directly linking the provision-of-services language to the specific populations served. Answering such questions from a racial-equity perspective requires organizational discourse.

Organizational Discourse

Chapter 3 examined conversations about race and nervousness at the individual level. It is also important to consider the importance of conversations about race at the organizational level, as this is an equally important factor in the nervous area of government. Racial dialogues occur in a larger institutional context that has unequal power and differential racial identity development (Schwartz 1971). For example, the consideration of the following questions is important to structuring organizational conversations about race: Who participates in the dialogue? Where is the conversation held? Is the conversation a single event or an ongoing subject of focus? How is the conversation facilitated? What is the mix or structure and spontaneity within the conversation? And, what is the organizational goal of the conversation? (Miller and Donner 2000).

As discussed by Hardy, Lawrence, and Phillips (1998), there is an important link between talk and action. As summarized in Figure 4.4,

> Certain individual and collective identities react to particular information and events; frame issues in distinctive ways; and are predisposed to certain kinds of actions which reinforce identities that are experienced as negative. Skills accord us both the right and the ability to take particular actions. Emotions generate the energy to act or not to act. These are not neatly self-contained categories. . . . The interplay of these factors leads to actions and, while complex, it is possible to conceptualize the conversational foundations of action in this way. (Hardy, Lawrence, and Phillips 1998, 73)

Race talk and organizational action are inextricably linked. Talk and action are not separate entities, nor do they form a linear sequence. "Through conversation, relationships between individuals are established, shared meanings are developed, and contested meanings are made visible" (Woodilla 1998, 31). As Hardy, Lawrence, and Phillips (1998) explain, "Not only are individual identities created, so, too, are collective identities" (69). The agency's collective identity shapes the racial equity actions the organization is subsequently willing to take. Dialogue among individuals within an organization often forms the basis for the creation of new ideas and innovative approaches that lead to important institutional knowledge discovery and organizational change. "Talk is integral to action at several levels. It is itself a form of action. It can facilitate subsequent forms of action through establishing common understandings as to what is required, by whom, and under a specified timeframe. It facilitates future

Figure 4.4   **The Links Between Organizational Talk and Organizational Action**

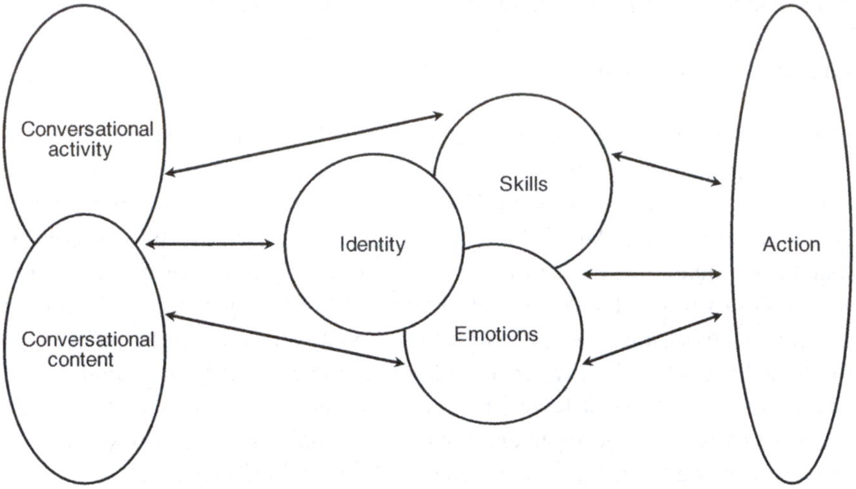

Source: Hardy, Lawrence, and Phillips 1998, 73.

action through its contribution to relationship-forming among organizational members. And, talk is essential to establishing meanings of terms and characteristics of success" (Dunford and Palmer 1998). Organizational discourse is most effective when it is purposively intended to promote constructive agency action based on data-driven evidence. Examining client service data by race identifies specific opportunities for   ganizational learning to occur.

Organizational Learning and High Performance

Organizational learning is most appropriately viewed as a method by which organizations can effect organizational change and continual self-improvement. It provides a model of agency self-correction in implementing organizational values and goals.

> Organizational learning is a collection of processes by which organizations improve their ability to accomplish their objectives by analyzing their past efforts. Learning organizations scrutinize unsatisfactory results to discover the reasons behind them and make cause-effect inferences about how to alter their outcomes. . . . In a learning organization, problems are openly acknowledged, causes are intensively investigated, and procedures are corrected. New techniques are searched out, all in order to bring results more closely in line with agency expectations, external mandates, and professional or personal values. (Mahler 2009, 18)

In order to advance racial equity within public sector organizations, the organization must be willing to openly examine its past and current performance in its distribution of public service and in its implementation of public policy. A learning cycle begins with the realization among at least some organization members that there is an important disconnect between organizational results and organizational mission (Mahler 2009). As partners with elected officials in a democratic society, public sector organizations share an important responsibility to make sure there is "justice for all." "Individual administrators and the public administration community must recognize that social equity problems persist and that public administrators should take action to alleviate and correct these problems as they develop, analyze, manage and deliver public programs" (Johnson and Svara 2011, 4). A core part of this action involves an unwavering willingness of public administrators to engage in critically examining their current practices, procedures, and outcomes through a racial-equity lens. Public administrators will experience nervousness as they work through these organizational analyses. However, the knowledge base that is acquired by directly examining racial inequities provides a data-driven foundation to guide future change.

Organizational learning offers significant rewards in the area of knowledge acquisition and work. However, organizational culture can seriously impede knowledge management (KM).

> Thus, "good" cultural values such as sharing, openness, and trust will lead to positive KM behaviors, (e.g., knowledge contribution and sharing), whereas "bad" values will lead to dysfunctional KM behaviors (e.g., information hoarding) and, hence, undesirable outcomes. . . . (Alavi, Kayworth, and Leidner 2006, 197)

Creation of organizational knowledge regarding racial equity requires the ability to share information, examine organizational processes, and examine this knowledge with the goal of making existing knowledge useful to advancing racial equity in the administration of public series. The public sector agency can then develop application-based processes oriented toward specifi knowledge use (Alvai, Kayworth, and Leidner 2006).

Learning takes practice, and structural changes in the public sector are realized over time. Organizational learning will also involve missteps and bumps along the way. Changing agency routine is not always smooth or error-free. As Mahler states, "The eventual test of learning, and its value to any organization, is that it improves performance and that those improvements, the lessons learned, are dependably practiced throughout the organization" (Mahler 2009, 211). Ideally, public sector organizations can become high-performing organizations in the area of racial equity. The organization will begin to hold itself accountable to high standards for promoting racial equity, and this expectation will permeate the organization, becoming a core component of the public service culture. Team building often fosters adoption of a high level of performance as a "norm." "The idea is that groups with a high standard of performance will pressure individual members to perform at a high level" (Carroll and Tosi 1977, 146). Entrepreneurial in approach, high-performing organizations are not limited by nervousness but rather foster innovation, creativity, and risk-taking. "This is what it means in the end to institutionalize new inferences and solutions to problems" (Mahler 2009, 211).

Conclusion

This chapter examined several factors within organizations that can inhibit or enhance an organization's ability to navigate the nervous area of government. The delivery of public administration occurs in an important organizational context. The culture of the organization, as well as its implementation of organizational values and goals, socialization, leadership, change, and discourse, as well as its commitment to organizational learning and high performance outcomes, are complex factors that impact racial equity in the provision of public services. As discussed at the individual level, confronting issues of racial equity at the organizational level embodies emotion and nervousness as well. The promotion of common public sector equity values (particularly by leaders in public administration), articulation of specific goals, understanding of discourse language, and a commitment to direct examination of agency practices, procedures, and outcomes and how they explicitly affect the diverse publics served are all critical in achieving racial equity and a commitment from public administrators to provide justice for all. While navigating the nervous area of government may seem daunting for many organizations, some public sector organizations at the federal, state, and local level are doing so. The next three chapters provide case studies of governmental organizations undertaking this critical work.

References

Alavi, Maryam, Timothy R. Kayworth, and Dorothy E. Leidner. 2006. "An Empirical Examination of the Influence of Organizational Culture on Knowledge Management and Practices." *Journal of Management Information Systems* 22 (3): 191–224.

Avery, Derek R., Patrick F. McKay, David C. Wilson, and Scott Tonidandel. 2007. "Unequal Attendance: The Relationships Between Race, Organizational Diversity, Cues, and Absenteeism." *Personnel Psychology* 60 (4): 875–902.

Beyer, Janice M. 1981. "Ideologies, Values, and Decision Making in Organizations." In *Handbook of Organizational Design: Remodeling Organizations and Their Environments,* ed. Paul C. Nystrom and William H. Starbuck, 166–202. Oxford University Press: London.

Carroll, Stephen J., and Henry L.Tosi. 1977. *Organizational Behavior*. Chicago: St. Clair Press.

Chao, Georgia T., and Henry Moon. 2005. "The Cultural Mosaic: A metAtheory for Understanding the Complexity of Culture." *Journal of Applied Psychology* 90 (6): 1128–40.

Claver, Enrique, Juan Llopis, José L. Gascó, Hipólito Molina, and Francisco J. Conca. 1999. "Public Administration: From Bureaucratic Culture to Citizen-Oriented Culture." *International Journal of Public Sector Management* 12 (5): 455–64.

Deal, Terrence E., and Allan A. Kennedy. 1982. *Corporate Cultures: The Rites and Rituals of Corporate Life*. Reading, MA: Addison-Wesley.

Deetz, Stanley A., Sarah J. Tracy, and Jennifer Lyn Simpson. 2000. *Leading Organizations Through Transition*. Thousand Oaks, CA: Sage.

Dunford, Richard, and Ian Palmer. 1998. "Discourse, Organizations and Paradox." In *Discourse and Organization,* ed. David Grant, Tom Keenoy and Cliff Oswick, 214–21. London: Sage.

Etzioni, Amitai. 1964. *Modern Organizations*. Englewood Cliffs, NJ: Prentice-Hall.

Goffman, Erving. 1959. *The Presentation of Self in Everyday Life*. New York: Doubleday.

———. 1967. *Interaction Ritual*. Hawthorne, NY: Aldine.

Hardy, Cynthia, Thomas B. Lawrence, and Nelson Phillips. 1998. "Talk and Action: Conversations and Narrative Interorganizational Collaboration." In *Discourse and Organization,* ed. David Grant, Tom Keenoy, and Cliff Oswick, 65–83. London: Sage.

Hochschild, Arlie Russell. 1983. *The Managed Heart*. Berkeley: University of California Press.

James, Lawrence R., Lois A. James, and Donna K. Ashe. 1990. The Meaning of Organizations: The Role of Cognition and Values. In *Organizational Climate and Culture*, ed. Benjamin Scheider, 40–84. San Francisco: Jossey-Bass.

Johnson, Norman J., and James H. Svara. 2011. "Social Equity in American Society and Public Administration." In *Justice for All: Promoting Social Equity in Public Administration*, ed. Norman J. Johnson and James H. Svara, 3–25. Armonk, NY: M.E. Sharpe.

Mahler, Julianne G. 2009. *Organizational Learning at NASA: The Challenger and Columbia Accidents*. Washington, DC: Georgetown University Press.

Marcoulides, George A., and Ronald H. Heck. 1993. Organizational Culture and Performance: Proposing and Testing a Model. *Organization Science* 4 (2): 209–25.

Miller, Joshua, and Susan Donner. 2000. "More Than Just Talk: The Use of Racial Dialogues to Combat Racism." *Social Work with Groups* 23 (1): 31–53.

Neugeboren, Bernard. 1991. *Organization, Policy, and Practice in the Human Services*. New York: Haworth Press.

O'Reilly, Charles. 1989. "Corporations, Culture, and Commitment: Motivation and Social Control in Organizations." *California Management Review* 50 (2): 9–25.

Ritti, Richard R., and G. Ray Funkhouser. 1982. *The Ropes to Skip and the Ropes to Know*. Columbus, OH: Grid.

Schein, Edgar H. 1968. "Organizational Socialization and the Profession of Management." In *Industrial Management Review* 9 (2): 1–15.

———. 1970. *Organizational Psychology*. Englewood Cliffs, NJ: Prentice-Hall.

———. 1978. *Career Dynamics: Matching Individual and Organizational Needs*. Reading, MA: Addison-Wesley.

————. 1985. *Organizational Culture and Leadership*. San Francisco: Jossey-Bass.

Schwartz, William. 1971. "The Use of Groups in Social Work Practice." In *The Practice of Group Work,* ed. William Schwartz and Serapio R. Zalba, 3–24. New York: Columbia University Press.

Shafritz, Jay M., and J. Steven Ott. 1992. "Organizational Culture and Symbolic Organization Theory." In *Classics of Organization Theory,* 3d ed., ed. Jay Shafritz and J. Steven Ott, 481–89. Belmont, CA: Wadsworth.

Sheppard, Blair H., Roy J. Lewicki, and John W. Minton. 1992. *Organizational Justice: The Search for Fairness in the Workplace.* New York: Lexington Books.

Sutton, Robert I. 1991. "Maintaining Norms About Emotional Expression: The Case of Bill Collectors." *Administrative Science Quarterly* 36 (2): 245–68.

Tagiuri, Renato, and George H. Litwin, eds. 1968. *Organizational Climate: Explorations of a Concept.* Boston: Division of Research, Harvard Graduate School of Business.

Testa, Mark R., and Lori J. Sipe. 2011. "The Organizational Culture Audit: A Model for Hospitality Executives." Paper presented at the International Council on Hotel Restaurant and Institutional Education Conference. Denver, CO, July 29, 2011, 1–16.

Van Maanen, John Eastin. 1976. "Breaking In: Socialization to Work." In *Handbook of Work, Organization, and Society,* ed. Robert Dubin, 67–130. Chicago: Rand McNally.

————. 1979. "The Self, the Situation, and the Rules of Interpersonal Relations." In *Essays in Interpersonal Dynamics*, ed. Warren Bennis et al., 43–101. Pacific Grove, CA: Brooks/Cole.

Woodilla, Jill. 1998. "Workplace Conversations: The Text of Organizing." In *Discourse and Organization,* ed. David Grant, Tom Keenoy, and Cliff Oswick, 31–50. London: Sage.

5 SEATTLE'S RACE AND SOCIAL JUSTICE INITIATIVE

Lots of people told me not to do this—it will only make people angry. But, I thought we had a responsibility to do it.

—Greg Nickels (2012), former mayor of Seattle

This chapter offers an empirical, applied examination of the preceding conceptual discussions by examining the City of Seattle's pioneering journey in navigating a nervous area of government—race and social justice. It captures the City's mission to prioritize justice in the services it provides. Through the City's ongoing efforts to analyze the treatment and experiences of the public they serve, their dominant concern is to develop and deliver governmental services in a manner that prioritizes racial justice.

As prominently stated on the City's website, "The Seattle Race and Social Justice Initiative (RSJI) is a citywide effort to end institutionalized racism and race-based disparities in City government. RSJI builds on the work of the civil rights movement and the ongoing efforts of individuals and groups in Seattle to confront racism. The Initiative's long term goal is to change the underlying system that creates race-based disparities in our community and to achieve racial equity" (Seattle Office for Civil Rights 2012a).

There are at least three important aspects of the RSJI. First, it is an initiative designed by local government to eliminate institutional racism in the provision of local government services. Seattle officials and administrators have acknowledged that institutional racism exists in the services provided to citizens, and they are committed to its elimination. Second, the RSJI has been actively sustained since its inception in 2004, despite leadership changes at the highest levels of local government. And, third, the RSJI is having a significant impact, both within the City of Seattle and among local governments throughout the United States.

Data to examine each of these areas are primarily based on twenty-three individual or small group interviews conducted during July 2012 with current and former City of Seattle employees. Additional data were derived from publicly available electronic and print documents. Together, these data offer a direct, empirical examination of the RSJI. It details how the initiative began, challenges encountered along the way, key contributions to date, and efforts to sustain and institutionalize this work.

Beginning Seattle's Race and Social Justice Initiative

Led by the Seattle Office of Civil Rights and an interdepartmental city team, the Seattle Race and Social Justice Initiative is an effort by Seattle city government to realize the vision of racial equity. Like elsewhere in the United States, Seattle is a city divided by race. For example;

- The unemployment rate for African American men in Seattle today matches the unemployment rate across the country during the Great Depression.
- Immigrant and refugee communities experience severe inequities in housing, jobs, education, and health.
- Although statistics for Asian–Pacific Islander communities often appear strong, combining these diverse communities into a single category often masks inequities.
- Only about half of Samoan, Native American, Latino, and African American students graduate from Seattle public schools.
- African Americans without a conviction record have a harder time getting hired than a white person with a conviction record.
- Almost a third of Native Americans live in poverty. (Race and Social Justice Initiative 2012c, 1).

The work of the initiative is guided by a core set of eight principles (see Table 5.1). These principles establish an explicit focus on race and institutional racism; require the initiative to begin with the City of Seattle itself by "getting our own house in order"; prioritize achieving real results; and embrace a commitment to long-term sustainability.

Discussing the beginning of anything, particularly a policy initiative, is challenging because the "starting point" is subjective. While it is factually accurate to state that the Seattle Race and Social Justice Initiative began in 2004, it was preceded by an important, larger context within Seattle and the United States more generally. This larger context includes a history of racial minorities and white allies working decades upon decades to make important strides for racial justice. In 1989, voters in the city of Seattle elected Norman Rice as the city's forty-ninth mayor—its first (and still only) African American mayor. Rice served as mayor of Seattle from 1990 to 1998, which followed his eleven years of elected service on Seattle's City

Table 5.1

Principles of the Race and Social Justice Initiative

- Focus explicitly on race and institutional racism. Although the initiative acknowledged other systemic inequities based on class, gender, ability, or sexual orientation, RSJI would train its lens on racism because of its centrality in Seattle's experience and the breadth and depth of disparities based on race.
- Define institutional racism as "organizational programs, policies or procedures that work to the benefit of white people and to the detriment of people of color, usually unintentionally or inadvertently." RSJI would not be another diversity or cultural competence program; it would view itself as a successor to that work.
- Focus on root causes and solutions. Previously, government typically had responded to inequities—when it responded at all—by developing programs and services to ameliorate the effects of racism. The initiative would focus on changing the underlying system that creates and maintains inequities.
- Concentrate initially within Seattle city government. The first priority would be to "get our own house in order"; in other words, to address institutional racism within city government as a necessary first step before engaging the community more broadly. Only when the City felt the initiative had gained some internal traction would it expand the focus to address race-based inequities in the external community.
- Achieve results. Racism is a learned behavior that can be unlearned though analysis, strategic organizing, and intentional changes in policies, practices, and procedures.
- View the initiative as a long-term project. There would be no rush for a quick fix. RSJI would be planned and presented as an ongoing commitment to a new way of doing business.
- Be accountable to communities of color. RSJI's success would be measured by its results: racial equity in the lives of the people who live and work in Seattle.
- Use a community-organizing model to move the work forward. RSJI would concentrate on strategically developing critical mass among City employees; "widening the circle" of participants who understood the goals and strategies of the initiative and could begin to put it into practice.

Source: Bronstein et al. 2011.

Council. Rice's political legacy included several areas of advancing racial equity within Seattle. "As a member of the Finance and Budget Committee, he worked for more equitable utility rates by Seattle City Light, the city owned utility, lobbied for the passage of the Women and Minority Business Enterprise Ordinance, and called for Seattle companies to end their investments in apartheid-dominated South Africa. Rice also worked to lower crime in Seattle and supported the use of city funds to help impoverished Seattle residents" (Mack 2011).

Mayor Rice was succeeded by Paul Schell, whose one term as Seattle's mayor from 1998 to 2002 brought considerable criticism from Seattle's voters following the Mardi Gras riots, which resulted in the beating death of twenty-year-old Kristopher Kime in Pioneer Square as he tried to help a stranger. Police stood on the sidelines and did not intervene, as they were instructed by the police chief not to enter the riot zone. Ultimately, Mayor Schell did not fire the police chief and he lost public support (Brunner 2002). "It was the first time in over 65 years a Seattle Mayor had failed to survive a primary election" (Egan 2001).

Perhaps less publicly known, Mayor Schell reached out to the People's Institute for Survival and Beyond, a New Orleans–based organization, to start citywide discussions on race. These discussions, called City Talks, ushered in public dialogue about race in Seattle. The People's Institute focused on understanding racism in the context of organization and communities. As its website states, "The People's Institute for Survival and Beyond focuses on understanding what racism is, where it comes from, how it functions, why it persists and how it can be undone. [The] workshops utilize a systemic approach that emphasizes learning from history, developing leadership, maintaining accountability to communities, creating networks, undoing internalized racial oppression and understanding the role of organizational gate keeping as a mechanism for perpetuating racism" (People's Institute for Survival and Beyond 2013).

The People's Institute worked with the Seattle community to have open discussions about race. As a former Seattle Office of Civil Rights (SOCR) director, explained,

> So we had a meeting with Mayor Schell and the People's Institute. I don't think many people knew about that. And we talked about what we were trying to do within the city and how we wanted to get it started. . . . Before that [Schell] didn't realize how deeply employees felt about it, how the city was divided. Because we're the "city-of-Seattle-nice," so it was below the surface. . . . So that [City Talks] laid the groundwork for when Mayor Nickels then came to office and said, "I want to address this.

Although Mayors Rice and Schell both supported racial justice, they both faced important impediments. In particular, in 1998 Washington became the second state to enact anti-affirmative-action legislation. Passed by more than 58 percent of voters, Initiative 200 (I-200) ended affirmative action by prohibiting the state from granting preferential treatment to "any individual or group on the basis of race, sex, color, ethnicity, or national origin in the operation of public employment, public education, or public contracting." It seemed rather unlikely that Seattle would become a leader of racial equity in government just a few years later. Ironically, as one City of Seattle employee asserted, I-200 actually was a catalyst of the Race and Social Justice Initiative: "So, all of the affirmative action programs were out. All of that was outlawed . . . you know, nothing happens in a vacuum. I think this [Race and Social Justice Initiative] was also a consequence of that legislation."

Implementing Seattle's Race and Social Justice Initiative

In 2001, Greg Nickels was elected as Seattle's fifty-first mayor and served for two terms (2002–2010). Prior to his own elected political career as a member of King County City Council, Nickels served as a legislative assistant to former Seattle City Council member and mayor Norman Rice from 1979 to 1987.

Nickels called for the RSJI at the beginning of his first term as mayor after his experiences on the campaign trail revealed a racial chasm in residents' perceptions of city government (Bronstein et al. 2011, 159). As Nickels talked with residents during the campaign, he realized that the perceptions of Seattle largely varied by race. "I learned that children had very different experiences in school based on location. We live within an 80-mile space—there shouldn't be such different educational expectations in an area that small," In remarks at a conference in 2012 Nickels reflected. "I don't want to be mayor of that city. We need to confront and consider our past as we outline our path going forward."

As the City of Seattle launched the RSJI under Mayor Nickels's administration, he faced extensive caution against moving forward, particularly with such a strong focus on race. "Lots of people told me not to do this—it will only make people angry. But, I thought we had a responsibility to do it," Nickels said.

> Language is really important to the conversation. Equity is an important value, but Race and Social Justice is a harder name and I wanted it to be clear. In any conversation, if people can talk about anything other than race, they will. So this was important. We needed a structure to keep the focus directly there. (Washington State Democratic Chairs Organization 2012)

Mayor Nickels hired a director of innovation for the City of Seattle to conceptualize and direct the initiative. As the then-director of innovation recalled, "I had a sort of humorous job description of myself in the City of Seattle as the master of the ill-defined job. There was a weird job that they wanted somebody to take. Somehow, I ended up taking that job by virtue of some ability I have in facilitation and keeping groups together in emotionally loaded situations."

As he explained to the mayor,

> In a year, every white person in this organization is going to see me as a threat or as a predator or as an irritant. And every person of color is going to see me as an Uncle Tom because I'm not doing this right. So I said, "Is this that job you're asking me to do?" And, he said, "Yep, that's pretty much the job we're asking you to do." . . . I asked the mayor over and over again, is this about race or is this about something else, because it was called the Race and Social Justice Initiative. And he said, "This is about race."

And, so, the RSJI's pioneering journey began.

"When Seattle introduced the Race and Social Justice Initiative in 2005, no U.S. city had even undertaken an effort that focused explicitly on institutional racism" (Race and Social Justice Initiative 2013, 3). With clear principles and a direct focus on race, the next item of business was full implementation across the city of Seattle. In the early stages, citywide implementation of the Race and Social Justice Initiative was largely focused on two primary items: (1) race and social justice training for all City of Seattle employees, and (2) the development and submission of racial equity plans by all City of Seattle agencies under the mayor's authority.

This responsibility fell to the SOCR, which was tasked with overseeing the initiative, including monitoring departments' progress and developing and coordinating citywide employee training (Bronstein et al. 2011). For everyone in Seattle government, this was largely uncharted territory. There were no roadmaps or best practices on eliminating institutional racism in government.

Acknowledging Institutional Racism

Prior to the RSJI, the SOCR was largely a complaint-driven, case-by-case operation. "SOCR was a typical urban civil rights agency whose bread-and-butter mission was to enforce fair housing, employment, and other antidiscrimination laws within Seattle's city limits" (Bronstein et al. 2011, 159). The Race and Social Justice Initiative required a completely different approach and strategy. Even some staff within SOCR were nervous about the initiative. As a SOCR staff member explained,

> But it [RSJI] was pretty vague, I'd think you'd say, because we were splashing around. We didn't know quite what we were asking. What did it mean to say, all right, we're going to train City of Seattle employees to understand institutional racism so that they could spot it and then do something about it. What did that mean? I didn't know what it meant. And I was sitting at the table.

The same staff member recalled initially being nervous about the entire name of the initiative—Seattle's Race and Social Justice Initiative—and then gradually overcoming this feeling:

> I'm embarrassed to report this, but let's be real—I was the person who said, "Well, is there another term we could use other than racism, because that's a trigger for a lot of white people? And, if there's another term we can use, we would—you know, it might be better—we might get faster traction without kicking up as much dust. . . ." Sitting around that table after several weeks, I got used to it enough that it no longer twinged me.

The use of the term "institutional racism" was also a red flag for the City Attorney's Office. As a member of the SOCR staff recalled,

> I have to say that I think for the City of Seattle we had a lot of nervousness at the beginning. And prior to being with the OCR, I was with the Human Services Department where we were doing a lot of racial equity work before there was even a citywide initiative. This was fifteen years ago. And it's interesting because at that time the law department told us that we could not use the term "institutionalized racism." That, in essence, we would be acknowledging that there's racism within our institution. And, of course, our response was, "No, duh, you know. So how are we going to change if we're not really willing to acknowledge it?"

The director of innovation recalled a similar reaction.

> I remember when we first started to talk about institutionalized racism. People were just, like incensed. The city attorney's office said, "You can't use the words *institutionalized racism.*" And, I said, "But why?" And they said, "Because if you admit that we have institutionalized racism and then somebody sues us, you will have already admitted us, and there's no way for us to win that suit."

However, Mayor Nickels was an unrelenting champion of the RSJI *and* its specific language of institutional racism. With clear, unwavering support from the Mayor's Office, the Initiative pressed forward, ultimately receiving support from both City Council and the City Attorney's Office

> The initiative had one big advantage: a captive audience. A mandate from the mayor meant that departments could not simply refuse to implement

the initiative. Employees who attended antiracism training could not walk out with impunity. This was work time, after all, and participants were answering to their supervisors, who were responsible to their directors, who were responsible to the mayor. (Bronstein et al. 2011, 161)

As Mayor Nickels explained, "Political capital is a muscle, not a well. Use it to change for the better, not to focus on reelection. Initially, there was no consensus from council that it was a good idea. We decided we would forge through and hopefully they would come along, and they did. . . . Some [City of Seattle] departments resisted, some were eager. We had an opportunity to lead and create an example, so we gave it a try. We were really ahead of the climate issue nationally."

Citywide Employee Training on Race and Racism

In addition to members of the SOCR staff, the initiative introduced a citywide core team comprising forty people representing most city departments. "Core team members received intensive training on institutional racism, group facilitation, problem solving, and strategic action planning. Core team members worked with change teams, department managers, and line staff to implement the initiative" (Bronstein et al. 2011, 159).

Through the course of these deliberations, the SOCR developed the infrastructure for the race and social justice training. Based largely around the PBS documentary series *Race: The Power of an Illusion*, completion of the race and social justice training was mandatory for all employees of the City of Seattle, with senior management completing the training first. According to Larry Adelman, the series' executive producer, the documentary makes visible "the underlying social, economic, and political conditions that disproportionately channel advantages and opportunities to white people" (Adelman 2003).

Seattle Public Utilities (SPU) agreed to pilot the training, becoming the first large department to launch this train the trainer–based initiative. This eight-hour training session, delivered to small groups of twenty employees, served as the basic training curriculum for SPU's 1,400 employees (Bronstein et al. 2011). And, the training required sustained commitment— taking a few years to deliver the training to nearly all employees. Each training session introduced and demonstrated the impact of institutional racism and white privilege to City of Seattle employees, many of whom had not previously directly engaged these topics, particularly when led by their employer. By all accounts, the trainings were very emotional. As one facilitator recalled,

Some people were silent. Some angry. You know, why are we doing this? This doesn't make sense. I don't think there's differences between races. You know, why are they bringing up these issues?

A retired senior administrator recalled,

And to say they were emotional meetings is probably an understatement. Some of them got exceedingly emotional. . . . The white privilege training was uncomfortable. The person [facilitator], I think, did a good job. But look, I'm a sixty-three-year old, and I'm white, and I've been around forever, and I came from a middle-class family. To sit there and to deal with kind of the unfairness that's been created and to accept some responsibility for that—it's uncomfortable. Whether I was the one that was instigating it or not, it's still uncomfortable because you sit through all that. And you see traits . . . sometimes in what's happened of things that you did. Have you kind of fed that system of privilege a little bit because of the system you were brought up in? And, I think that's where you get the uncomfortable moments.

Another manager explained,

When we first starting doing the workshops around Race—The Power of Illusion and putting groups of people in the room to confront these concepts, there were a lot of people learning about institutional racism for the first time. There were various dynamics in the room. I can remember in this room talking about how we need to expect issues to arise from that, and that you can't do the work without cracking open a few eggs and having discomfort and even—I think there were cases where conflict erupted in the room. You know, stuff happened. And we all sat here and said, "That's good and that's right, and we need to ride it out. I think that's an important message for others, too."

Working through the emotional tensions of institutional racism was a difficult but necessary component to the City of Seattle's goal of eliminating racism in the provision of government services. It is essential to working through a nervous area of government. As one employee said, it is a critical part of the organizational life cycle of change necessary to advance racial equity in government organizations:

Starting [the RSJI] was very difficult. The beginning was really hard—to be in those discussions. . . . Part of the life cycle is that you're going to have tensions between white people and people of color. So you really are doing a circular learning where you're continuing to go back and reinforce the learning that they've got, add additional tools and skills. And, it's okay to not get it right the first time or not to fully understand it. . . . As more and more people understand the concept [institutional racism], and they understand kind of how things happened, you get more and more discussion. So there's an element of that where people loosen up and they're more willing to talk about it.

The RSJI trainings required employees to directly understand and critically consider the impact of institutional and structural racism, defined as "policies, practices and procedures that work to the benefit of white people and to the detriment of people of color, often unintentionally or inadvertently" and "a history and current reality of institutional racism across multiple institutions. This [impact] combines to create a system that negatively impacts communities of color" (Race and Social Justice Initiative 2012c, 2). As a senior agency head remarked,

> Anger, concern, fear—maybe you'd characterize it as nervousness. But [the training] opened up issues that have been for the last couple of decades kind of pushed aside. . . . And boy, the term *racist* does create a lot of hot buttons. But the institution continues to protect the people of power that have always been there the last thirty or forty years. And, look, that's the way I got ahead. If I go back to the '70s when I started in government, how did I get ahead? Well, I knew the managers in power. Gee, they were all white and they were all old. And, I happened to be on their good side, so I got pulled along in the system. So, I saw it firsthand and I benefited from i

The implementation of the mandatory RSJI training received unwavering commitment and support from the top level of leadership in the City of Seattle, despite resistance to attending expressed by some employees. The City's rationale for making the race and social justice training mandatory was to ensure that all City employees had a basic understanding of institutional racism and the mission of the Seattle Race and Social Justice Initiative (Bronstein et al. 2011). As an RSJI trainer explained, "[Some] people didn't like it being mandatory. A lot of people didn't like that. . . . Even some people of color didn't like that it was mandatory and that they had to be there. That was just the reality of it. But, I think it was necessary to get us all through it so we could have some common footing."

A clear benefit of the training, coupled with the sustained commitment to racial justice work, is the normalizing of conversations about race. An

SOCR staff member explained, "So, now we create the framework to have the conversation. It will be uncomfortable. And we're not trying to make it uncomfortable. We're just trying to make it possible so that people can get their work done, which is to talk about how race might impact the City's policies so that we can then identify the different ways we can do this work."

But the discomfort decreased over time. As another SOCR staff member commented, "So, I think that initial nervousness has abated somewhat. And part of our goal has been to normalize conversations about race and racism. . . . We have largely passed that hurdle. . . . I think the City took its time to give people a chance to get comfortable talking about race."

Developing Agency Plans

Since 2005, all City of Seattle departments have been required to develop and implement work plans. Primary elements of these work plans were included in the annual performance evaluations of agency heads (Race and Social Justice Initiative 2008). "Each department created its own Change Team—a group of employees from all levels within the department that guided and supported the department's work plan implementation and RSJI activities" (Bronstein et al. 2011, 160).

Predictably, some agencies were eager to develop RSJI work plans, while others resisted. As a City of Seattle employee recalled,

> You can't say that your agency has nothing [no institutional racism]. So you're charged with identifying what you're willing to admit to. But you have to admit to something or it just sounds bogus. And, so that's what some agency heads did. They identified maybe a handful of issues that they could address, things that did not appear to be as heinous. And, quite often, at least at first, this was the low-hanging fruit. . . . And we'd have these monthly meetings and quarterly reports. . . . So these reports had to be made to the City Council members and the City Council subcommittees. And the City Council meetings are televised. They [agency heads] had to respond and be as inclusive and enlightened as possible, and so it was a whole lot of peer pressure—just sort of this indirect push toward the goals that are set.

As this same employee explained, City agencies were and continue to be at different points. "It's like triage in a real sense. Some need a general practitioner and some need a neurosurgeon. There are some agencies that really need the help, so we send in an expert or group of experts to assist them."

From an organizational culture perspective, one challenge in developing the agency plans was overcoming the passive-aggressive resistance (earlier termed "city-of-Seattle-nice"). For the most part, administrators and managers did not oppose the initiative directly, but some employed passive-aggressive techniques. As an SOCR staff member and City of Seattle employee explained,

> I think in Seattle the biggest threat is the bobble head phenomena where you can have people sort of nodding their head and then just keep doing the same old, same old. That's a passive form of resistance.

> They [agency directors and managers] did not push back like that. They did not rail. But they were resistant in actually adopting a program work plan, saying that it would negatively impact their budget or a number of other different excuses.

As departments began to address the initiative in the first year, the RSJI coordinating team looked for commonalities across departments to promote efficiency and synergy in addressing issues that cut across all City departments. Bronstein et al. (2011) list the following five common areas of work that became known as the Central Concerns:

- Workforce Equity: Improve diversity of our workforce on all levels and across functions.
- Economic Equity: Change purchasing and contracting practices to increase participation by people of color.
- Immigrant and Refugee Services: Improve access to services for immigrant and refugee communities.
- Public Engagement: Improve access and influence of communities of color.
- Capacity Building: Increase the knowledge and tools used by city staff to achieve race and social justice. (2011, 160)

Exhibit 5.1 provides an early example of a work plan from the Environmental Justice and Service Equity Division at Seattle Public Utilities (SPU) in 2006. This plan involved the agency's analyzing the extent to which its services are provided equitably across, race, income groups, and geographic locations.

In addition to the agency work plans, agencies were required to apply a Race and Social Justice budget and policy filter to their operations (an example of this filter is discussed in chapter 8). Exhibit 5.2 displays Mayor Nickels's memo directing agencies to use the budget and policy filte .

Exhibit 5.1

Example of a Race and Social Justice Work Plan

Service Equity Team Study (SETS)
Pilot Project
Workscope Final Draft
December 31, 2006

I. Project Purpose

A. Support the City's economic equity goal as it relates to the mayor's Race and Social Justice Initiative by helping ensure that SPU's service levels are equitably met across race, income groups, and geographic locations.

B. Make recommendations to ensure that SPU rate payers across race, income groups, and geographic locations receive services that fall within the range of adopted levels of service.

C. Identify cost issues involved in providing the same levels of service citywide.

II. Approach and Methodology

A. Conduct a three-month pilot study to examine service delivery by census block to determine whether there is a relationship between service levels provided and ethnicity, income or geographic location.

B. Select service levels with easily accessible, valid data, which for this pilot study include solid waste, wastewater and drinking water.

C. Based on adopted service levels for each of the three selected LOBs, examine the following by census block group:

Drinking water: # of water outages per year

Wastewater: # of sewer backups per year

Solid waste: # of missed garbage can pickups per year including repeat misses

D. Customer Service: customer satisfaction measures relating to the selected service levels to see if there are identifiable patterns between service provision and customer satisfaction.

III. Deliverables

- Executive Team Briefing on Workscope
- Written Report
- AMC Briefing

IV. Schedule

January–March 2007: Conduct Study

January 2007: Brief E-Team (to be scheduled)

March 15, 2007: Draft Report

March 30, 2007: Final Report

April 2007: Brief AMC (date to be confirmed)

Source: City of Seattle Public Utilities Department 2007.

Exhibit 5.2

Mayor Nickels' Budgets and Policy Filter Memo

Gregory J. Nickels
Mayor of Seattle
M E M O R A N D U M

DATE: March 11, 2008

TO: Department Directors

FROM: Mayor Greg Nickels

SUBJECT: Important Changes to the Budget Issue Paper process

I am pleased to announce changes to the Budget Issue Paper (BIP) process that will have a profound effect on the city's ability to implement and sustain the Race and Social Justice Initiative.

The Race & Social Justice Executive Change Team has proposed two Policy & Budget Filter questions that will be added to the BIP template. The Policy & Budget Filter questions will ensure equitable city policies and practices by reviewing BIP proposals within the framework of the Race & Social Justice Initiative and by screening for potential unintended consequences of increased inequity. Departments will be required to respond to these questions in each of the BIPs they submit to DOF for review. DOF Staff will be required to provide feedback to Departments and recommendations to me.

In order to facilitate implementation of the new RSJI Policy & Budget Filter, a training session will be required for both Departmental Finance Analysts and Development of Finance Analysts. The trainings will be hosted by members of the RSJ Executive Change Team and located in City Hall's Boards & Commission Room, L280 on the following dates and times:

DOF Analyst Training:	Department Finance Training
Monday, April 7th, 1:30-3:00 p.m.	Tuesday, April 8th, 2:30-4:00 p.m.
City Hall	City Hall
Boards & Commissions Room L280	Boards & Commissions Room L280

As you know, fairness and inclusion are the cornerstones of my priorities for the City of Seattle. All of us who work in city government have a role to play in achieving race and social justice for everyone, and the budget process is central to this effort.

I look forward to this next stage of work in advancing the Race and Social Justice Initiative. Thank you.

Seattle City Hall, 7th Floor, 600 Fourth Avenue, P.O. Box 94749, Seattle, WA 98124-4749
Tel (206) 684-4000 • TDD (206) 615-0476 • Fax (206) 684-5360 • www.seattle.gov/mayor
An equal employment opportunity, affirmative action employer. Accommodations for people with disabilities provided upon request.

Source: Seattle Office for Civil Rights. 2008. *Race and Social Justice Budget and Policy Filter Supplemental Toolkit.* March 31. ww.racialequitytools.org/ resourcefiles/nelson.pdf

The agency work plans and the budget filter forced agencies to examine the capacity of their agency and understand the impact of institutional racism within their specific unit. A member of the SOCR team stated,

> The goal there was to get people to the point where they could look at their work—whatever that was, whatever their lines of business were as a department, as a work unit—and begin to work on achieving racial equity rather than professionally racial inequity in their work. So that meant understanding what institutional racism was and being able to recognize it in actual situations because that's the first step toward being able to develop a plan to change

Results from the Seattle Race and Social Justice Initiative

Seattle's Race and Social Justice Initiative included unwavering support from senior administrators, extensive employee training, and the development and implementation of agency work plans. But what are the results so far? What specifically is the City of Seattle doing to eliminate institutionalized racism? Table 5.2 lists some of its key accomplishments. As this table suggests, the results are widespread across city government.

Consistent with the RSJI, the accomplishments largely relate to internal City of Seattle operations, programs, and services. They are also aligned with the fiv central concern areas identified in the initiative: workforce equity, economic equity, immigrant and refugee services, public engagement, and capacity building. For example, in regard to workforce equity, Seattle has reduced the number of unnecessary criminal background checks conducted as part of hiring processes, requiring those only if they directly relate to the position being filled. The Seattle Fire Department and the Seattle Department of Transportation consider equity when giving overtime assignments. The City of Seattle's work in the area of economic equity is largely focused on promoting more women and minority contractors. This has resulted in a tripling of the use of women- and minority-owned business enterprises (WMBEs) in nonconstruction goods and services from $11 million to $23 million from 2006 to 2011. In regard to immigrant and refugee services, the City of Seattle translated documents about City services into thirty languages. The home page of the Seattle Race and Social Justice Initiative provides materials in Amharic, Cambodian, Chinese, Korean, Oromo, Somali, Spanish, Tagalog, Tigrigna, and Vietnamese (Race and Social Justice Initiative 2012a). In terms of public engagement, the Office of Housing helped save the John C. Cannon House in the Central Area from foreclosure and to maintain community-based ownership. This house provides assisted living for Medicaid recipients, many of whom are African American. Finally, in regard to capacity building, the City of Seattle remains committed to equipping its workforce with training in the area of

Table 5.2

Accomplishments of the Seattle Race and Social Justice Initiative

- Boiler inspectors from the Department of Planning and Development carry translation cards to help them conduct boiler inspections with business owners who speak little or no English.
- The Department of Information Technology surveyed Seattle residents' use of the Internet, cell phones, and other technology, and analyzed the information by race and ethnicity. Tracked over time, the City will use these measures to improve customer services, shape the City's information technology systems, and increase communities of color's access to new technologies.
- The Seattle Office for Civil Rights released the results of fair housing testing in 2011, which revealed widespread racial discrimination in housing application procedures. Six property managers were charged with illegal discrimination based on the test results.
- The City Attorney's Office now seeks sentences of 364 days (rather than 365 days) for gross misdemeanors, thereby avoiding a potential deportation trigger under federal law for any noncitizen. The Washington State Legislature followed Seattle's example and instituted the same policy across the state. The City Attorney's Office also assessed and made changes to laws having a disproportionate impact on communities of color. For example, the City Attorney discontinued prosecuting simple possession of marijuana and driving while license suspended third degree for nonpayment, and drafted a new wage theft law adopted by the City Council and the mayor. The Office provides Continuing Legal Education antiracism training to lawyers throughout the community.
- The Office of Housing helped save the John C. Cannon House in the Central Area from foreclosure and to maintain community-based ownership. Cannon House provides assisted living for Medicaid recipients, many of whom are African Americans.
- The Seattle Department of Transportation used a race and social justice lens to develop its Pedestrian Master Plan.
- The City of Seattle has more than tripled the use of women- and minority-owned business enterprises (WMBEs) in nonconstruction goods and services since the initiative began, from $11 million to $34 million.
- The City's Personnel Department wrote new rules to create more equitable out-of-class work opportunities for City employees. The City's Workforce Equity Committee developed best practices for filling out-of-class positions and trained supervisors to use best practices to achieve racial equity.
- The Seattle Fire and Police Departments are making concerted efforts to ensure communities of color are aware of recruiting, testing, and hiring opportunities.
- The City has reduced the number of unnecessary criminal background checks conducted as part of hiring processes. Background checks now occur only if they directly relate to the position being filled. The change was made to increase employment opportunities for people of color, who are disproportionately represented in the criminal justice system.
- Seattle Public Utilities has reduced the requirement for a college education in positions where a college degree is not actually necessary, after the utility analyzed the impact of a college education requirement on workforce equity.
- The Seattle Fire Department and the Seattle Department of Transportation consider equity when giving overtime assignments. The Fire Department has rewritten its hiring and promotional interview questions to ensure that applicants recognize the diversity of the community.

- Seattle City Light has incorporated the Race and Social Justice Initiative in its succession planning to reduce racial disparities among management and professional and line staff.
- Over 8,000 City employees have participated in Race and Social Justice training, including training in inclusive outreach and public engagement. Most departments have trained all their employees.
- In an RSJI Employee Survey in October 2010, 83 percent of the 5,200 respondents said they believe it is valuable to examine the impact of race, and more than 3,000 employees stated they are actively involved in promoting RSJI changes in their workplace.
- All City departments have change teams that support implementation of departments' annual work plans. A core team works across departments on citywide issues.
- The Office of Arts and Cultural Affairs' smART ventures and neighborhood/community arts funding programs create cultural bridges with communities of color—65 percent of the funding goes to underserved communities. Arts and Cultural Affairs also works with partnering agencies to sponsor community outreach.
- The Department of Planning and Development partners with communities of color to review the department's website. User groups review, test, and give input to determine final website design.
- Policies first introduced in 2007 require all City departments to provide free language interpretation to customers on request and to develop translations of key service information in the six most common languages spoken by Seattle residents.
- The Department of Neighborhoods uses Public Outreach Liaisons (POLs) to engage underrepresented communities in civic processes. Bilingual and bicultural advocates work directly with immigrant and refugee communities and other underrepresented groups to increase access to information about community events and provide language interpretation at the events themselves.
- Translated documents about City services extend to the City's website, which offers program and service information in thirty languages. The Seattle Channel website offers videos in Spanish, Cantonese, Mandarin, and Vietnamese on residential recycling, food and yard waste, and how to recycle electronic equipment.

Source: Race and Social Justice Initiative 2012a.

---

racial equity. Since the inception of the Race and Social Justice Initiative, more than 8,000 City of Seattle employees have completed the RSJI training (virtually the entire City workforce), and nearly 40 percent of employees indicate they are actively involved in promoting RSJI changes in their workplace.

Sustaining the Work

In August 2009, Mayor Nickels lost his primary bid for a third term. The political leadership in Seattle would change. The Seattle Race and Social Justice Initiative began largely as a Mayor Nickels initiative. Was it sustainable beyond his administration? "The two remaining candidates for mayor were political newcomers who were unfamiliar with the initiative" (Bronstein et al. 2011, 171). The RSJI coordinating team arranged briefings on the initiative for both candidates, and they met with Seattle City councilmembers (Bronstein et al. 2011). In November 2009, Councilmember Bruce Harrell agreed to sponsor a resolution affirming support for the initiative. The news release is provided in Exhibit 5.3. In brief, Resolution 31164 is "a resolution affirming the City's race and social justice work and directing City Departments to use available tools to assist in the elimination of racial and social disparities across key indicators of success, including health, education, criminal justice, the environment, employment, and the economy; and to promote equity within the City workplace and in the diversity of City services" (City Council of the City of Seattle 2009).

In addition to strong support from City Council, in November 2009 Seattle elected a new mayor, Mike McGinn, who quickly embraced the Race and Social Justice Initiative (Bronstein et al. 2011).

> As the mayor grappled with significant revenue shortfalls in 2010/2011 caused by the severe nationwide recession, he also made it clear to departments that he expected them to use the Racial Equity Toolkit to analyze the impact of budget reductions on both the public and city employees. Due to the severity of the budget shortfall, it was clear that there would be RSJI impacts, but by using the toolkit, city staff would be more likely to develop strategies to mitigate the impacts of these cuts. (Bronstein et al. 2011, 172)

Additionally, in April 2010, Mayor McGinn issued Executive Order 2010–5, Outreach to Women and Minority Owned Businesses, which strengthens the City's commitment to utilize women- and minority-owned businesses and outlines steps for departments to ensure citywide accountability (Seattle Office for Civil Rights 2012a)

The City of Seattle further sustains the RSJI by hosting an annual conference—Governing for Racial Equity—focused on how governments, particularly at the local level, can promote, measure, and evaluate racial equity. More than 450 individuals attended the two-day conference held in December 2012. The conference was organized around the following thematic tracks: Structural Racism, Partnerships, Collective Impact; Public Policy That Supports Racial Equity; Communicating About Race; Racial Equity Impact Assessment Tools; Building Capacity; and Inclusive Outreach and Public Engagement (Seattle Office for Civil Rights 2012b)

The passage of Resolution 31164 and Mayor McGinn's strong support of the RSJI expanded the initiative to a solid City of Seattle endeavor, rather than a mayoral initiative. As one City of Seattle administrator put it,

> The City turned a corner when it stopped being a mayoral initiative. So this came out under Mayor Nickels. And then Mayor Nickels lost when he was running for the third term. And, as with many mayoral initiatives, there's a question about whether or not that initiative is going to survive and transfer

Exhibit 5.3
Seattle City Council Resolution 31164 News Release
Council News Release

FOR IMMEDIATE RELEASE:
11/30/2009 3:01:00 PM

FOR MORE INFORMATION CONTACT:
Michael Jerrett, Harrell's Office, 206–684–8804

Councilmember Bruce Harrell

Council Passes Resolution Directing Race and Social Justice Work to Continue
City Employees and Department Heads Commit to Heighten Efforts

SEATTLE   Today the City Council passed a Race and Social Justice Resolution intended to heighten the City of Seattle's awareness of institutional racism and social disparities. The Resolution, sponsored by Councilmember Bruce Harrell, seeks to carry forward and strengthen the initiative begun by Mayor Nickels. Councilmember Harrell believes that "Mayor Nickels had the vision and courage to drive this important work which demonstrated his recognition that race and social disparities continue to exist throughout our city. The initiative can result in a healthier and more efficient work environment and better city services to all communities."

Department heads, change teams, city employees and community leaders were all on hand to support the legislation. Deputy Mayor Tim Ceis, on behalf of the Mayor and the City's executive team, expressed their gratefulness that this important work will continue.

The Resolution states the strategies and tools to address racial and social disparities and describes the goals of improving workforce equity, contracting equity and best practices to achieve equal access to city services.

"This work must continue because all people in Seattle benefit when we demonstrate inclusiveness in how we make decisions, how we provide basic city services and how we manage change. This is the first piece of legislation on this issue and Seattle's commitment in this area has already been nationally recognized," says Mayor Nickels.

A key component of the work going forward was the 2009 establishment of a Race and Social Justice Community Roundtable. This group consists of individuals from community organizations, business, philanthropy, education and others with the mission of extending this work beyond city government and into the community. Councilmember Harrell "looks forward to working with the Roundtable and moving this effort beyond City government."

Council meetings are cablecast live on Seattle Channel 21 and Webcast live on the City Council's website at http://www.seattle.gov/council/. Copies of legislation, archives of previous meetings, and news releases are available on http://www.seattle.gov/council/. Follow the Council on Twitter at twitter.com and on Facebook at Seattle City Council.

Source: Harrell 2009.

to a new administration. t o both the new mayor and the c ity c ouncil's credit, they owned it. So that was huge. . . . t hey could have said, "t hat's the old mayor, we're done with that, we've got a new campaign," but they didn't. t hat's when this effort got institutionalized across the city. t hat was a huge watershed moment for the Race and Social Justice i nitiative.

A City of Seattle Race and Social Justice trainer concurred:

> When I saw one of the first ordinances, I said, Wow, this is solidified. It's
> not just an action plan that will go away in a year. This is what we plan to
> do. We put it in law that we're going to do it. It's in the ordinance. . . . But
> beyond that, we know why we're going to do it. We see the benefits of doing
> it. And that makes us want to do it more. It continues the momentum.

Conclusion

Examination of the Seattle Race and Social Justice Initiative yields fiv
primary conclusions: First, unwavering commitment from senior leadership
is a must. In its formative stage, the RSJI had unrelenting support from then
Seattle mayor Greg Nickels. The mayor provided the political muscle and
infrastructure to support key citywide implementation. Seattle's City Council
and current mayor as of this writing, Mike McGinn, continue to provide strong
support to the RSJI. The initiative has expanded from its initial characterization as Mayor Nickels's initiative to a City of Seattle initiative.

Second, internal examination of institutional racism *in government* is an
appropriate first step. A fundamental approach of the RSJI included a direct
and candid assessment of how policies and practices within City of Seattle
government work to benefit white people and to the detriment of people of
color. "The Initiative works within City government to and with community
leaders to get to the root cause of racial equity: institutional racism" (Race
and Social Justice Initiative 2012b). The informal internal motto of RSJI
expressed repeatedly by interviewed City of Seattle employees is the need to
"get our own house in order first.

Additionally, in order to be successful over the long term, racial equity
efforts need to be supported by ordinary government employees, not only
those who are passionate about racial justice work. As an SOCR staff
member noted,

> We learned early on not to go down the road that racial equity often takes
> you . . . it's the role of fire-breathing radicals on the right or left to always
> say unless you're with me, you're nowhere at all. We just didn't buy that.
> We were really clear. We're government. We're representing everybody. . . .
> There's always going to be committed radicals who want to do this; this is
> their passion. But I believe that nothing will change institutionally if you
> only catch the most radical. . . . It can't just rely on a handful of leaders.
> It's got to be the actual mediocre person who doesn't care about this. Ul-
> timately, the goal is to get people to do racial equity work who don't care

about it. We shouldn't think of ourselves as special for doing this. Rather, we should view this as regular government stuff.

Third, beginning racial equity work in government is hard. Nervousness peaks here. As illustrated in the case of Seattle, implementing an initiative characterized by government ownership of institutional racism met initial resistance from multiple parties—employees, administrators, even the City Attorney's Office. Emotions in the training sessions ranged from support and enthusiasm to anger and resentment. Some administrators initially utilized passive aggressiveness to avoid engaging the RSJI and its required work plans. Directly navigating these uncomfortable, emotion-laden areas is an important and necessary part of the process. It provides a common grounding in the concept of institutionalized racism in government and the responsibility of government to eliminate it. Discussing race and institutional racism is difficult. Without an appropriate structure, the focus on race can easily shift to other, more comfortable topics, such as income and poverty. Leaders of the initiative were committed to keeping the focus on race, both in the naming of the initiative and in its implementation.

Fourth, normalizing discussions about race and institutional racism is an early indicator of progress. Over time, more and more employees of the City of Seattle became comfortable talking about key concepts such as institutional racism and white privilege. This facilitated direct racial equity impact analysis of the policies, practices, and services provided by the City. The normalizing of discussion about race and institutional racism provided an opportunity for organizational change and learning to occur.

Fifth, results of institutional racism work will take time. It does not happen quickly, but with sustained commitment, significant changes occur. As highlighted in Table 5.2, the City of Seattle has realized widespread improvements in racial equity. With employee training, agency plans, and strong accountability and performance reporting mechanisms, substantial outcomes in the area of racial equity occur. Yet, as one City of Seattle employee articulated, with the appropriate systems in place, racial equity work can thrive relatively quickly.

> When I go out and give a presentation on this [RSJI], I liken this to looking at the Soviet Union and thinking the Cold War will be going on for the next two or three hundred years. And in one swoop, it disappeared. And it doesn't require 100 percent agreement either. . . . I think social change comes quickly if you have the right elements in place. Institutions are not as invulnerable as we think. There are critical moments in their lives when you can literally transform the organization. . . . So, it's all a matter of languaging [*sic*] and strategy.

Importantly, an analysis of the Seattle Race and Social Justice initiative provides an empirical, on-the-ground case of several of the individual and organizational elements presented in earlier chapters. The RSJI experience captures the significance of organizational leadership, the development and implementation of organizational justice values and goals, the need to expand the boundaries of organizational socialization to include broader dimensions of racial equity, the emotional (and avoidance) dimension of race talk, especially at work, the critical linkage between race talk and organizational action, and the importance of accountability in fostering organizational learning within the nervous area of racial equity in government.

References

Adelman, Larry. 2003. "Statement from the Executive Producer." About the series *Race: The Power of an Illusion* (California Newsreel). www.pbs.org/race/000_About/002_04-about.htm (accessed April 16, 2013).

Bronstein, Elliott, Glenn Harris, Ron Harris-White, and Julie Nelson. 2011. "Eliminating Institutional Racism Within Local Government: The City of Seattle Race and Social Justice Initiative." In *Government Is Us 2.0*, ed. Cheryl Simrell King. Armonk, NY: M.E. Sharpe. 157–173.

Brunner, Jim. 2002. "The Measure of a Mayor." *Seattle Times*, January 13. http://seattletimes.com/pacificnw/2002/0 13/cover.html.

City Council of the City of Seattle. 2009. Resolution Number 31164. November 30.

City of Seattle Public Utilities Department. 2007. *The Environmental Justice & Service Equity Division at Seattle Public Utilities—How Did That Happen and What Did They Do?* The State of Environmental Justice in America 2007 #112006-2. www.ejconference.net/images/White_Diangson.pdf (accessed April 19, 2013).

Egan, Timothy. 2001. "Primary Voters Reject Seattle Mayor After One Term." *New York Times,* September 9. www.nytimes.com/2001/09/20/us/primary-voters-reject-seattle-mayor-after-one-term.html.

Harrell, Bruce. 2009. "Council Passes Resolution Directing Race and Social Justice Work to Continue." News release, November 30. www.seattle.gov/council/news-detail.asp?ID=10355&Dept=28 (accessed January 10, 2013).

Mack, Dwayne. 2011. "Rice, Norm (1943–)." In *An Online Reference Guide to African American History,* ed. q uintard Taylor. Seattle: BlackPast.org. www.blackpast.org/?q=aaw/rice-norm-1943.

Nickels, Gregory. 2012. Remarks. Governing for Racial Equity Conference, Seattle University, Seattle, WA. December.

The People's Institute for Survival and Beyond. 2013. Website. www.pisab.org (accessed April 16, 2013).

Race and Social Justice Initiative. 2008. *2008 Report: Looking Back, Looking Forward.* Seattle: Seattle Office for Civil Rights. www.seattle.gov/rsji/docs/Jan20FINAL-RSJIrept.pdf (accessed April 16, 2013).

———. 2012a. *Accomplishments 2009–2011.* Seattle: Seattle Office for Civil Rights. www.seattle.gov/rsji/docs/RSJIAccomplishments2009-2011.pdf (accessed April 16, 2013).

————. 2012b. *Advance Opportunity. Achieve Equality.* Seattle: Seattle Office for Civil Rights. www.seattle.gov/rsji/docs/2-pager.pdf (accessed April 16, 2013).

————. 2012c. *Racial Equity in Seattle: Race and Social Justice Initiative Three-Year Plan 2012–14.* Seattle: Seattle Office for Civil Rights. www.seattle.gov/rsji/docs/RacialEquityinSeattleReport2012-14.pdf (accessed April 16, 2013).

————. 2013. *Employee Survey 2012.* March. Seattle: Seattle Office of Civil Rights. www.seattle.gov/rsji/docs/Report-2012Survey_FINAL.pdf.

Seattle Office for Civil Rights. 2008. *Race and Social Justice Budget and Policy Filter Supplemental Toolkit.* March 31. www.racialequitytools.org/resourcefiles nelson.pdf.

————. 2012a. About RSJI. www.seattle.gov/rsji/about.htm (accessed April 16, 2013).

————. 2012b. Governing for Racial Equity Conference 2012. www.seattle.gov/rsji/GRE/conference12.htm (accessed January 18, 2013).

Washington State Democratic Chairs Organization. 2012. Biography for Gregory J. Nickels. http://wp.chairs.wa-democrats.net/ (accessed April 16, 2013).

6 ASSESSING AGENCY PERFORMANCE: THE WISCONSIN EXPERIENCE

Examining racial disparities in welfare programs is not an easy task. As John Rohr states in his classic work *Ethics for Bureaucrats,* "It is perhaps no exaggeration to say that questions of race, in one form or another, have been the most important issues in American politics" (1989, 99). Having governmental agencies take an active role in researching racial disparities of their programs is an important, but complex, task. It is important because under Title VI, Section 601 of the Civil Rights Act of 1964, "No person in the United States, shall, on the ground of race, color or national origin, be excluded from the participation in, be denied the benefits of, or be subjected to discrimination under any program or activity receiving Federal financial assistance." This prohibition includes intentional discrimination, as well as procedures, criteria, or methods of administration that appear neutral but have a discriminatory effect on individuals because of their race, color, or national origin. It is important for governmental agencies not only to respond to allegations of racial discrimination but also to *routinely self-assess* whether racial disparities exist in the services they provide. Race analysis is an important dimension in gauging social equity within public policy. "Race analysis is the systematic application of the tools of historical and cultural analysis to understand the social and economic circumstances facing blacks and other racial minority group members" (Myers 2002, 170).

Assessing racial disparities is qualitatively different from assessing other outcomes, such as comparing agency performance by region or by subgroups (for example, single-parent families vs. married families). It is different because there is an important emotional and historical context that intervenes. Why would agencies want to self-assess racial disparities of their programs given the wide array of emotions such an assessment could invoke?

Agencies should initiate this type of an assessment because it promotes good government. As defined by Lawrence Mead, good government involves making and implementing effective policy (2004, 213). Therefore, "good government" should also include assessing the implementation of public policy for racial disparities. The behavioral aspects of good welfare reform policy cut both ways: Clients have behavioral expectations in terms of seeking employment and reporting earnings. Agency staff have behavioral expectations to not discriminate in the implementation of their programs. Good government should monitor both sets of expectations.

This chapter is focused on the following question: How can government agencies assess whether racial disparities exist in their programs? Specifically, what is the *process* they can use to facilitate such a study? After discussing the concept of social equity as it relates to public administration and establishing important historical context for why examining racial discrimination in welfare administration is important, this chapter analyzes the work of a steering committee tasked with assessing racial disparities in the sanctioning of Wisconsin's welfare clients. It offers an examination of how public policies can be assessed for racial disparities.

Public Administration and Social Equity

A fundamental component of the promotion of good government is the examination of social equity. Issues of equity and justice are fundamental concerns of public administrators. Public administrators face the constant struggle of evaluating the country's social climate and ensuring equity in governance (Akram 2004). Like the United States, public administration has moved slowly in applying principles of justice. In fact, equity or fairness in public services was the last established "pillar" of the field—and it still remains secondary in emphasis behind economy, effectiveness, and efficienc .[1]

Assessing Social Equity in Governmental Services

A core challenge to achieving social equity in the delivery of governmental services is to identify an approach to social equity assessment. A useful framework to launch this type of assessment includes five key actions: (1) identifying the purpose of the department, the services it provides, and for whom these services are provided; (2) providing an assessment of agency procedures to identify equity issues; (3) conducting an assessment of the nature and distribution of benefits and services externally; (4) conducting an assessment of the quality of services provided; and (5) assessing the outcomes impacted by the department's performance. This chapter offers a case study of how the Division of Workforce Solutions in Wisconsin conducted an assessment of racial disparities in its welfare program and offers a conceptual model, as well as lessons learned, that may be useful for other agencies concerned with assessing the social equity of their services.

Contemporary Welfare Policy and Race

The Personal Responsibility and Work Opportunity Reconciliation Act of 1996 eliminated Aid to Families with Dependent Children (AFDC) as an entitlement and created a block grant for states to provide time-limited cash assistance for needy families. These state programs are funded under the Temporary Assistance for Needy Families (TANF) federal block grant program. States may use their TANF funding in any manner "reasonably calculated to accomplish the purposes of TANF" (U.S. Department of Health and Human Services 1996). States have broad discretion under TANF to determine eligibility, method of assistance, and benefit levels. The discretionary setting of TANF is very different from that of AFDC, because (1) the Department of Health and Human Services must determine that a state's plan is legally complete, but does not otherwise have authority to approve or disapprove a plan, and (2) it is not clear whether there is any consequence if a state fails to follow its plan (Greenberg and Savner 1996).

Based on the historical relationship between race and welfare in the United States, several areas of TANF policy are particularly relevant and should be systematically evaluated to ascertain racial bias. These areas include case management including client assessment; access to training, community work experiences, and education; availability of support services such as child care and transportation assistance; the issuance of sanctions; labor market opportunities and earnings; time limits; and lack of uniformity in political subdivisions (Gooden 1999).

Case Management

Case management is a key component of any welfare reform plan. An analysis of clients' experiences with their case managers facilitates better understanding of the nature of a program's "treatment" in practice. Case managers become agents of the policymakers and give a program model its concrete meaning. They operationalize their relationship between the client and the program by applying, in specific situations, legislative and regulatory directions about who must participate, in what activities they should participate, and what support services they should receive (Doolittle and Riccio 1992). How case managers complete these tasks will have a great effect on the program outcomes experienced by their clients. In delivering policy, public-service workers or "street-level bureaucrats" have substantial discretion in their work. They are entrusted to make decisions about people that affect their life chances (Lipsky 1980). In this case, these chances involve the likelihood of self-sufficienc . A pilot research study that examined the promotion of education services by caseworkers among black and white clients in two rural Virginia counties found

41 percent of white clients reported that their caseworker continued to promote education, compared to none of the black clients (Gooden 1998, 28).

Sanctioning

Under TANF, caseworkers may issue a financial sanction for welfare clients who do not comply with program rules and work activities without good cause. Deciding whether to issue a sanction or to excuse nonparticipation based on good cause is an area of caseworker discretion. A study of five panhandle counties in Florida found blacks were much more likely to be sanctioned for noncompliance than their white counterparts (61 percent versus 48.4 percent) (Clarke, Jarmon, and Langley 1999, 130).

Exiting Welfare

Recent research on welfare leavers suggests that racial differences also occur. Clarke, Jarmon, and Langley found a 35 percent differential in post-welfare poverty figures, with white respondents reporting a mean income of $10,403, compared with $6,736 for blacks (1999, 122). When examining employer demand for welfare recipients in four urban areas, Holzer and Stoll found that "relative to their white counterparts, black and Hispanic welfare recipients are less likely to be hired in suburban and/or smaller establishments, and for blacks, in the retail trade industries" (2000, 26). Using employer survey data with 170 firms in the Chicago area, Wilson found that 74 percent expressed negative views of inner-city blacks (1996, 112).

There are also some studies that suggest favorable outcomes for minorities under TANF. Studies in Arizona, Georgia, and Ohio suggest that the percentages of blacks that are employed exceed the percentages of whites that are employed and even report somewhat higher quarterly earnings (Savner 2000). Holzer and Stoll (2000, 35) also report employer demand for all racial groups of welfare recipients is somewhat higher in minority-owned businesses and that contact with the relevant local agencies is associated with substantial increases in demand for white and black recipients when initiated by agencies and especially for Hispanics when initiated by firms

The Case of Wisconsin

Wisconsin Works, commonly called "W-2," replaced Aid to Families with Dependent Children and was designed to promote economic self-sufficiency via labor market engagement. The Division of Workforce Solutions (DWS) in the Department of Workforce Development (DWD) administers W-2, although providers under state contract administer W-2 at the local level. As a response to a legal complaint to the U.S. Department of Health and Human Services filed in 2002 by the American Civil Liberties Union (ACLU) and the Milwaukee Branch of the National Association for the Advancement of Colored People (NAACP)[2] and external research[3] suggesting some racial groups may be sanctioned at a higher rate than others in the W-2 program, the Division of Workforce Solutions (DWS) issued a preliminary report, "Analysis of W-2 Sanctions by Race 2001 and 2002."

Sanctioning is the reduction or discontinuation of financial support based on participant noncompliance with program rules and guidelines. The impact of sanctions is real because it affects the overall grant amount, duration of grant reduction, and overall remaining eligibility for benefit receipt. Agencies and caseworkers have considerable discretion in issuing sanctions.

The DWS report found differences in sanctioning rates by race/ethnicity across a number of agencies throughout the state. Prior to the release of the DWS study, a study by the Institute for Wisconsin's Future reported that 42 percent of black and 45 percent of Hispanic W-2 recipients were sanctioned, compared to 24 percent of white recipients (Mulligan-Hansel and Fendt 2002). Another study by the Wisconsin Legislative Audit Bureau (LAB) indicated that black W-2 recipients were sanctioned at twice the rate of white recipients (47 percent vs. 23 percent) (Wisconsin Legislative Audit Bureau 2002). The DWS analysis also found some racial differences in sanctioning rates, and the department decided to examine the issue more in depth. In doing so, the department clearly articulated its commitment to a critical examination of the racial issue: "This is a very complex issue and will require additional research beyond the exploratory analysis presented here. However, based on this review, the [DWS] has determined that the issue warrants further study in order to identify potential problems with more precision. . . . The Department is committed to forthrightly addressing issues that may arise from this research" (DWS 2003).

The DWS established a steering committee to provide guidance to the study. The steering committee reflected a broad range of knowledge, technical skills, and perspectives on the W-2 program. It included W-2 agency administrators, representatives of client advocacy groups, state administrators, and academics with experience in research methods and knowledgeable of W-2.

The charge to the steering committee was to develop the research questions for the study, to approve an overall methodology that would be used to address those questions, to review the research products developed, to draw conclusions about the research results, and to make recommendations to the DWS administrator. The original scope of the study was threefold: (1) to develop more sophisticated measures of sanction rates and analytical techniques to better understand where racial/ethnic disparities exist and the magnitude of these disparities; (2) to determine whether policy or variations in the interpretation of policy may contribute to disparities in sanction rates by race/ethnicity; and (3) to determine if variations in placement type and assignment to activities may contribute to disparities in sanction rates by race/ethnicity (Department of Workforce Development 2004, 4).

Although the general task of utilizing a steering committee to guide the research was fairly standard, the explicit focus on race was not. Over the course of more than a year, the steering committee and its technical work groups provided guidance to the study and examined racial disparities through a very diverse committee of people who held differing perspectives on the issue at hand. The approach of DWS and the steering committee provides a useful case study to better understand how public agencies can self-assess racial disparities in their poverty programs.

This is a qualitative study based primarily on interviews with DWD administrators and members of the steering committee conducted during March 2005. Most interviews were conducted individually and lasted between sixty and ninety minutes. Interviewing the members of the steering committee provides valuable information because the steering committee was a very broad and diverse group. Its membership included members of advocacy groups, local agency staff, state administrators, and academic researchers. The interview protocol included questions about how the study evolved and how the steering committee conducted its work, resolved disputes, and formulated its recommendations. All respondents were assured of confidentialit . Appendix 6.1 provides the interview protocol. A content analysis of these interviews was performed using a qualitative software data analysis package. From this data analysis, themes were identified that became the basis for a conceptual model to facilitate the analysis of racial disparities by state agencies.

Findings from Wisconsin Works

Drawing on the results of the content analysis, eight key findings were identified. They are summarized here with supporting quotations from the staff interviews.

1. Advocacy groups were important in elevating racial analysis on the agency agenda.

By all accounts, a motivating force behind the DWD study was the formal complaint filed by the ACLU and the NAACP. It seems unlikely that DWD would have committed to a study of this magnitude absent this preceding event, suggesting a critically important role of advocacy groups. As a steering committee member reflected

The complaint to the Office of Civil Rights was originally a disability complaint. But, then we stumbled onto data that had racial issues. Our primary focus initially was on disabilities, then race secondarily. But, we had the Legislative Audit Bureau report, so there really was a converging set of events that led to this study.

Another member of the steering committee agreed:

Having the NAACP at the table, has not allowed them to forget or brush away race. . . . The conversation is just different when a black person is there. I'm sorry but it makes a difference. It's one thing to talk about these things, but when a black person is there, there's a different reaction. Having that representation is important; otherwise, the conversation can slip into this "we're all the same" discussion. A voice from this group was important.

2. Examining racial disparities within a governmental agency is a "nervous area of government." However, over time, both the steering committee and agency administrators became more comfortable engaging issues of race.

There was universal consensus across agency administrators and other steering committee members that engaging issues of race is uncomfortable. Specific comments included:

What was interesting to me was to listen to the explicit conversations about race. It's interesting to see how nervous and uncomfortable people are talking about race. Their first reaction is, "You're accusing me of being a racist." Don't accuse me of being a racist. But, you have the data, so why the protest?

Many of the agencies were defensive. They kept saying, "You're calling me a racist." We had to ensure them that we are not talking about your specific [caseworker], we're talking about a policy structure that does not consider racial discrimination. How could anyone find this unimaginable

Yes, we had to focus on the impact, rather than the source.

Yes, people were horribly uncomfortable talking about race.

The sanctions study was one of the most hot button topics studied. There is a lot of defensiveness when you start talking about race. . . . Sometimes the process was painfully laborious, but in the end it was a very positive process. We need to be public about this [analysis of racial disparities].

It forced more thinking about this. It's easy to describe devolution and discretion theoretically. But, to break it down to discreet decision-making, it brings home the wild west nature of the program—injustice can happen.

Perhaps a senior DWD administrator summed it up best:

Examining racial disparities is a "nervous area of government." There's a tension. You want to do a good job. In order to do that, you must do the analysis. But, it's hard because an agency doesn't want to look like it's doing a bad job.

It is not surprising that steering committee members and agency administrators felt uncomfortable engaging issues of racial disparities. However, an important additional finding was that as the months progressed, committee members became more comfortable engaging issues of race. An administrator commented:

The process took much longer than anyone anticipated. We began to form a common basis and form common ground. In the end, people just said what they thought. They didn't have to worry about having a department person there or whatever. State workers could criticize the state. We just all told it like it was. It became a much more comfortable process. . . . Discrimination is likely occurring at all levels—by the individual person, by the agency, or due to policy intent. We need to ferret all of that out and examine a lot of assumptions.

This suggests an important finding for public sector agencies that embark upon racial disparities analysis. If the agency administrators understand that there will initially be discomfort in discussing race but decide to stay committed to racial analysis over the long term, concrete progress in analysis can occur.

3. The composition of the steering committee was important. It gave legitimacy to the study.

The fourteen-member steering committee reflected a broad range of knowledge, technical skills, and perspectives on the W-2 program. It included W-2 agency administrators, representatives of client advocacy groups, state administrators, and academics with experience in research methods and knowledgeable of W-2. The committee met at least once a month, with several work group meetings in between, as well as distribution of materials to the full group by e-mail. Specific tasks of the committee included developing research questions for the study, overseeing the analyses that were conducted, reviewing the research products that were developed, drawing conclusions about the research results, and making recommendations to DWS. The steering committee was supported by technical work groups that were responsible for guiding the specific analysis and for presenting research findings to the committee.

There was a strong consensus that the composition of the steering committee gave legitimacy to the study. The agency intentionally selected solid people from the variety of perspectives represented on the steering committee.

> Having solid, well-respected people regardless of sector was important. We made sure we had solid advocates, solid W-2 agency people, solid researchers. We didn't want to have the charge that we selected solid members from one sector and put them in a setting with weak members from other settings. We had strong, solid people on the entire team.

Over time, the quality of the composition of the steering committee led to some appreciation of alternative viewpoints. Although original positions were not radically altered, alternative positions were better understood.

> The steering committee was cumbersome. There was grandstanding at some points. Someone would make some point and then someone else would rebut it. . . . But, people at the table had "ah-ha" moments. *Discretion is important.* (original emphasis)

4. Agency leadership is important. DWD's willingness to commit time and resources to a study involving racial disparities was critical to overall project success.

Respondents universally acknowledged that the DWD committed a significan amount of time and resources to the study. DWD's commitment was twofold. Senior leadership sent strong signals of the study's importance, and they assigned well-respected lower-level administrators to work more closely on the study. By all accounts, the chief administrator of the Division of Workforce Solutions had an unwavering commitment to this study. In conducting racial analysis of public policies and programs, senior leadership matters. Respondents offered positive comments regarding the agency's ability to show senior support, but to minimize politicizing the study.

[A senior administrator] was very supportive in us taking a look at the facts and not to get involved in the political process. The top folks are always going to be strategizing politically. But, the line bureaucrat wants to do the best job they can. These folks have a strong vested interest in making improvements in their areas.

Staff were assigned to the study with appropriate skills. They did not give this to the limelight [political staff], but rather to the real worker bees. The study had sufficient expertise

[A senior administrator] said you have to do something about this. Having a core person within the agency take ownership right away was important. Right away, she made sure the Secretary took a position and launched a study.

In fairness, I think the state spent more time on this study than they do on most. It did exceed our expectations. It was given a lot of time and space. There was a real sense of commitment.

5. The steering committee agreed upon specific methodology, which increased buy-in for the results.

Initially, the steering committee had several discussions about the research design and specific research methodology. The committee considered case file review, matched-pair testing, caseworker observation, and analysis of administrative data. Ultimately, the committee agreed to examine administrative sanctioning data for the entire state, and to rely primarily upon regression analysis. Although there are myriad ways to analyze any phenomenon, it was important that the group work through this process and collectively decide on a research approach.

Within DWD there was considerable discussion about whether the methodology was legitimate. There is this tension they were working out internally. Some folks thought they had a finding—others insisted you guys just don't know how to read the numbers. It's good to have a clear understanding of the methods if you're planning to do the study.

Lots of [methodological] decisions to make, setting up equations, figuring out interaction effects of variables.

Academic researchers were particularly helpful here.

> The academic research side was very useful. They were helpful in explain-
> ing methodological concerns to the advocates. They were willing to discuss
> these issues. The Department did not have to broker this discussion. The
> Department would not have been viewed as an appropriate broker of the
> data.

It was important that the group agree upon the methodological approach
prior to the presentation of findings. Once the agreed-upon methodological
approach was in place, there was a consensus to accept the findings. This
was important for several reasons. It avoided "analysis paralysis," which
can ultimately serve as an inhibitor to reaching consensus on any findings. It
did not allow people to pick and choose the methodology based on the final
results, and it facilitated buy-in from the entire steering committee regarding
the research findings. The transparent nature of the methodological discussion
also allowed all committee members to participate in the discussion, be aware
of the trade-offs, and eliminate the "I didn't agree with the methodology"
excuse for not accepting the findings

6. When developing recommendations, removing the messenger from the message yielded positive results.

A challenging task of the steering committee was to develop a core set of
recommendations. This became challenging because both DWS and the
steering committee felt that, for the recommendations to be taken seriously, it
was important to have consensus around the recommendations. However, in
developing the recommendations, it was apparent early on that it was difficul
to disassociate the recommendation from the recommender.

The steering committee relied upon a facilitator who had not been involved with the project. The facilitator had three major objectives: (1) refine
how the report findings, the summaries, and the policy recommendations
were finally worded; (2) identify the priority recommendations that they
could agree upon as a full committee; and (3) identify a second tier of recommendations that received a majority of the committee votes, and include
them as a separate set of recommendations. As one person commented:
"Concern about group sign-off was a real concern. No one wanted two sets
of recommendations going forward. First of all, what is the Secretary sup-
posed to do with that?"

The facilitator relied upon Group Systems, a facilitation software package. The product allowed sixteen users to participate simultaneously and
anonymously. Although the members were in the same room together,

each member had an individual computer where he or she could provide input on an anonymous basis. Multiple voting processes were used through the process of formulating final recommendations. These included yes/no votes, ranking, and recommendations by a particular sector (advocate, state employees, W-2 agencies, etc.).

The facilitator commented:

> One of the key aspects of the facilitation software is that people key in their comments on an anonymous basis. They also appreciate that Group Systems allowed them to capture their exact comments as they typed it in. They could state things as they felt it should be stated. . . . At the end people were delighted. The process was long and their ideas were not always chosen, but their participation mattered. It was a valuable participation effort. I think everyone felt that their comments were fully considered.

She continued:

> We used multiple methods to identify the priorities. As first we ranked them. People could see the rankings on a spreadsheet. They were quite intrigued with that. The group decided as a group not to use the first round of rankings. We also ranked by sector (advocates, state workers, W-2 agencies). Those fell out pretty much as expected. We also used the yes/no function. We used multiple methods to work on the recommendations.

The neutral but guiding role of the facilitator was also very important.

> I made every effort to remain neutral. The recommendation had to be based on the group's decision. And a key point was that this wasn't going to work if the facilitator was not neutral. It is key to make sure you don't allow people to take the floor for too long. I stressed that comments should be succinct. Group Systems could capture it. It's fine to state your issue, but you cannot take up the whole agenda.

The timing of the facilitator was also important. The facilitator was brought in at the end of the process, with a specific task of assisting the group in developing their recommendations. The facilitator had not been privy to or biased by earlier discussions of the steering committee.

Ultimately, the use of Group Systems and a facilitator forced the steering committee into making specific decisions

In the end, after using several methods [to formulate recommendations] and doing several revisions, collecting comments back from e-mail, the final method we used was yes/no. You either had to say up or down whether you supported the recommendation. The voting structure we used took a long time. I can live with that. I think it helped people with the final product

A senior administrator commented, "Group Systems provides an equal opportunity for input and mediates the chatty types. It eliminates the people who like to browbeat one way or the other." Through use of the Group Systems software, the steering committee ultimately agreed upon a core set of nineteen recommendations in the areas of case manager and supervisor training, changes in policy statute, changes in implementation practices, increased monitoring of agency behavior, and analysis (see Table 6.1). As a senior DWD administrator commented, "This establishes the research agenda."

7. The study took a long time, but the process itself was viewed as a clear strength.

The steering committee and associated work groups worked intensively for over a year. As one may expect, some meetings were more productive than others. However, ultimately, the commitment of time itself seemed to be an important variable in promoting study buy-in and acceptance. As committee members commented:

I'm not a patient person. So, when I saw this concept of a slow process, I was not thrilled. But, I did appreciate that more. There are times when a slow process can be helpful.

The entire process was very time consuming, but also extremely valuable.

It was time consuming working through the recommendations. We realized that some people were against some of the recommendations based on a minor point. We were able to clarify some misunderstandings. It did shift my opinion on the use of a consensus project.

8. Ultimately agency administrators viewed the examination of racial disparities to be a very important undertaking. They encourage other agencies to not be afraid to engage in racial analysis.

Public sector agencies may be reluctant to embark upon racial disparities analysis of their programs for many reasons. At best, it can be an uncomfortable analysis to

Table 6.1

Wisconsin Works Sanction Study Recommendations

Priority Recommendations (based on group consensus)

Training	• Provide training to case managers and supervisory staff to increase awareness of diversity issues. Identify, analyze, and share the results of research from other states that examines the impact of case managers' decision-making on sanctioning, with the goal of reducing differential impacts.
	• Develop policy and staff training to emphasize the need for accommodations for participants with health conditions (or children with disabilities) that preclude full-time participation. Those accommodations can include but are not limited to reducing required participation hours.
	• Evaluate W-2 training curriculum to determine how discretionary aspects of W-2 policy are trained. Determine if training outcomes are consistent with stated law, administrative rule, and policy. Focus training to ensure that all FEPs [case managers] and supervisory staff understand policy and appropriately use guidelines when exercising discretion.
Policy/Statute	• Provide more guidance through policy in the area of granting "good cause." Guidelines should include reasons similar to those specified in Learnfare. The "good cause" process should be made accessible to people with a variety of barriers, and specify documentation for "good cause" and time frame. Agency practice must comply with state policy guidelines.
	• Emphasize through policy that assessment, including formal assessment, is an ongoing process and not a one-time event. Establish a trigger that requires that additional assessments and intensive case management would be offered to participants who receive severe or repeated sanctions, or to establish if they are employed full-time.
	• Restore the fair hearing process (would require a statutory change).
	• Establish a definition of what activities can be sanctioned. Only work activities should be sanctionable. Activities related to health needs would not be sanctionable. Train staff to assist customers on compliance.

(continued)

116

Table 6.1 (continued)

Practice/ Implementation	• Identify best practices that reduce inappropriate sanctioning to be implemented with agencies statewide. Determine if there are case management strategies or practices that lead to inappropriate sanctions. • Develop an action plan of ways to improve case management, including targeted training, policy clarification, and system reporting tools that can help FEPs. • Hold periodic roundtables for FEPs and supervisory staff to review case scenarios and discuss as a group where the individual should be placed in W-2, with the goal of increasing uniformity in decision-making statewide.
Monitoring	• Monitor adverse actions by race and require agencies with a high level of disparities to provide explanations. • Continue to monitor "significant sanction" cases through the DWS BW-2 Regional Offices to ensure appropriate outcomes for all participants. • Increase BW-2 regional staff to ensure adequate case management monitoring can be continued.
Analysis	• Analyze why people of color are much more likely to be placed in CSJs [community service jobs] than white participants. • Conduct a comprehensive study of sanctions, strikes, and other adverse actions by race in the [next] biennium. • Analyze the significant changes in racial disparities between 2001, 2002, and 2003 and seek to identify patterns or factors that may have contributed to the reduction or increase. This could be used to develop best practices that could be implemented in Wisconsin, as well as other states. • Examine the findings related to Native American participants, whose sanction rates are also much higher than white participants. • Approve the proposal to evaluate the W-2 screening and assessment process. • Create and release a standardized annual report of sanctions by race.

Source: Department of Workforce Development 2004, 32–35.

undertake. At worst, it can lead to public embarrassment or legal action by exposing internal agency shortcomings. Importantly, however, senior administrators at DWD recognized a larger, overarching concern of providing administrative justice, fairness, and equity. A senior administrator commented:

> I've been involved in government for many, many years and seen many, many studies. I've been through all types of investigations. The fallout never concerns me. What concerns me is that we do whatever we can to improve the integrity of our services and improving that—making a positive impact on people's lives—that we're helping them. If a report points something out that we are doing wrong, then so be it. To find there's discrimination in our program is not a surprise. I am very aware that discrimination exists. When a white male convicted felon is more employable than an African-American male that has no negatives, there are major racial disparities. It has always amazed me that more people haven't taken to the street when it comes to racial disparities. Documented discrimination in W-2 and racial disparities is not a surprise. . . . Agency appreciation of research is critical. You can't work in a "no bad news" environment.

Other senior administrators agreed.

> I think we are in a better position having done the study itself. It shows a willingness of the agency to look at what it is doing.

> Of course, we have had many, many studies. I've seen in years past when negative studies never saw the light of day. But, this isn't the case now. The agency understands the importance of this type of research.

> Don't be reluctant to do a study. Get your stakeholders onboard and ensure them that it is not a witch-hunt. If there is a problem, let's see what we can do to fix it

Conceptual Model for Racial Disparities Analysis Within Agencies

Findings from the Wisconsin case study offer an important understanding of one agency's experience in examining racial disparities. But, in order to reduce social inequities in the administration of public services and benefits more generally, a conceptual model is warranted. How might other agencies approach a similar type of racial disparities analysis? Figure 6.1 proposes a useful model.

Figure 6.1   **Conceptual Model for Agency Examination of Racial Disparities**

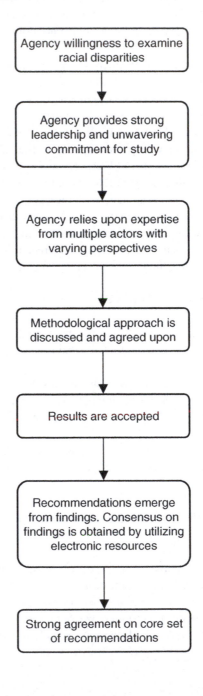

First, and perhaps most important, the agency must be willing to examine racial disparities. Wisconsin's DWD analysis was preceded by a legal complaint by the Office of Civil Rights. This need not be the case. In order to advance good government and social equity, agencies should routinely assess whether the benefits and services they provide suggest racial disparities. Second, such a study of racial disparities must have solid support from senior agency administration. Administrators must send clear messages regarding their unwavering commitment to undertake such a study and to devote significant agency time and expertise to conducting race-related research in a rigorous and thoughtful manner. Third, it is important for the agency to rely upon multiple sources of expertise. In the case of DWD, the steering committee was composed of well-respected administrators, line staff, policy researchers, and advocates. This gave the study credibility and fostered buy-in for the research findings. Fourth, the study's research design and overall methodology should be thoroughly vetted and decided in advance of the findings. Following careful consideration of the research design, the methodological approach should be considered valid. In the case of Wisconsin, input from external, academic public policy researchers was very helpful and reduced skepticism of the agency's methodological approach. Fifth, findings should be accepted. In a study of this type, employing a steering committee comprising multiple stakeholders with varying perspectives is helpful. In the absence of such a deliberative process, fin - ings may be viewed as suspect. The deliberative and transparent process, coupled with a solid agreement upon the methodological approach, should result in acceptable findings. Sixth, utilizing software packages such as Group Systems to separate the message from the messenger can promote maximum participation, limit overbearing personalities, and provide a useful means to facilitate a consensus set of recommendations. Finally, developing consensus on a core set of recommendations is important for future agency action. Ultimately, two sets of recommendations are not valuable to agency decision makers in determining next steps.

Conclusion

Examining racial disparities is important to the overall distribution of public services. Such an examination allows public sector agencies (and their contractors) to gauge the fairness of the benefits and services they provide. In order to promote social equity and good government associated with public service delivery, assessing racial disparities should become common practice. An examination of the work of the DWD welfare sanction study in Wisconsin provides a useful, close-up view of the processes involved in such an agency's undertaking. The lessons from Wisconsin should prove very valuable for other public sector agencies that decide to engage in similar research. Of course, the investigative process is only one step in ensuring social equity. To reverse social inequities or maintain existing social equities, agency administrators also must implement core recommendations in a timely manner. Yet, an important first step is still an agency's willingness to embark upon the discovery process.

Appendix 6.1

Interview Protocol

Opening Question

1. The DWS has been examining racial disparities for the past three years. How has it generally been going?
2. How would you assess your overall level of involvement with this study? [Probe: continuous, sporadic, specific areas]

Study Development (Background and Context)

3. Can you walk me through how the study evolved? Why did you decide to examine racial disparities in the sanctioning of welfare clients?
4. Who were the key people (or organizations) who were instrumental in getting this study on the map?
5. How did they decide to initiate the study?
6. What was the original scope and time frame for the study? How were the scope and time frame decided?
7. Originally, what did you hope to accomplish or learn from this study?
8. Did you encounter any obstacles or difficulties in getting this study initiated? If so, what were the difficulties? How did you resolve them? [Identify each difficulty and resolution technique until no more difficulties are named by the interviewee.]
9. In getting the study initiated, were there aspects that were easier (or went smoother) than you originally anticipated?
10. Overall, how would you evaluate the *initiation* phase of the study? What suggestions would you have for other agencies if they were seeking to develop a similar study?

How the Study Was Conducted (Implementation)

11. Once the decision was made to conduct a racial disparities study, how did you decide the research design (or how to conduct the study)?
12. What level of support did DWS internally provide to the study? [Probes: departments/units, personnel, expertise, budget]
13. Did you find this level of support adequate? Why or why not?
14. How did it compare to the types of support DWS typically provides to internal research studies?

15. DWS established a steering committee to provide guidance on the study. Were there other approaches considered? If so, please describe them. Why were these approaches rejected?
16. How did you determine the membership of the steering committee? What role (or purpose) did you envision for the steering committee?
17. How did you decide which tasks would be performed by DWS and which tasks would be conducted by the steering committee?
18. What were the main contributions of the steering committee? How were they helpful?
19. What were the main weaknesses or shortcomings of the steering committee?
20. Did the scope and time frame originally envisioned for the study change over time? If so, why and how so?
21. In designing this study, did you encounter difficulties that you felt were unique to this study because the focus was on examining racial disparities? If so, what? How did you get through these challenges?
22. Overall, how would you evaluate the research design phase of this study?
23. What research design suggestions would you have for other agencies if they were seeking to conduct a similar study?

Anticipated Changes Resulting from Study [Impacts]

24. I have reviewed a draft of the final report resulting from this study. Did you feel the study offered accurate findings?
25. What do you feel are the most important findings from this study?
26. In what ways did the findings confirm what you initially thought?
27. In what ways were the findings surprising?
28. What did you learn from this study? Specifically, what do you know about racial disparities in W-2 sanctioning that you did not know before this study was conducted?
29. Are there any questions that you had hoped this study would address, that still remain? If so, what?

Overall Evaluation and Assessment

30. Wisconsin is widely viewed as an innovator in developing U.S. welfare policy. When this study is publicly released, other organizations, researchers, or advocacy groups may be interested in conducting a similar analysis. What advice would you give them? What can they learn from the Wisconsin experience? [Probe: If you had to design a "to do" and "not to do" list, what items would you place on each list?]

Notes

1. The National Academy of Public Administration's Board of Directors adopted social equity as the fourth pillar of public administration, along with economy, efficienc , and effectiveness. See National Academy of Public Administration (2005).

2. American Civil Liberties Union and NAACP Complaint to U.S. Department of Health and Human Services, Office for Civil Rights, Docket No. 05023078, filed February 22, 2002.

3. See, for example, Mulligan-Hansel and Fendt (2002); Wisconsin Legislative Audit Bureau (2002, 5).

References

Akram, R. 2004. *Social Equity and the American Dream. Standing Panel on Social Equity in Governance.* Washington, DC: National Academy of Public Administration.

Clarke, Leslie L., Brenda Jarmon, and Merlin Langley. 1999. "q ualitative Study of WAGES: People Who Have Left WAGES." Florida Inter-University Welfare Reform Collaborative, Fall.

Department of Workforce Development. 2004. Wisconsin Works (W-2) Sanctions Study. State of Wisconsin, DWD.

Division of Workforce Solutions. 2003. "Analysis of W-2 Sanctions by Race 2001 and 2002." Madison, Wisconsin, March 6.

Doolittle, Fred, and James Riccio. 1992. "Case Management in Welfare Programs." In *Evaluating Welfare and Training Programs.* Charles Manske and Irv Garfinkel eds. Cambridge: Harvard University Press.

Gooden, Susan Tinsley. 1998. "All Things Not Being Equal: Difference in Caseworker Support Toward Black and White Welfare Clients." *Harvard Journal of African American Public Policy*: 23–33.

———. 1999. "The Hidden Third Party: Welfare Recipients' Experiences with Employers." *Journal of Public Management and Social Policy* (Summer): 69–83.

Greenberg, Mark, and Steve Savner. 1996. "A Detailed Summary of Key Provisions of the Temporary Assistance for Needy Families Block Grant of HR. 3734: The Personal Responsibility and Work Opportunity Reconciliation Act of 1996." Center for Law and Social Policy: Washington, DC.

Holzer, Harry J., and Michael Stoll. 2000. "Employer Demand for Welfare Recipients by Race." Institute for Research on Poverty, Discussion Paper no. 1213–00.

Lipsky, Michael. 1980. *Street-Level Bureaucracy: Dilemmas of the Individual in Public Services.* New York: Russell Sage Foundation.

Mead, Lawrence. 2004. *Government Matters: Welfare Reform in Wisconsin.* Princeton, NJ: Princeton University Press.

Mulligan-Hansel, Kathleen, and Pamela S. Fendt. 2002. *Unfair Sanctions: Does W-2 Punish People of Color?* Milwaukee: Institute for Wisconsin's Future, University of Wisconsin (October).

Myers, Samuel L., Jr. 2002. "Presidential Address: Analysis of Race as Policy Analysis." *Journal of Policy Analysis and Management* 21(2): 169–190.

National Academy of Public Administration. 2000. "Standing Panel on Social Equity in Governance." Issue Paper and Work Plan, November.

———. 2005. Strategic Plan. Spring.

Rohr, John. 1989. *Ethics for Bureaucrats: An Essay on Law and Values.* New York: Marcel Dekker.

Savner, Steve. 2000. "Welfare Reform and Racial/Ethnic Minorities: The q uestions to Ask." *Poverty and Race* 9, (4, July/August): 3–5.

U.S. Department of Health and Human Services. 1996. Major Provisions of the Personal Responsibility and Work Opportunity Reconciliation Act of 1996 (P.L. 104–193). Washington, DC.

Wisconsin Legislative Audit Bureau. 2002. *Sanctioning of Wisconsin Works (W-2) Participants (Report 01–07).* December 10.

Wilson, William Julius. 1996. *When Work Disappears: The World of the New Urban Poor.* New York: Knopf.

7 MAKING RACIAL EQUITY WORK VISIBLE: THE U.S. ENVIRONMENTAL PROTECTION AGENCY

> *If we talk about the environment, for example, we have to talk about environmental racism—about the fact that kids in South Central Los Angeles have a third of the lung capacity of kids in Santa Monica.*

> —Danny Glover (van Gelder 2001)

This chapter focuses on racial equity at the federal level through an examination of the U.S. Environmental Protection Agency. An analysis of this federal agency provides an important description of a long-term public sector organizational focus designed to promote justice by operating within the nervous area of government. An examination of the operations of the EPA offers a useful example of how a focus on equity may be structurally embedded into the operations of a public sector agency. This examination is guided by analyzing information about the EPA that is publicly available on its official website. For any organization, information readily accessible via the Web offers strong signals to the general public about its priorities. Through public outlets such as official websites, governmental agencies transmit important messages regarding organizational values and priorities to the public at large. As Jeffrey Roy states, "The face of e-government is quite literally the Web site. . . . A Web page provides information in a digital format; a portal is a port of entry into a widening set of possibilities" (2003, 393). Websites also disseminate important information about the operations of government (Tolbert and Mossberger 2006).

While the public communication of any organizational value does not ensure its implementation, it does send an important operational and societal message. In essence, public communication of equity within a governmental agency is best viewed as an important and necessary condition, rather than a sufficient and exhaustive one. If a public sector organization values equity, there should be publicly visible evidence of this commitment through, for example, the organization's mission statement, leadership priorities, strategic plan, operational programs and activities, and e-governance activities.

With a particular focus on the Office of Environmental Justice within the EPA, the equity work of this agency is publicly visible. This analysis is intentionally limited to an examination of the EPA's work that is readily accessible on its official website. While acknowledging that the digital divide remains an important equity issue itself, an organization's website is its single most important information portal, offering the greatest visibility to an infinite number of viewers. An examination of materials accessible via an organization's website communicates important signals about the prominence and importance of its equity work.

About the EPA

The U.S. Environmental Protection Agency was established on December 2, 1970, by President Richard Nixon, largely in response to elevated concerns regarding environmental pollution. The original organization of the EPA included a director of equal opportunity:

> The Director, Equal Opportunity, shall be the principal adviser to the Administrator with respect to equal opportunity and civil rights programs and policies. The Director shall supervise and direct an Office of Equal Opportunity, which shall exercise leadership and provide services and advice to all of the organizational elements of the Agency and with respect to all programs and activities of the Agency. The Office shall direct activities required to carry out the Agency's responsibilities to assure compliance with Title VI of the Civil Rights Act and with the executive orders providing for equal opportunity in employment practices in Federally-assisted construction contracts. (U.S. EPA 1970)

However, environmental justice was not a primary focus of the EPA until the early 1990s (Murray and Hertko 2011).

The EPA's emphasis on racial equity was influenced largely by the environmental justice movement that gained force in the 1980s and 1990s. Several thousand groups merged in the United States to oppose inequities in the distribution of environmental hazards and the direct threat to public health of nearby communities (Bullard 1993). In 1991, the First National People of Color Environmental Leadership summit adopted seventeen "principles of environmental justice" (Goldman 1996). The racial equity focus within the EPA today is a direct result of this important preceding environmental justice context. As a direct result of this movement, the EPA's racial equity work is contained within the more common term in the environmental field, "environmental justice." While environmental justice is a broader term, the specific work of the EPA has a clearly identifiabl focus on issues involving racial equity for communities of color in the United States, including a specific focus on tribal and indigenous peoples

Establishing the Office of Environmental Justice

As discussed in chapter 1, motivators from an organization's external environment can serve as a catalyst for racial equity work within the organization. These motivators originate from a political, legal, economic, or moral trigger (or a combination thereof). The establishment of the EPA's Office of Environmental Justice (OEJ) resulted from important legal and political triggers, including significan actions of politicians and environmental justice researchers and advocates. For decades preceding the formal establishment of the OEJ, several "studies found disproportionate exposure to air pollution, water pollution, pesticides and other toxic chemicals, and in overall measures of environmental quality" among minority and low-income communities in the United States (Ringquist and Clark 1999, 76). (See, for example, Asch and Seneca 1978; Gianessi and Peskin 1980; Davies et al. 1972.) The cumulative effect of these studies, coupled with strong political and advocacy interests, led to the establishment of OEJ. As described on the U.S. Environmental Protection Agency's website,

> Early in 1990, the Congressional Black Caucus, a bi-partisan coalition of academicians, social scientists and political activists, met with EPA officials to discuss their findings that EPA was unfairly applying its enforcement inspections and that environmental risk was higher in racial minority and low-income populations. In response, the EPA Administrator created the Environmental Equity Workgroup in July 1990 to address the allegation that "racial minority and low-income populations bear a higher environmental risk burden than the general population."
>
> The Workgroup produced a final report "Reducing Risk in All Communities" Volumes I and II in June 1992, which supported the allegation and made ten recommendations for addressing the problem. One of the recommendations was to create an office to address these inequities. The Office of Environmental Equity was established November 6, 1992. The name was changed to Office of Environmental Justice in 1994. (U.S. E A 2011b)

The focus of the Environmental Equity Workgroup was specifically on racial and income inequities. Then-EPA administrator William K. Reilly, a member of President George H. W. Bush's administration, charged the workgroup with four primary tasks:

Task One: Review and evaluate the evidence that racial minority and low-income people bear a disproportionate risk burden.

Task Two: Review current EPA programs to identify factors that might give rise to differential risk reduction, and develop approaches to correct such problems.

Task Three: Review EPA risk assessment and risk communication guidelines with respect to race and income related risks.
Task Four: Review institutional relationships, including outreach to and
consultation with racial minority and low-income organizations, to assure that EPA is fulfilling its mission with respect
to these populations. (U.S. EPA 1992, 1–2)

The workgroup's final report was issued to Reilly, and environmental
equity workgroup chair Robert M. Wolcott noted in his letter to Reilly (see
Exhibit 7.1), "The evidence indicates that minority and low-income populations are disproportionately exposed to lead, selected air pollutants, hazardous
waste facilities, contaminated fish tissue and agricultural pesticides in the
workplace. The extent and nature of the problem may not be known in every
case, but EPA can help lead the way in clearly defining the problems" (EPA
1992). Wolcott's statement both acknowledged the disproportionate impacts
of environmental hazards on minority communities and committed the EPA
to important racial equity work.

Established in 1992, the U.S. Environmental Protection Agency's Office of
Environmental Justice "oversees the integration of environmental justice into
EPA's policies, programs, and activities throughout the Agency; serves as the
point of contact for environmental justice outreach and educational activities;
provides technical and financial assistance. The Office also serves as the lead
on the Interagency Working Group of other federal agencies to incorporate
environmental justice into all federal programs" (EPA 2013d). Importantly,
the EPA website offers a brief historical account that directly acknowledges
the connection between the environmental justice movement, the creation of
the Office of Environmental Justice, and the EPA's contemporary focus on
environmental justice (see U.S. EPA 2013c).

EPA Mission, Leadership, and Strategic Planning

Mission and Purpose

An effective mission statement offers a clear and concise description of what an
organization does. It defines the organization's reason for existence and identifie
areas of importance. Weiss (1996) emphasizes the importance of a mission in
framing and motivating the work of individuals within the agency. The Government Performance and Results Act (PL 103–62) requires federal departments
and agencies to write a mission statement before developing strategic plans and
measuring performance related to that mission (Kravchuk and Schack 1996; U.S.
General Accounting Office 1996). As Weiss and Piderit state, "Mission statements

Exhibit 7.1

Environmental Equity Workgroup Report to EPA Cover Letter

UNITED STATES ENVIRONMENTAL PROTECTION AGENCY

May 29, 1992

Mr. William K. Reilly
Administrator
U.S. Environmental Protection Agency
Washington, D.C. 20460

Dear Mr. Reilly:

In July of 1990, you established the Environmental Equity Workgroup. You directed the Workgroup to review the evidence that racial minority and low-income communities bear a disproportionate environmental risk burden. You asked the Workgroup to make recommendations for Agency action on environmental equity issues. The following report contains a summary of the information collected and the Workgroup's recommendations.

The literature relating environmental risk to race and income is limited although highly suggestive. It spans a wide spectrum of environmental problems and population groups exposed. The evidence indicates that racial minority and low-income populations are disproportionately exposed to lead, selected air pollutants, hazardous waste facilities, contaminated fish tissue and agricultural pesticides in the workplace. The extent and nature of the problem may not be known in every case, but EPA can help lead the way in clearly defining the problems.

The report is the final product of a collective effort by many individuals and offices across the Agency. It is a first step. We welcome and encourage public debate on the report and the issue. Any effort to address environmental equity issues effectively must include all segments of society: the affected communities, the public at large, industry, people in policy-making positions and all levels and branches of government.

We have been delighted and inspired by the enthusiasm and attention that environmental equity issues have received. Concern for the issues has come from a diversity of people and institutions, both within and outside the Agency. Diversity spawns the innovative and effective solutions needed to address this complex and engrained problem.

Sincerely,

Robert M. Wolcott   Warren A. Banks
Chair   Special Assistant
Environmental Equity   Workgroup Office of the Administrator

Source: U.S. Environmental Protection Agency 1992, 2.

Exhibit 7.2

**Purpose Statement of the
U.S. Environmental Protection Agency**

EPA's purpose is to ensure that:

- all Americans are protected from significant risks to human health and the environment where they live, learn, and work;
- national efforts to reduce environmental risk are based on the best available scientific information;
- federal laws protecting human health and the environment are enforced fairly and effectively;
- environmental protection is an integral consideration in U.S. policies concerning natural resources, human health, economic growth, energy, transportation, agriculture, industry, and international trade, and these factors are similarly considered in establishing environmental policy;
- all parts of society—communities, individuals, businesses, and state, local, and tribal governments—have access to accurate information sufficient to effectively participate in managing human health and environmental risks;
- environmental protection contributes to making our communities and ecosystems diverse, sustainable, and economically productive; and
- the United States plays a leadership role in working with other nations to protect the global environment.

Source: U.S. Environmental Protection Agency 2013g.

make explicit organizational goals and priorities, leading to better communication with employees about what they should be doing" (1999, 196).

As articulated by the Environmental Protection Agency, "The mission of EPA is to protect human health and the environment" (U.S. EPA 2013g). As Exhibit 7.2 details, directly following the EPA's mission statement is a broader statement of purpose.

Within the EPA's statement of purpose, three of the seven statements directly communicate an organizational commitment to equity. The first statement emphasizes the EPA's commitment to protect *all* Americans regardless of where they live, learn, or work (emphasis added). The third statement prioritizes the EPA's commitment to enforce federal laws *fairly* (emphasis added). The fifth statement captures the organization's commitment to all parts of society, and with a specific reference to tribal governments (U.S. EPA 2013g).

EPA Administrator Core Priorities

The EPA's core priorities provide an empirical example of the importance of leadership in prioritizing equity in government. Agency administrators communicate important messages about agency priorities and can wield important influence to achieve broad and specific goals. In January 2010, EPA administrator Lisa Jackson established seven core agency priorities, shown in Exhibit 7.3. These priorities include:

1. taking action on climate change;
2. improving air quality;
3. ensuring the safety of chemicals;
4. cleaning up our communities;
5. protecting America's waters;
6. expanding the conversation on environmentalism and working for environmental justice;
7. building strong state and tribal partnerships. (U.S. EPA 2010b)

Equity is a direct area of emphasis in three of the seven priority areas. Areas 6 and 7 are specifically focused on equity. Within Area 6, Jackson acknowledges the historical environmental inequities confronting communities of color, and she states, "We must include environmental justice principles in all of our decisions." Area 7 directly acknowledges the importance of establishing strong state-tribal partnerships and the need for the EPA to "support Tribal capacity." As stated in Area 4, "Cleaning Up Our Communities," Jackson notes, "I am committed to maximizing the potential of our brownfields program, particularly to spur environmental cleanup and job creation in disadvantaged communities" (U.S. EPA 2010b).

Strategic Plan

Strategic plans offer important roadmaps of specific areas of focused priorities to guide an organization's work. Strategic planning has been defined as "a disciplined effort to produce fundamental decisions and actions that shape and guide what an organization is, what it does, and why it does it" (Bryson 1988, 5). "It blends futuristic thinking, objective analysis, and subjective evaluation of goals and priorities to chart future courses of action that will ensure the long-run vitality and effectiveness of the organization (Poister and Streib 1999, 309).

Directly linked to the EPA's mission and leadership, the EPA Strategic Plan FY 2011–2015 also offers an emphasis on equity. The plan identifies cross-cutting fundamental strategies that explicitly align with the core priority areas of environmental justice and state-tribal partnerships. Exhibits 7.4 and 7.5 offer specific examples derived from the EPA's Strategic Plan that focus directly on promoting environmental justice.

Exhibit 7.3

Priorities for EPA's Future

Taking Action on Climate Change: Last year saw historic progress in the fight against climate change, with a range of greenhouse gas reduction initiatives. We must continue this critical effort and ensure compliance with the law. We will continue to support the President and Congress in enacting clean energy and climate legislation. Using the Clean Air Act, we will finalize our mobile source rules and provide a framework for continued improvements in that sector. We will build on the success of ENERGY STAR to expand cost-saving energy conservation and efficiency programs. And we will continue to develop common-sense solutions for reducing GHG emissions from large stationary sources like power plants. In all of this, we must also recognize that climate change will affect other parts of our core mission, such as protecting air and water quality, and we must include those considerations in our future plans.

Improving Air Quality: American communities face serious health and environmental challenges from air pollution. We have already proposed stronger ambient air quality standards for ozone, which will help millions of American breathe easier and live healthier. Building on that, EPA will develop a comprehensive strategy for a cleaner and more efficient power sector, with strong but achievable emission reduction goals for SO_2, NOx, mercury, and other air toxics. We will strengthen our ambient air quality standards for pollutants such as PM, SO_2, and NO_2 and will achieve additional reductions in air toxics from a range of industrial facilities. Improved monitoring, permitting, and enforcement will be critical building blocks for air quality improvement.

Assuring the Safety of Chemicals: One of my highest priorities is to make significant and long overdue progress in assuring the safety of chemicals in our products, our environment, and our bodies. Last year I announced principles for modernizing the Toxic Substances Control Act. Separately, we are shifting EPA's focus to address high-concern chemicals and filling data gaps on widely produced chemicals in commerce. At the end of 2009, we released our first-ever chemical management plans for four groups of substances, and more plans are in the pipeline for 2010. Using our streamlined Integrated Risk Information System, we will continue strong progress toward rigorous, peer-reviewed health assessments on dioxins, arsenic, formaldehyde, TCE, and other substances of concern.

Cleaning Up Our Communities: In 2009 EPA made strong cleanup progress by accelerating our Superfund program and confronting significant local environmental challenges like the asbestos Public Health Emergency in Libby, Montana, and the coal ash spill in Kingston, Tennessee. Using all the tools at our disposal, including enforcement and compliance efforts, we will continue to focus on making safer, healthier communities. I am committed to maximizing the potential of our brownfields program, particularly to spur environmental cleanup and job creation in disadvantaged communities. We are also developing enhanced strategies for risk reduction in our Superfund program, with stronger partnerships with stakeholders affected by our cleanups.

Protecting America's Waters: America's waterbodies are imperiled as never before. Water quality and enforcement programs face complex challenges, from nutrient loadings and stormwater runoff, to invasive species and drinking water contaminants. These challenges demand both traditional and innovative strategies. We will continue comprehensive watershed protection programs for the Chesapeake Bay and Great Lakes. We will initiate measures to address post-construction runoff, water quality impairment from surface mining, and stronger drinking water protection. Recovery Act funding will expand construction of water infrastructure, and we will work with states to develop nutrient limits and launch an Urban Waters initiative. We will also revamp enforcement strategies to achieve greater compliance across the board.

Expanding the Conversation on Environmentalism and Working for Environmental Justice: We have begun a new era of outreach and protection for communities historically underrepresented in EPA decision-making. We are building strong working relationships with tribes, communities of color, economically distressed cities and towns, young people, and others, but this is just a start. We must include environmental justice principles in all of our decisions. This is an area that calls for innovation and bold thinking, and I am challenging all of our employees to bring vision and creativity to our programs. The protection of vulnerable subpopulations is a top priority, especially with regard to children. Our revitalized Children's Health Office is bringing a new energy to safeguarding children through all of our enforcement efforts. We will ensure that children's health protection continues to guide the path forward.

Building Strong State and Tribal Partnerships: States and tribal nations bear important responsibilities for the day-to-day mission of environmental protection, but declining tax revenues and fiscal challenges are pressuring state agencies and tribal governments to do more with fewer resources. Strong partnerships and accountability are more important than ever. EPA must do its part to support state and tribal capacity and, through strengthened oversight, ensure that programs are consistently delivered nationwide. Where appropriate, we will use our own expertise and capacity to bolster state and tribal efforts.

Source: U.S. Environmental Protection Agency 2010b.

Note: Priorities established by EPA Administrator Lisa P. Jackson on January 12, 2010.

Exhibit 7.4

Working for Environmental Justice and Children's Health

Goal
Work to reduce and prevent harmful exposures and health risks to children and underserved, disproportionately impacted low-income, minority, and tribal communities, and support efforts to build healthy, sustainable green neighborhoods.

Description of problem
All populations—including minority, low-income, and indigenous populations—that are vulnerable to environmental pollution are at risk of having poor health outcomes. These vulnerabilities may arise because of higher exposures to pollution in places where they work, live, and play, and/or diminished abilities to withstand, cope with, or recover from environmental pollution. Children are often most acutely affected by environmental stressors.

Example EPA specific actions
- In our regulatory capacity, implement the nation's environmental laws using the best science and environmental monitoring data to address the potential for adverse health effects from environmental factors in disproportionately impacted, overburdened populations and vulnerable age groups. EPA programs will incorporate environmental justice and children's health considerations at each stage of the Agency's regulation development process and in implementation of environmental regulations.
- Apply the best available scientific methods to assess the potential for disproportionate exposures and health impacts resulting from environmental hazards on minority, low-income, and indigenous populations, women of child-bearing age, infants, children, and adolescents, to support EPA decision making, and to develop the tools to assess risk from multiple stressors.
- Engage communities in our work to protect human health and environment. EPA will align multiple community-based programs to provide funding and technical assistance to communities to build capacity to address critical issues affecting children's health and disproportionately impacted populations.

Source: U.S. Environmental Protection Agency 2010a.

Exhibit 7.4 captures the EPA's goal of promoting environmental justice and health protection. Within this area, the EPA Strategic Plan states, "Environmental justice and children's health protection will be achieved when all Americans, regardless of age, race, economic status, or ethnicity, have access to clean water, clear air, and healthy communities" (EPA 2010a, 30). Exhibit 7.5 acknowledges the importance of EPA partnerships with tribal governments. "EPA will strengthen its state, tribal, and international partnerships to

---

Exhibit 7.5

Strengthening State, Tribal, and International Partnerships

Goal
Deliver on our commitment to a clean and healthy environment through consultation and shared accountability with states, tribes, and the global community for addressing the highest-priority problems.

Description of approach
Successful partnership will be based on four working principles: consultation, collaboration, cooperation, and accountability. By *consulting*, we will engage our partners in a timely fashion as we consider approaches to our environmental work so that each partner can make an early and meaningful contribution toward the final result. By *collaborating*, we will not only share information, but we will actively work together with our partners to use all available resources to reach our environmental and human health goals. As our work progresses, we will *cooperate*, viewing each other with respect as allies who must work successfully together if our goals are to be achieved. Through shared *accountability*, we will ensure that environmental benefits are consistently delivered nationwide.

Example EPA specific actions
- Focus on increasing tribal capacity to establish and implement environmental programs while ensuring that our national programs are as effective in Indian country as they are throughout the rest of the nation.
- Enhance our effort as we work with tribes on a government-to-government basis, based upon the Constitution, treaties, laws, executive orders, and a long history of Supreme Court rulings.
- Strengthen our cross-cultural sensitivity with tribes, recognizing that tribes have cultural, jurisdictional, and legal features that must be considered when coordinating and implementing environmental programs in Indian country.

Source: U.S. Environmental Protection Agency 2010a.
Note: Emphasis added by author.

---

achieve our mutual environmental and human health goals. . . . The relationship between the United States Government and federally-recognized tribes is unique and has developed throughout the course of the nation's history" (U.S. EPA 2010a, 34–35).

Implementing the Work: Operational Structure, Programs, and Activities

As aforementioned, within the EPA, much of environmental justice work is implemented through the Office of Environmental Justice. The EPA defines environmental justice as the following:

Environmental Justice is the fair treatment and meaningful involvement of
all people regardless of race, color, national origin, or income with respect
to the development, implementation, and enforcement of environmental
laws, regulations, and policies. EPA has this goal for all communities and
persons across this Nation. It will be achieved when everyone enjoys the
same degree of protection from environmental and health hazards and
equal access to the decision-making process to have a healthy environment in which to live, learn, and work. (U.S. EPA 2013b)

Within the EPA Office of Environmental Justice, there are several important
indicators of the organizational implementation of environmental justice work.
Such indicators include the National Environmental Justice Advisory Coun-
cil; Plan EJ 2014; Environmental Justice Grants and Programs; the Federal
Interagency Working Group on Environmental Justice; Environmental Justice
Achievement Awards; Community Outreach Teleconferences; and Tribal and
Indigenous Peoples Environmental Justice Policy. The EPA's activity in each
of these areas is profiled belo .

National Environmental Justice Advisory Council

The National Environmental Justice Advisory Council (NEJAC) was established in 1993 with the purpose of obtaining independent consensus advice
and recommendations from a broad spectrum of stakeholders involved in
environmental justice (U.S. EPA 2012f). As a federal advisory committee,
the NEJAC was chartered to provide the administrator with advice and
recommendations on integrating environmental justice considerations into
the agency's programs, policies, and day-to-day activities. The NEJAC
consists of representatives of community-based groups, business and industry, academic and educational institutions, state and local governments,
tribal governments and indigenous organizations, and nongovernmental and
environmental groups. The twenty-six–member council includes members
from academia, community groups, industry and business, nongovernmental
environmental organizations, state and local governments, and tribal governments and indigenous groups. The council meets publicly and provides
a forum for discussions about integrating environmental justice into EPA
priorities and initiatives (U.S. EPA 2012e).

The charter of NEJAC details its major objectives.

The major objectives will be to provide advice and recommendations about
EPA efforts to:

a. Integrate environmental justice considerations into Agency programs, policies, and activities
b. Improve the environment or public health in communities disproportionately burdened by environmental harms and risks
c. Address environmental justice to ensure meaningful involvement in EPA decision-making, build capacity in disproportionately-burdened communities, and promote collaborative problem-solving for issues involving environmental justice
d. Strengthen its partnerships with other governmental agencies, such as other Federal agencies and state, tribal, or local governments, regarding environmental justice issues
e. Enhance research and assessment approaches related to environmental justice. (U.S. EPA 2012e)

The National Environmental Justice Advisory Council has delivered a large body of recommendations and reports on a wide variety of environmental justice topics. Table 7.1 provides examples of some of the recommendation reports provided to the EPA by NEJAC.

Plan EJ 2014

On February 11, 1994, President William J. Clinton signed Executive Order 12898, *Federal Actions to Address Environmental Justice in Minority Populations and Low-Income Populations*, to focus federal attention on the environmental and human health conditions of minority and low-income populations with the goal of achieving environmental protection for all communities. The order mandated federal agencies to develop environmental justice strategies to help federal agencies address disproportionately high and adverse human health or environmental effects of their programs on minority and low-income populations. The order is also intended to promote nondiscrimination in federal programs that affect human health and the environment. It aims to provide minority and low-income communities access to public information and public participation in matters relating to human health and the environment (EPA 2013c). One of the primary impacts of Executive Order 12898 was that it significantly elevated environmental justice as a "scientifically acceptable" area of research (Bowen and Wells 2002, 690).

Building on the intention of Executive Order 12898 and in recognition of its twentieth anniversary (the EJ office was established in 1994) the EPA's Plan EJ 2014 is a strategy that permeates environmental justice work into the day-to-day operations of the EPA, at both its headquarters and its regional offices.

Table 7.1

Reports of the National Environmental Justice Advisory Council

- *Environmental Justice, Urban Revitalization, and Brownfields: The Search for Authentic Hope,* December 1996
- *El Plan Modelo Para Participacioón Pública,* February 2000
- *A Regulatory Strategy for Siting and Operating Waste Transfer Stations,* March 2000
- *Environmental Justice in the Permitting Process: A Report from the National Environmental Justice Advisory Council,* July 2000
- *Guide on Consultation and Collaboration with Indian Tribal Governments and the Public Participation of Indigenous Groups and Tribal Members in Environmental Decision Making,* November 2000
- *Environmental Justice and Community-Based Health Model Discussion,* February 2001
- *Integration of Environmental Justice in Federal Programs,* May 2002
- *Fish Consumption and Environmental Justice,* November 2002
- *Advancing Environmental Justice Through Pollution Prevention,* June 2003
- *Meaningful Involvement and Fair Treatment by Tribal Environmental Regulatory Programs,* October 2004
- *Environmental Justice and Federal Facilities: Recommendations for Improving Stakeholder Relations Between Federal Facilities and Environmental Justice Communities,* November 2004
- *Ensuring Risk Reduction in Communities with Multiple Stressors: Environmental Justice and Cumulative Risks/Impacts,* December 2004
- *Future Mechanisms to Enhance Stakeholder Involvement and Engagement to Address Environmental Justice,* August 2006
- *The 2005 Gulf Coast Hurricanes and Vulnerable Populations: Recommendations for Future Disaster Preparedness/Response,* August 2006
- *Unintended Impacts of Redevelopment and Revitalization Efforts in Five Environmental Justice Communities,* August 2006
- *NEJAC Initial Letter Regarding the Environmental Justice Strategic Enforcement Assessment Tool,* December 2007
- *Strengthening the Participation of Business and Industry in Environmental Justice, Green Business, and Sustainability,* September 2008
- *Recommendations for EPA's State Environmental Justice Cooperative Agreement Initiative,* October 2008
- *Advice Letter Rejecting the Use of Variances for Small Drinking Water Systems,* August 2009
- *Reducing Air Emissions Associated with Goods Movement: Working Towards Environmental Justice,* November 2009
- *Recommendations for EPA's Community Action for a Renewed Environment (CARE) Program,* April 2010
- *Strategies to Enhance School Air Toxics Monitoring in Environmental Justice Communities,* April 2010
- *Recommendations for Nationally Consistent Environmental Justice Screening Approaches,* May 2010
- *Request to Provide Advise on EPA's Draft Strategic Plan 2011–2015,* August 2010
- *NEJAC Comments on Plan EJ 2014,* May 2011
- *Enhancing Environmental Justice in EPA Permitting Programs,* May 2011
- *Recommendations for Ensuring Long-Term Engagement of Communities in Gulf Coast Ecosystem Restoration,* July 2011

- *Recommendations for EPA's Community Action for a Renewed Environment (CARE) Program,* November 2011
- *Recommendations for the Prevention of Chemical Plant Disasters,* March 2012
- *Model Guidelines for Public Participation: An Update to the 1996 NEJAC Model Plan for Public Participation,* January 2013
- *Recommendations for the Work Draft of EPA Policy on Environmental Justice for Tribes and Indigenous Peoples,* January 2013
- *Recommendations for Fostering Environmental Justice for Tribes and Indigenous Peoples,* January 2013

Source: U.S. Environmental Protection Agency 2013f.

As noted by EPA administrator Lisa Jackson,

> *Plan EJ 2014* offers a road map that will enable us to better integrate environmental justice and civil rights into our programs, policies, and daily work. The plan focuses on agency wide areas critical to advancing environmental justice, including rulemaking, permitting, compliance and enforcement, community-based programs, and our work with other federal agencies. It also establishes specific milestones to help us meet the needs of overburdened neighborhoods through our decision making, scientific analysis, and rulemaking. (U.S. EPA 2011a, ii)

Plan EJ 2014 has three major sections: (1) Cross-Agency Focus Areas, (2) Tools Development Areas, and (3) Program Initiatives. The Cross-Agency Focus Areas include: Incorporating Environmental Justice into Rulemaking; Considering Environmental Justice in Permitting; Advancing Environmental Justice Through Compliance and Enforcement; Supporting Community-Based Action Programs on Environmental Justice; and Fostering Administration-Wide Action on Environmental Justice. Plan EJ 2014's Tools Development Areas focus on: (1) Science, (2) Law, (3) Information, and (4) Resources. The EPA developed and is implementing a plan for each of these areas. The agency also developed a draft supplemental plan on Advancing Environmental Justice through Title VI of the Civil Rights Act of 1964 (EPA 2011a).

In February 2013, the EPA issued a Plan EJ 2014 86-page progress report (see EPA 2013h for the report's URL) report documenting the agency's significant accomplishments in meeting the commitments made in EJ 2014

Environmental Justice Grants and Programs

The Office of Environmental Justice operates seven specific grant sources specifically focused on environmental justice. Exhibit 7.6 offers a more detailed view of one of these programs, the Environmental Justice Small Grants Program. As its website details, the Environmental Justice Small Grants Program provides financial assistance to eligible organizations to build collaborative

Exhibit 7.6
Environmental Justice Small Grants Program

Overview

Established in 1994, Environmental Justice Small Grants Program established the small grant program to provide financial assistance to community-based organizations and local and tribal governments that work on local solutions to address local environmental or public health issues. Since the program's inception, the EPA has awarded nearly $23 million to 1,253 grant recipients who have educated and empowered their communities to understand and address exposure to multiple environmental harms and risks.

FY2012 Example Projects

- *The Yakutat Tlingit Tribe Researches the Impact of Dioxin Contamination on Subsistence Resources Near Yakutat, Alaska*

The Yakutat Tlingit, a federally recognized tribe located on the Gulf of Alaska, plans to research the impact of toxic substances on area marine wetlands. Historically, the project area, Ankau Saltchucks, provided up to 30% of the Tribe's food supply. Dioxin contamination has limited the food supply, disrupted a significant source of traditional foods, and had a negative impact on Tribal cultural practices. Tribal members will be involved in a sampling effort to determine the nature, extent, and sources of the contamination with an emphasis on determining if there are uncontaminated areas that are safe for Tribal subsistence activities. This project will also build community capacity through outreach, involvement, and education of Tribal members and others.

- *Coalition Addresses Adverse Impacts of Freight Transportation on Minority Communities*

The Clean Air Coalition of Western New York will educate community leaders in Buffalo about the adverse health impacts of freight transportation on communities closest to freight transport hubs. The project will build the capacity of local leaders to understand and advocate for solutions to reduce their community's disproportionate exposure to diesel exhaust. This project also educates residents about the possible health risks from exposure to pollution associated with high freight traffic. Residents will learn how to take air samples and share air quality data with the broader community.

(continued)

Exhibit 7.6 *(continued)*

• *North Carolina Immigrant Farmworkers Learn About Federal Worker Protection Standards*

Toxic Free NC seeks to improve the health and safety of migrant and seasonal farmworkers through education about pesticide exposure by creating a plain-language analysis of EPA's Worker Protection Standards available in both Spanish and English. The project will develop and deliver a series of training sessions throughout North Carolina. These sessions will cover workers' rights as they relate to pesticides in the workplace and EPA's proposed revisions to the Worker Protection Standard. The project hopes to encourage immigrant and low-income workers to become engaged in local and federal rulemaking processes that may impact their health, safety, and welfare.

Source: U.S. EPA 2012a.

partnerships, to identify the local environmental and/or public health issues, and to envision solutions and empower the community through education, training, and outreach.

The Environmental Justice Collaborative Problem-Solving Cooperative Agreement Program provides financial assistance to eligible organizations working on or planning to work on projects to address local environmental and/or public health issues in their communities, using the EPA's "Environmental Justice Collaborative Problem-Solving Model."

The Environmental Justice Cooperative Agreements in Support of Communities Directly Affected by the Deepwater Horizon Oil Spill in the Gulf of Mexico provides funding to local nonprofit community-based organizations—including faith-based organizations, environmental justice networks, and local Native American tribal governments in affected regions—to assist local communities facing environmental justice challenges and help develop educational materials and strategies on how to address and adapt to the spill's long-term effects.

The State Environmental Justice Cooperative Agreements Program provides funding so that eligible entities may work collaboratively with affected communities to understand, promote, and integrate approaches to provide meaningful and measurable improvements to the public health and/or environment in the communities.

The Environmental Justice Showcase Communities Project provides EPA Regional Office funding to bring together governmental and nongovernmental organizations to pool their collective resources and expertise on the best ways to achieve real results in communities.

The EPA's National Clean Diesel Funding Assistance Program issues competitive grants through EPA Regional Offices to fund implementation of diesel emission-reduction technologies on school buses, vessels and equipment used in ports, construction, and agriculture, among other areas. Eligible entities include units of government, including federally recognized tribes and nonprofit organizations whose principal purpose is promotion of transportation or air quality (U.S. EPA 2012c).

Federal Interagency Working Group on Environmental Justice

Established in 1994 under Executive Order 12898, the role of the Federal Interagency Working Group on Environmental Justice (EJIWG) is to guide, support, and enhance federal environmental justice and community-based activities. Chaired by the EPA, the EJIWG comprises multiple federal agencies and White House offices, including the Department of Agriculture; Department of Commerce; Department of Defense; Department of Education; Department of Energy; Department of Health and Human Services; Department of Homeland Security; Department of Housing and Urban Development; Department of the Interior; Department of Justice; Department of Labor; Department of Transportation; Department of Veterans Affairs; General Services Administration; and Small Business Administration (U.S. EPA 2013e).

Environmental Justice Achievement Awards

Since 2008, the EPA's National Achievements in Environmental Justice Awards Program has recognized partnerships that address local environmental justice concerns and result in positive environmental and human health benefits in communities. Recipients include academic institutions, community-based organizations, nongovernmental and environmental organizations, state and local governments, and tribal governments and indigenous organizations (U.S. EPA 2012b).

Community Outreach Teleconference

The Office of Environmental Justice hosts quarterly environmental justice community outreach calls. As the website describes, the purpose of these calls is to provide information to participants about the agency's EJ activities and maintain an open dialogue with EJ advocates. As the EPA continues to advance Plan EJ 2014, the agency hopes these calls will better inform the public about the EPA's EJ work and enhance opportunities to take advantage of federal activities (U.S. EPA 2013i). The website contains links to audio files and transcripts of quarterly conference calls since November 2010

Tribal and Indigenous Peoples Environmental Justice Policy

The Office of Environmental Justice has developed two work groups (one composed of external stakeholders and one composed of EPA employees) to focus on the following four primary areas of policy: (1) how the EPA is to incorporate environmental justice into its environmental capacity-building and implementation policies and programs for federally recognized tribes; (2) how the EPA is to incorporate environmental justice into its direct implementation of federal environmental programs in Indian country; (3) how the EPA is to work effectively with tribal community–based organizations, state-recognized tribes, tribal members, and other indigenous peoples to address their EJ concerns, within or outside Indian country; and (4) how the EPA is to work with other federal agencies to address federally recognized tribes, state-recognized tribes, tribal community–based organizations, tribal members, or nonmembers on reservations environmental justice issues (U.S. EPA 2013a).

Environmental Justice 2.0: Environmental Justice in Action

An examination of the Office of Environmental Justice's website also reveals several other information sources and tools available to the public upon request—for example, the Environmental Justice listserv designed to provide EPA-related information on environmental justice topics. One prominent feature of the listserv is Greenversations, an e-governance blogging effort designed to promote environmental justice work and feedback. From mid-April 2012 through mid-February 2013, there were forty blogs on a variety of environmental justice topics (U.S. EPA 2012d). Several of the blogs also included short, informational videos. Table 7.2 captures the topics by date. The range of written responses per blog ranged from a low of zero to a high of 26. Additionally, each blog received an average of 307 likes. Some specific blog written comments include (positive and negative)

> Great video!! I learned a lot about Asthma rates and it was good to see a community organization that was able to bring change to their neighborhood. (July 13, 2012)

> . . . EPA has never actually supported citizen involvement. The EPA has always teamed up with the states and industry to undermine and suppress ordinary citizens and taxpayers, not just here, but all over the U.S. I'm very upset by the EPA's refusal to listen to us. (August 14, 2012)

> I have attended a couple of the meetings on the Gulf Coast and have found that the EPA was very engaged with communities. (October 29, 2012)

Table 7.2

EPA Environmental Justice in Action Blog

Blog Title	Date
A San Diego Showcase for Equitable Development and Environmental Justice	4/16/2012
Federal EJ Strategies Mark a Major Development in the Advancement of Environmental Justice	4/16/2012
How Can You Help Environmental Justice Communities Create an Oasis in a Food Desert?	4/16/2012
National Environmental Justice Conference and Training Program Focuses on Making a Difference in Communities	4/16/2012
Welcome to EPA's New Environmental Justice Blog	4/17/2012
What Environmental Justice in Action Is All About	4/17/2012
Learning About Environmental Justice in Aotearoa/New Zealand	4/26/2012
New Strategies for Environmental Justice: Green Zones	5/3/2012
Addressing Environmental Justice Concerns in Indian Country	5/10/2012
Using the Toxic Release Inventory to Build Power in Communities	5/17/2012
Environmental Justice: From Strategic Planning to Action	5/24/2012
Learning Lessons in Tremé	6/1/2012
Taking Steps to Protect your Family from Lead Exposure	6/7/2012
Check Out Our New Video Series Commemorating 20 Years of the Agency Working on Environmental Justice	6/14/2012
Nuestras Raíces: How We Turned Environmental Justice into Action	6/22/2012
Help Expand the Conversation on Permitting	6/28/2012
Building Bridges for Sustainability and Environmental Justice	7/5/2012
Tire Initiative to Eliminate Dumping (TIRED)—Don't Dump on Us!	7/13/2012
A Breath of Fresh Air After 35 Years	7/19/2012
Environmental Justice in the Pews	8/2/2012
Follow Our 20th Anniversary Video Series!	8/2/2012
EPA Seeking Feedback on Beta Tool to Address Community Environmental Issues	8/9/2012
Empowering Citizens Is What Environmental Justice Is All About	8/16/2012
Public Health Solutions to Advance Environmental Justice	8/23/2012
You Are the True Expert About Your Community	9/7/2012
(Re)trofit Design: From the Ground Up	9/13/2012
Environmental Justice from a Physician's Perspective	9/20/2012
Clean Water Is Environmental Justice	9/27/2012
One Prescription for Healthier Brownfield Communities—A Community Clinic, Please!	10/4/2012
Tox Town: A Great Tool for Learning About Chemicals in Our Environment	10/12/2012
Do You Know if Your Waterway Is Polluted?	10/25/2012
After the Storm	11/2/2012
My Journey as a Student in Understanding and Assessing the Impacts of Pesticides	11/15/2012
Building a Bridge Between Environment and Equity	11/29/2012
Are You Getting the Basic Amenities Your Taxes Paid For?	12/7/2012
Come Learn About Environmental Justice and Equitable Development at New Partners for Smart Growth!	1/11/2013
Environmental Justice Is About Government Engaging with Communities on a Personal Level	1/18/2013
You Can Help Make Better Government Policies	2/1/2013
Reducing Pollution for All American Families	2/14/2013

Source: U.S. EPA 2012d. Older blogs (hosted on http:/blog.epa.gov) may be found by searching for the titles using the Google search engine.

Conclusion

This chapter examines the publicly visible work of the EPA, with a primary focus on the agency's environmental justice work that is readily accessible via the agency's official website. This analysis suggests several useful themes relating to the public communication of an agency's work in a nervous area of government such as racial equity. First, it is important for the agency to acknowledge the important historical context that guides its work. The EPA clearly links its environmental justice work to the larger context of the environmental justice movement of the 1970s and 1980s, the influence of members of the Congressional Black Caucus, researchers, and advocacy groups. Additionally, the EPA acknowledges the important influence of Executive Order 12898 signed in 1994 by President Clinton. This context largely guides the environmental justice work of the EPA. The EPA should also include similar context regarding its interaction with tribal governments. Public sector agencies need to identify and acknowledge the key foundational influences that shape their racial equity work

Second, the EPA's environmental justice work permeates the agency. The agency's commitment to environmental justice is clearly evident in its mission statement, leadership, strategic plan, and operational structure, programs, and activities. Its work is also focused, thematic, and well aligned. The EPA's website effectively communicates its past accomplishments, present goals and directives, and future aspirations. Its work also suggests an openness to including innovative approaches by engaging environmental justice work through more contemporary means, such as blogging (U.S. EPA 2012d). All of these efforts convey a sustained commitment to the EPA's work in the nervous area of government.

Third, racial equity work need not adopt a one-size-fits-all approach. The EPA engages in an array of activities designed to promote environmental justice work, with a mix of environmental justice work internal to the EPA, work with external actors, and collaborative initiatives.

Most importantly, this chapter's focus on the EPA challenges every public sector organization to consider what public messages regarding racial equity are conveyed in its agency's public domain. Is its equity approach explicit or obscure? Does the website reflect the organization's value and prioritization of racial equity work? Is racial equity work clearly linked to mission, leadership, strategic plans, and agency programs and activities? The answers to these questions communicate clear messages to the public about an agency's overall value system, organizational priorities, and tangible record in racial equity work.

Chapters 5–7 provided an analysis of governments that are making significant contributions in a nervous area of government. They are actively engaging racial equity work though the public sector. The next section considers some of the important work that remains.

References

Asch, Peter, and Joseph Seneca. 1978. "Some Evidence on the Distribution of Air quality." *Land Economics* 54 (3): 278–97.

Bowen, William M., and Michael V. Wells. 2002. "The Politics and Reality of Environmental Justice: A History and Considerations for Public Administrators and Policy Makers." *Public Administration Review* 62 (6): 688–98.

Bryson, John M. 1988. *Strategic Planning for Public and Nonprofit Organizations: A Guide to Strengthening and Sustaining Organizational Achievement.* San Francisco: Jossey-Bass.

Bullard, Robert D. 1993. "Anatomy of Environmental Racism and the Environmental Justice Movement." In *Confronting Environmental Racism: Voices from the Grassroots,* ed. Robert Doyle Bullard, 15–40. Boston: Southend Press.

Davies, John E., et al. 1972. "The Role of Social Class in Human Pesticide Pollution." *American Journal of Epidemiology* 96 (5): 334–41.

Gianessi, Leonard, and Henry Peskin. 1980. "The Distribution of the Costs of Federal Water Pollution Control Policy in the U.S." *Land Economics* 56 (1): 85–102.

Goldman, Benjamin A. 1996. "What Is the Future of Environmental Justice?" *Antipode* 28 (2): 122–41.

Kravchuk, Robert, and Ronald Schack. 1996. "Designing Effective Performance Measurement Systems Under the Government Performance and Results Act." *Public Administration Review* 56 (4): 348–59.

Murray, Sylvester, and Mark D. Hertko. 2011. "Environmental Justice and Land Use Planning." In *Justice for All: Promoting Social Equity in Public Administration,* ed. Norman J. Johnson and James H. Svara, 192–206. Armonk, NY: M.E. Sharpe.

Poister, Theodore H., and Gregory D. Streib. 1999. "Strategic Management in the Public Sector: Concepts, Models, and Processes." *Public Productivity & Management Review* 22 (3): 308–25.

Ringquist, Evan J., and David H. Clark. 1999. "Local Risks, States' Rights, and Federal Mandates: Remedying Environmental Inequities in the U.S. Federal System." *Publius* 29 (2): 73–93.

Roy, Jeffrey. 2003. "The Relational Dynamics of E-Governance: A Case Study of the City of Ottawa." *Public Performance & Management Review* 26 (4): 391–403.

Tolbert, Caroline J., and Karen Mossberger. 2006. The Effects of e-Government on Trust and Confidence in Government. *Public Administration Review* 66 (3): 354–69.

U.S. Environmental Protection Agency. 1970. Information about Order 1110.2 establishing the EPA. http://www2.epa.gov/aboutepa/epa-order-11102.

———. 1992. Environmental Equity: Reducing Risk for All Communities. Report, June. EPA 230-R-92-008. Washington, DC: EPA.

———. 2010a. *Fiscal Year 2011–2015 EPA Strategic Plan: Achieving Our Vision.* Report, September 30. Washington, DC: EPA. http://nepis.epa.gov/Exe/ZyPDF. cgi?Dockey=P1008YOS.PDF (accessed May 1, 2013).

———. 2010b. Seven Priorities for EPA's Future. http://www2.epa.gov/aboutepa/ seven-priorities-epas-future (accessed May 1, 2013).

———. 2011a. *Plan EJ 2014.* September. Washington, DC: EPA. www.epa.gov/ environmentaljustice/resources/policy/plan-ej-2014/plan-ej-overview.pdf (accessed May 1, 2013).

———. 2011b. "What Is the Origin of Environmental Justice at EPA?" http://compliance.supportportal.com/link/portal/23002/23009/Article/32786/What-is-the-origin-of-Environmental-Justice-at-EPA (accessed May 1, 2013).

————. 2012a. Environmental Justice Small Grants FY2012 Summaries by Region. Office of Enforcement and Compliance Assurance, December 6. www.epa.gov/environmentaljustice/resources/publications/grants/ej-smgrants-recipients-2012.pdf (accessed February 18, 2013).

————. 2012b. Environmental Justice Achievement Awards. www.epa.gov/environmentaljustice/awards/index.html (accessed May 1, 2013).

————. 2012c. Grants & Programs. www.epa.gov/environmentaljustice/grants/index.html (accessed May 1, 2013).

————. 2012d. Greenversations (EPA's collection of public blogs). www.epa.gov/greenversations/ (accessed February 18, 2013).

————. 2012e. National Environmental Justice Advisory Council. Fact sheet, July. www.epa.gov/environmentaljustice/resources/publications/factsheets/fact-sheet-nejac.pdf (accessed May 1, 2013).

————. 2012f. United States Environmental Protection Agency Charter: National Environmental Justice Advisory Council. www.epa.gov/environmentaljustice/resources/publications/nejac/nejac-charter-2012.pdf (accessed May 1, 2013).

————. 2013a. Developing a Tribal and Indigenous Peoples Environmental Justice Policy. www.epa.gov/environmentaljustice/indigenous/index.html (accessed May 1, 2013).

————. 2013b. "Environmental Justice." www.epa.gov/environmentaljustice/index.html (accessed March 22, 2013).

————. 2013c. Environmental Justice: Basic Information. www.epa.gov/environmentaljustice/basics/ejbackground.html (accessed May 1, 2013).

————. 2013d. Environmental Justice Key Terms. www.epa.gov/region7/ej/definitions.htm (accessed May 1, 2013).

————. 2013e. Federal Interagency Working Group on Environmental Justice. www.epa.gov/environmentaljustice/interagency/index.html (accessed May 1, 2013).

————. 2013f. NEJAC Advice and Recommendations. www.epa.gov/environmentaljustice/nejac/recommendations.html#recommendations (accessed May 1, 2013).

————. 2013g. "Our Mission and What We Do." http://www2.epa.gov/aboutepa/our-mission-and-what-we-do (accessed May 1, 2013).

————. 2013h. Plan EJ 2014 Progress Report. EPA Report no. EPA-300-R-13-001, February. www.epa.gov/environmentaljustice/resources/policy/plan-ej-2014/plan-ej-progress-report-2013.pdf.

————. 2013i. q uarterly Environmental Justice Outreach Teleconference. www.epa.gov/environmentaljustice/events/ej-outreach-calls.html (accessed May 1, 2013).

U.S. General Accounting Office. 1996. *Executive Guide: Effectively Implementing the Government Performance and Results Act.* Report no. GAO/GGD-96-118. www.gao.gov/assets/80/76262.pdf (accessed May 1, 2013).

van Gelder, Sarah. 2001. "Danny Glover: An Interview by Sarah van Gelder." *YES!* March 31. www.yesmagazine.org/issues/working-for-life/danny-glover-an-interview-by-sarah-van-gelder.

Weiss, Janet A. 1996. "Public Management and Psychology." In *The State of Public Management,* ed. Donald F. Kettl and H. Brinton Milward, 118–42. Baltimore: Johns Hopkins University Press.

Weiss, Janet A., and Sandy Kristin Piderit. 1999. "The Value of Mission Statements in Public Agencies." *Journal of Public Administration Research and Theory* 9 (2): 193–223.

8 ASSESSING RACIAL EQUITY IN GOVERNMENT

In order to get beyond racism, we must first take account of race. There is no other way.

—Harry A. Blackmun (1978)
(University of California v. Bakke)

Assessing the performance management and accountability dimensions of racial equity is central in the delivery of public services. It provides a direct and systematic examination of both processes and outcomes related to agency practice, policies, and behavior. It also promotes transparency in the impacts and consequences of government action. Examining the role of performance management and accountability relative to racial equity fosters an examination of advantaged and disadvantaged clients, structural causes of inequities, and ways of reducing racial disparities in publicly provided services.

Ideally, accountability in government offers the promise of democracy, justice, ethical behavior, and performance (Dubnick 2005). Each of these outcomes is particularly important with regard to assessing racial equity. Democracy is fostered through transparency and openness in agency behavior (O'Donnell 1998; Schedler, Diamond, and Plattner 1999). Justice is advanced through impartiality, objectivity, and protection from abuse of power (Ambos 2000; Elster 2004). Ethical behavior is promoted through oversight of the behavior of public servants (Dubnick 2005; Morgan and Reynolds 1997), and improved performance is cultivated through an increased emphasis on the effectiveness and efficiency of government service (Berman and West 1995; Hatry and Fisk 1971; Ridley and Simon 1943; Wholey 1983).

While the *E*s of effectiveness and efficiency are nearly synonymous with performance management, the *E* of equity is largely missing from assessments of performance management or, at best, receives far less attention than its counterparts. As Frederickson states, "In running the government the administrator's job was to be efficient (getting the most service for available dollars) or economical (providing an agreed-upon level of services for the fewest possible dollars). It should be no surprise, therefore, that issues of equity and injustice were not central to public servants or to public administration theorists" (1990, 228).

The initial reasoning went this way: To say that a service may be well man-aged and that a service may be efficient and economical, still begs these questions. Well managed for whom? Efficient for whom? Economical for whom? We have generally assumed in public administration a convenient oneness with the public. We have not focused our attention or concern to the issue of variations in social and economic conditions. It is of great convenience, both theoretically and practically, to assume that citizen A is the same as citizen B and that they both receive public services in equal measure. This assumption may be convenient, but it is obviously both il-logical and empirically inaccurate. (Frederickson 1990, 228)

Often equity is framed as a compromiser of efficienc . As Myers notes, "What is evident in our discipline, however, is the tension between the equity and efficiency criteria and the inherent trade-offs between the two" (2002, 170). Similarly, Patton and Sawicki contend, "In many instances programs that prove to be very efficient also prove to be very inequitable. The two criteria are seldom both maximized in the same program" (1993, 204). More recently, however, return-on-investment studies suggest there are significant economic costs of social inequity to society (Norman-Major and Wooldridge 2011). For example, Aaron and Temple (2007) performed a social return-on-investment study of youth-intervention programs in Minnesota. A primary finding was that intervention programs aimed at "at risk" youth can produce returns of up to $14 for every state dollar invested, realizing reductions in court costs, school dropout rates, adult crime prosecution, and expenditures on public assistance.

Racial Equity Analysis

Race analysis is defined as "the systematic application of tools of historical and cultural analysis to understand the social and economic circumstances facing blacks and other racial minority groups" (Myers 2002, 170). Modern racial equity analysis was pioneered by W. E. B. Du Bois (1899) in his seminal work, *The Philadelphia Negro*. Based on an in-depth sociological analysis of Negro life in Philadelphia's Seventh Ward, the then-largest concentrated area of African Americans, Du Bois identified and analyzed structural factors that provided a grounding frame of black life. As Bobo comments,

He [Du Bois] identified six specific types of effects of prejudice: 1) restric-tion of blacks to menial work roles; 2) vulnerability to displacement due to competition from native whites or white immigrants; 3) resentment of black advancement and initiative; 4) vulnerability to financial exploitation;

5) inability to secure quality education for children or to shelter them from societal prejudice and discrimination; and 6) a wide array of discourteous and insulting treatment in "social intercourse." (Bobo 2000, 191)

Building upon this work, with a more direct focus on government, Blauner (1972) found that racism had an independent institutional base that did not require prejudice in order to demonstrate effectiveness.

The processes that maintain domination—control of whites over non-whites—are built into the major social institutions. These institutions either exclude or restrict the participation of racial groups by procedures that have become conventional, *part of the bureaucratic system of rules and regulations*. Thus there is little need for prejudice as a motivating force. (Blauner 1972, 9–10, emphasis added)

An important foundation of racial equity analysis is previous and ongoing identification of illegal discrimination based on race. "Legally defined, disparate treatment racial discrimination occurs when an individual is treated less favorably—for example, is not hired for a job—because of his or her race. Disparate impact racial discrimination occurs if a behavior or practice that does not involve race directly has an adverse impact on members of a disadvantaged racial group without a sufficiently compelling reason" (National Research Council 2004, 40–41).

For example, in the area of U.S. education policy, "equity audits of school districts have been conducted by school districts (either voluntarily or under pressure by civic activists or ordered by the U.S. Department of Education Office of Civil Rights) as a way of determining the degree of compliance with a number of civil rights statutes that prohibit discrimination in education programs and activities receiving federal funding (Skrla et al. 2004, 138).

While considerable work remains in aggressively prosecuting illegal discrimination, there are many legislative and administrative actions that are not legally prohibited.

Government actions fall under a somewhat different set of legal rules. . . . Specifically, although the equal protection clause prohibits disparate treatment discrimination that fails to have the most compelling societal justification, the Constitution prohibits only intentional discrimination; evidence of disparate impact alone will not establish a violation. Thus, the Constitution does not restrict a government from engaging in acts that harm disadvantaged racial groups unless the harm is caused intentionally. Moreover, knowing that a certain practice will cause harm is not enough to render it an intentional act of discrimination barred by the equal protection clause. As the court has emphasized, a government is not prohibited from acting in spite of harm to members of disadvantaged racial groups; it is only banned from causing harm because of race. (National Research Council 2004, 52–53)

One important area, for example, is cumulative discriminatory effects.

Discrimination by real estate agents may result in housing segregation, which in turn affects educational quality (because of local tax financing of the schools) and long-term educational and labor market outcomes. Although discriminating real estate agents can be found liable for housing market discrimination, there is no legal mechanism to allocate blame for educational or labor market differences that such discrimination might induce. (National Research Council 2004, 41–42)

Assessing Racial Equity in Government

Fortunately, across multiple areas, government action is not guided by the narrow, minimalistic standard of avoiding illegal behavior, but by providing high-quality service to the public it serves. The same standard for excellence is instructive in analyzing government performance in providing services that are racially equitable. Government agencies should be motivated to analyze the racial equity dimensions of their services from an intrinsic goal to demonstrate high performance and accountability. Government agencies routinely engage in strategic planning, budget forecasting, and performance management practices designed to offer high-quality public service. Agencies monitor and strive to improve their performance in the areas of pothole repairs, snow removal, and the provision of online services, not because of legal requirements but because citizens and residents expect high-quality services. Racial equity in the provision of government services is driven not only by legal considerations, but by an organizational desire to employ fair practices in governmental performance.

Table 8.1 offers guiding criteria for defining best practices. As Keehley et al. suggest, "A best practice should address an activity that is resource intensive and has a significant impact on external customers" (1997, 26). In general, best practices are successful over time, innovative, yield recognized positive outcomes, are repeatable, have local importance, and are not linked to unique demographics.

Identifying a "best practice" relative to racial equity is preceded by an examination of evidence. Regardless of the specific quantitative or qualitative

Table 8.1

Best Practices Criteria

1. *Successful over time.* A best practice must have a proven track record.
2. *Quantifiable results.* The success of a best practice must be quantifiable.
3. *Innovative.* A program or practice should be recognized by its peers as being creative or innovative.
4. *Recognized positive outcome.* If quantifiable results are limited, a best practice may be recognized through other positive indicators.
5. *Repeatable.* A best practice should be replicable with modifications. It should establish a clear roadmap, describing how the practice evolved and what benefits are likely to accrue to others who adopt the practice.
6. *Has local importance.* Best practices are salient to the organization searching for improvement. The topic, program, process, or issue does not need to be identical to the importing organization, however.
7. *Not linked to unique demographics.* A best practice may have evolved as a result of unique demographics, but it should be transferable, with modifications, to organizations where those demographics do not necessarily exist.

Source: Keehley et al. 1997.

techniques employed, racial equity analysis generally aligns within one or more of the four broad approaches used to measure social equity: procedural fairness (due process), access (distributional), quality (process), and outcomes.

Procedural fairness involves the examination of problems or issues of procedural rights (due process), treatment in a procedural sense (equal protection), and the application of eligibility criteria (equal rights) for existing policies and programs. . . . Practices such as failure to provide due process before relocating low-income families as part of an urban renewal project, using racial profiling to identify suspects, or unfairly denying benefits to a person who meets eligibility criteria all raise obvious equity issues.

Access—distributional equity—involves a review of current policies, services, and practices to determine the level of access to services/benefits and analysis of reasons for unequal access. . . . Equity can be examined empirically—do all persons receive the same service and the same quality of service (as opposed to the procedural question of whether all are treated the same according to distributional standards in an existing program or service)—or normatively—should there be a policy commitment to providing the same level of service to all?

quality—process equity—involves a review of the level of consistency in the quality of existing services delivered to groups and individuals. . . . For example, is garbage pickup the same in quality, extent of spillage, or missed cans in all neighborhoods? Do children in inner-city schools have teachers with the same qualifications as those in suburban schools?

Outcomes involve an examination of whether policies and programs have the same impact on all groups and individuals served. Regardless of the approach to distribution and the consistency of quality, there is not necessarily a commitment to an equal level of accomplishment or outcomes. . . . Equal results equity might conceivably require that resources be allocated until the *same results* are achieved . . . a critical issue in consideration of equity at this level is how much inequality is acceptable and to what extent government can and should intervene to reduce the inequality in results. (Johnson and Svara 2011, 20–22)

Table 8.2 provides a sample social equity template that aligns with the areas noted above.

Such templates identify guiding questions for analysis. For example, in assessing procedural fairness, an appropriate guiding question relative to personnel actions is "Are processes for career development, advancement, awards, and recognition equitable?" For access equity, an example guiding question is, "Do budget allocations reflect a commitment to fair results among all stakeholders?" For quality equity, "Is the level, frequency, duration, etc. of service appropriate for specific stakeholders?" And for outcome equity, "Does the organization take action to improve disparities?"

Racial Equity Impact Assessments

While racial equity analysis is contained within the larger rubric of social equity analysis, it is useful for federal, state, and local governments to provide an assessment specific to race. "A Racial Equity Impact Assessment (REIA) is a systematic examination of how different racial and ethnic groups will likely be affected by a proposed action or decision" (Keleher 2009). Table 8.3 is a sample Racial Equity Impact Assessment Guide for Economic Policies and Public Budgets that provides questions specific to race that governmental agencies and policymakers can use to analyze current problems, develop proposed changes, or analyze current proposals.

Governmental agencies can then develop worksheets for specific racial equity impact analysis to examine the effect of proposed programs. In order to promote racial equity in government services, these tools are most appropriately utilized *prior* to program implementation. Exhibit 8.1 provides an example worksheet from the Streetlight Relamping Program within Seattle City Light. The worksheet requires agencies to answer ten standard questions regarding racial impacts of their proposed Streetlight Relamping program.

Table 8.2

Social Equity Analysis Template

Dimension	Guiding Questions for Analysis and Associated Outcome
Procedural fairness (due process)	• Does the organization employ fair and equitable processes to acquire a diverse, highly skilled workforce? • Are processes for career development, advancement, awards, and recognition equitable? • Are there processes to ensure appropriate information sharing among internal and external partners? • Are goals for contracting with minority- and women-owned businesses being supported and met?
Outcome	*Ensures equal protection and due process in personnel actions and business and operational dealings.*
Access (distributional equity)	• Do budget allocations reflect a commitment to fair results among all stakeholders? • Does the organization examine its outcomes in a manner that would permit it to identify inequities? • Are targeted interventions and other corrective actions taken to correct identified inequities? • Does the organization employ a culturally competent workforce capable of delivering services in a multicultural manner?
Outcome	*Ensures that appropriate allocations of resources are made so that fair results are realized by all stakeholders.*
Quality (process equity)	• Is the quality of service comparable for all stakeholders? • Is the level, frequency, duration, etc. of service appropriate for specific stakeholders? • Does the organization gather and analyze data, conduct periodic reviews, examine service delivery metrics, and so forth to identify service delivery deficiencies? • Does the organization undertake reviews and evaluations to determine whether its processes have a disparate or adverse impact upon a group of stakeholders? • Does the organization take action to address identified deficiencies and/or disparate or adverse impact?
Outcome	*Ensures consistent quality of service to all stakeholders.*
Outcome	• Does the organization collect and analyze data that would permit it to identify disproportionate results? • Does the organization examine causes of identified disparities? • Does the organization take action to improve such disparities?
Outcome	*Ensures the absence of disparities in processes, equal access, and procedural activities.*

Source: Johnson and Svara 2011.

Table 8.3

Racial Equity Impact Assessment Guide for Economic Policies and Public Budgets

Stage	Questions for Consideration
1. Analyzing current problems	A. What are the *adverse effects* that different disadvantaged racialized communities experience under current conditions, policies, practices, and expenditures?
	B. What are the *causes or contributing factors* (e.g., unfair policies and practices, inequitable or insufficient funding formulas) that produce or perpetuate the inequities?
	C. What *data or evidence* is available or can be collected to demonstrate the racial inequities, adverse effects, contributing causes, trends, and current needs?
2. Developing and advancing proposed changes	A. What steps can ensure *public input and participation* by the most disadvantaged racial communities and stakeholders in developing proposed policies and budgets?
	B. What *new policies, programs, funding streams* are needed to address the needs and inequities that different racialized communities face?
	C. What *changes in existing policies, programs, budgets* would reduce racial inequities?
	D. What *new opportunities* can be created to enhance equity, inclusion, and unity across different racial/ethnic groups?
	E. What specific equitable *outcomes* will this achieve, and what are the success indicators?
	F. How can these proposed changes be *effectively designed* in such a way to make them most viable, enforceable, and sustainable?
3. Analyzing current proposals	A. Will the proposal *reduce, limit, or eliminate programs* that are vital to or disproportionately needed by particular disadvantaged racial/ethnic communities?
	B. Will the proposal *increase, expand, or create programs* that are vital to or disproportionately needed by particular disadvantaged racial/ethnic communities?
	C. Will the proposal *miss or create opportunities* to benefit and unify people across different racial/ethnic communities?
	D. Will there be enough money allocated to address real racial inequities *with fair and sustainable revenue streams*?
	E. Will there be *adequate provisions to ensure success and fairness,* including sufficient public participation by stakeholders in development, implementation, and evaluation?
	F. What *modifications* in the proposal are needed to maximize racial equity and inclusion?

Source: Keleher 2009.

Exhibit 8.1
Racial Equity Impact Analysis Worksheet

1. Department and project title

Streetlight Relamping Program, Seattle City Light

2. Briefly describe the proposed action and the desired results.

Seattle City Light is implementing a group relamping program for street-lights. The proposal outlines the steps SCL wants to take to engage a contractor to begin replacing 21,000 street lights. Then the Utility will begin a rotating program to replace luminaries in Seattle and our franchise cities. At present, the Utility replaces streetlight bulbs as it becomes aware of outages from customers and other spotters. This practice is more expensive than group relamping, and customers frequently have long periods before the streetlight can be fixed.

3. Who are the racial/ethnic groups affected by this program, policy, or practice? How will each group be affected? What are the racial disparities related to this project?

All racial groups residing in our service area will be affected. Those living in areas with higher crime rates presumably will be safer with more illumination. The original plan was to have two sets of contractor crews work north and south from the Utility's midway point, Denny Way. In response to the RSJ [Race and Social Justice] analysis, the Utility decided to work from the southernmost line of the service area and relamp moving north from there. This way, more low-income and immigrant communities would be served first. The relamping program is intended to provide greater reliability in streetlight operations than the current process.

4. How does the proposed action expand opportunity and access for individuals (including immigrants and refugees)?

There are large immigrant populations in the southern part of the service area. Currently, City Light relies heavily on customers to report lights out. Immigrants who do not speak English fluently and may not be knowledgeable about City Services are less likely to phone in outage reports.

5. How does the proposed action promote racially inclusive collaboration and civic engagement? Is there community support for or opposition to the proposal? Why?

The project manager went to several community meetings ahead of time to explain the program. There were written messages translated into the seven most common languages used in the district.

6. How does the proposed action [e]ffect systemic change (address institutional racism)?

(continued)

Exhibit 8.1 *(continued)*

Traditionally, City Light began system and service improvements in the north part of the service area. These residents are generally white and more financially advantaged. This method of rolling out the project will bring improvements first to communities of color.

7. How does the proposed action educate on racial issues?

Mainly the learning has been internal to City Light by making the project managers and engineers more aware that the decisions they make can have consequences to low-income and racially diverse communities. One hopeful outcome may be developing better trust and expectations within communities of color.

8. How does the proposed action support workforce equity and/or contracting equity?

City Light will contract out for group streetlight repair work; we will be looking at HUBS. Contractor employees will work for prevailing wages.

9. How does this action help to achieve greater racial equity? Describe the resources, timelines, and monitoring that will help ensure success.

The contractor's work will be inspected by a City Light resident engineer. We will use those reports to monitor progress and quality of service.

10. Are there any unintended consequences on racial equity? Are there strategies to mitigate any negative impacts?

None expected.

Source: Race and Social Justice Initiative 2010.

This worksheet captures subtle aspects of street lighting. For example, the proposal discusses the impact of customers' language skills in phoning in outage reports under the current system. It also addresses the association between lighting and crime. Additionally, the response to question six discusses the City of Seattle's previous record in providing system and service improvements, which historically began such improvements in the north part of the service area, largely comprising a higher-income and white population. The proposed lighting program will alter this historical service sequence to improve the City of Seattle's service to communities of color.

Legislative Racial Equity Assessments

The utilization of racial equity assessments is extending beyond use at the agency level. In April 2007, the state of Iowa passed the nation's first minority

Exhibit 8.2

Minority Impact Statement Legislation, Iowa Code § 2.56 (2009)

1. Prior to debate on the floor of a chamber of the general assembly, a correctional impact statement shall be attached to any bill, joint resolution, or amendment which proposes a change in the law which creates a public offense, significantly changes an existing public offense or the penalty for an existing offense, or changes existing sentencing, parole, or probation procedures. The statement shall include information concerning the estimated number of criminal cases per year that the legislation will impact, the fiscal impact of confining persons pursuant to the legislation, the impact of the legislation on minorities, the impact of the legislation upon existing correctional institutions, community-based correctional facilities and services, and jails, the likelihood that the legislation may create a need for additional prison capacity, and other relevant matters. The statement shall be factual and shall, if possible, provide a reasonable estimate of both the immediate effect and the long-range impact upon prison capacity.

2. a. When a committee of the general assembly reports a bill, joint resolution, or amendment to the floor, the committee shall state in the report whether a correctional impact statement is or is not required.

   b. The legislative services agency shall review all bills and joint resolutions placed on the calendar of either chamber of the general assembly, as well as amendments filed to bills or joint resolutions on the calendar, to determine whether a correctional impact statement is required.

   c. A member of the general assembly may request the preparation of a correctional impact statement by submitting a request to the legislative services agency.

3. The legislative services agency shall cause to be prepared a correctional impact statement within a reasonable time after receiving a request or determining that a proposal is subject to this section. All correctional impact statements approved by the legislative services agency shall be transmitted immediately to either the chief clerk of the house or the secretary of the senate, after notifying the sponsor of the legislation that the statement has been prepared for publication. The chief clerk of the house or the secretary of the senate shall attach the statement to the bill, joint resolution, or amendment affected as soon as it is available.

4. The legislative services agency may request the cooperation of any state department or agency or political subdivision in preparing a correctional impact statement.

(continued)

Exhibit 8.2 *(continued)*

5. The legislative services agency, in cooperation with the division of criminal and juvenile justice planning of the department of human rights, shall develop a protocol for analyzing the impact of the legislation on minorities.
6. A revised correctional impact statement shall be prepared if the correctional impact has been changed by the adoption of an amendment, and may be requested by a member of the general assembly or be prepared upon a determination made by the legislative services agency. However, a request for a revised correctional impact statement shall not delay action on the bill, joint resolution, or amendment unless so ordered by the presiding officer of the chamber.

Source: State of Iowa 2008.

---

impact legislation (Exhibit 8.2). The passage of Iowa's legislation occurred following a Sentencing Project report that found that Iowa incarcerates African Americans compared to Caucasians at a ratio of 13 to 1. The national average is 5.6 to 1. This places Iowa in the top spot for the highest ratio of black-to white incarcerations of any state in the nation (Mauer and King 2007). According to Iowa's governor, Chet Culver, "while 2% of Iowa's population is African-American, 24% of Iowa's prison population is African-American" (Office of the Governor of Iowa 2008). Targeted at reducing racial disparities in the Criminal Justice system, "Iowa plans to utilize minority impact statements when new public offenses are created, when penalties for existing public offenses are changed, and when changes are made to sentencing, parole, or probation procedures" (Rossi 2010, 866).

After a legislative committee makes a determination that new correctional legislation may have an impact on a minority population, an impact statement will be prepared by one of the agencies or commissions previously mentioned. After an impact statement is prepared, and before the proposed legislation is voted on, the impact statement is sent to the legislative body for review. "Committee consideration of . . . [the racial impact statement] should be guided by two questions. First, do the crime control benefits of such a policy outweigh the consequences of heightened racial disparity?" That is, would an increase in racial disparity resulting from passage of the proposed legislation seem justified if looked at from a public safety viewpoint? "[S]econd, are there alternative policy choices that could address the problem at hand without such negative [racially disparate] effects? By answering these two questions, legislatures would direct sentencing policy more specifically toward the area of concern and would almost inevitably reduce the racial disparities" (Rossi 2010, 864-65).

Evaluating Racial Equity Performance

Equity evaluation is not calculated by a universal mathematic formula. Rather, it is similar to program evaluation or agency performance evaluation. The rating system offers a differentiation among inequitable policies and practices, ranging from an overall assessment of "inequitable" to "minimally inequitable." As Table 8.4 depicts, specific or general agency policies and practices should be evaluated against the four primary measures of equity: procedural fairness, access, quality, and outcome. Each dimension is assessed to derive an overall equity evaluation. If the evaluation results yield an assessment of "excellent" on each of the four dimensions of equity, then the agency policy or practice is "equitable." If the evaluation results yield an assessment of at least "good" on each of the four dimensions of equity, then the agency policy or practice is "minimally inequitable." If the evaluation results yield an assessment of at least "fair" on each of the four dimensions of equity, then the agency policy or practice is "moderately inequitable." If the evaluation results yield an assessment below fair on any one of the four dimensions of equity, then the agency policy or practice is "inequitable." Importantly, the overall equity assessment is based upon performance on *each* of the four dimensions of equity. For example, if a specific policy or practice is rated "excellent" on one equity dimension, such as procedural fairness, but rated "fair" on another equity dimension, such as quality, the overall evaluation is "moderately inequitable."

Similar to program evaluation, equity assessments may be determined by using a variety of quantitative and qualitative tools, such as regression analysis, residual differences analysis, hazard models, audit studies, geographic information systems (GIS) analysis, content analysis, and ethnography. Performing racial equity analysis alone is not predicated by a specific technique, but rather a thorough assessment along multiple dimensions as methodologically appropriate based upon the specific policy or practice

Conclusion

Government agencies that deliver public services in a democratic society should value and measure the equity of their work. Assessing equity within government is as important as assessing effectiveness and efficiency. To promote such appraisals, the use of racial equity assessment tools is increasing within government. Governments are providing internal monitoring and

Table 8.4

Racial Equity Ratings

Ratings	Criteria
Equitable	Excellent performance on each of the four equity dimensions (procedural, access, quality, and outcome)
Minimally inequitable	At least good performance on each of the four equity dimensions (procedural, access, quality, and outcome)
Moderately inequitable	At least fair performance on each of the four equity dimensions (procedural, access, quality, and outcome)
Inequitable	Below fair performance on one or more equity dimensions (procedural, access, quality, and outcome)

accountability of their racial equity performance, rather than relying solely upon external academic researchers and policy organizations to fill this gap. It is particularly important to assess racial equity impacts *prior* to the implementation of legislation or programs, rather than just following implementation. Similar to projecting the fiscal impact of a proposed policy or program, projecting the racial equity impact of a particular action is also critical.

Racial equity toolkits are designed to detect subtle aspects of racial inequities, which are more aligned with contemporary racial inequity practices. While blatant racism and discrimination still exist, on the whole they have decreased over time. Monitoring illegal discrimination remains important, but additional examination of more nuanced racial inequities is important as well. Doing only the former fails to systematically consider the nuances of racial inequities that permeate twenty-first-century governmental agencies

Evaluating agency performance in terms of racial equity is also a critical task. Routine racial equity analysis of agency performance can be effective in assessing policies and practices. While racial equity analysis in government is important, such systematic evaluation is also relatively new, unless it is legally required. Public administrators will need additional training in developing and conducting racial equity impact assessments. This suggests that the fields of public administration and public policy will need to better train public affairs professionals along these skill set dimensions. However, public administration programs must also examine areas of nervousness within their own organizational structures.

References

Aaron, Paul A., and Judy Temple. 2007. *Analyzing the Social Return on Investment in Youth Intervention Programs: A Framework for Minnesota.* St. Paul, MN: Wilder Research.

Ambos, K. 2000. "Judicial Accountability of Perpetrators of Human Rights Violations and the Role of Victims." *International Peacekeeping* 6 (2): 67–77.

Berman, Evan M., and Jonathan P. West. 1995. "Municipal Commitment to Total q uality Management: A Survey of Recent Progress." *Public Administration Review* 55 (1): 57–66.

Blauner, Robert A. 1972. *Racial Oppression in America.* New York: Harper & Row.

Bobo, Lawrence D. 2000. "Reclaiming a Du Boisian Perspective on Racial Attitudes." *Annals of the American Academy* 568: 186–202.

Dubnick, Melvin. 2005. "Accountability and the Promise of Performance: In Search of the Mechanisms." *Public Performance & Management Review* 28 (3): 376–417.

Du Bois, W. E. B. 1899. *The Philadelphia Negro: A Social Study.* Philadelphia: University of Pennsylvania Press. Republished in 1996 with an introduction by Elijah Anderson by the University of Pennsylvania Press.

Elster, Jon. 2004. *Closing the Books: Transitional Justice in Historical Perspective.* New York: Cambridge University Press.

Frederickson, H. George. 1990. "Public Administration and Social Equity." *Public Administration Review* 50 (2): 228–37.

Hatry, Harry P., and Donald Fisk. 1971. *Improving Productivity and Productivity Measurement in Local Government.* Washington, DC: Urban Institute.

Johnson, Norman J., and James H. Svara. 2011. "Social Equity in American Society and Public Administration. In *Justice for All: Promoting Social Equity in Public Administration,* ed. Norman J. Johnson and James H. Svara, 20–22. Armonk, NY: M.E. Sharpe.

Keehley, Patricia, Steven Medlin, Sue MacBride, and Laura Longmire. 1997. *Benchmarking for Best Practices in the Public Sector: Achieving Performance Breakthroughs in Federal, State, and Local Agencies.* San Francisco: Jossey-Bass.

Keleher, Terry. 2009. *Racial Equity Impact Assessments of Economic Policies and Public Budgets.* New York: Applied Research Center. www.racialequitytools.org/resourcefiles/keleher1.pdf

Mauer, Marc, and Ryan S. King. 2007. *Uneven Justice: State Rates of Incarceration by Race and Ethnicity.* Report, July. Washington, DC: The Sentencing Project.

Morgan, Peter W., and Glenn H. Reynolds. 1997. *The Appearance of Impropriety: How the Ethics Wars Have Undermined American Government, Business, and Society.* New York: Free Press.

Myers, Samuel L., Jr. 2002. "Analysis of Race as Policy Analysis." *Journal of Policy Analysis and Management* 21 (2): 169–90.

National Research Council. 2004. *Measuring Racial Discrimination.* Washington, DC: National Academies Press.

Norman-Major, Kristen, and Blue Wooldridge. 2011. "Using Framing Theory to Make the Economic Case for Social Equity: The Role of Policy Entrepreneurs in Reframing the Debate." In *Justice for All: Promoting Social Equity in Public Administration,* ed. Norman J. Johnson and James H. Svara, 209–27. Armonk, NY: M.E. Sharpe.

O'Donnell, G. 1998. "Horizontal Accountability in New Democracies." *Journal of Democracy* 9 (3): 112–26.

Office of the Governor of Iowa. 2008. "Governor Culver Signs Minority Impact Statement Bill into Law." Press release, April 17. www.allamericanpatriots.

com/48746401_iowa-governor-culver-signs-minority-impact-stateme (accessed April 22, 2013).

Patton, Carl V., and David S. Sawicki. 1993. *Basic Methods of Policy Analysis and Planning*. Upper Saddle River, NJ: Prentice Hall.

Race and Social Justice Initiative. 2010. Racial Equity Toolkit for Policies, Programs, and Budget. Seattle, WA: Seattle Office for Civil Rights. www.seattle.gov/rsji/docs/RSJIToolkit_3_10.pdf (accessed April 16, 2013).

Ridley, Clarence E., and Herbert A. Simon. 1943. *Measuring Municipal Activities: A Survey of Suggested Criteria for Appraising Administration*. Chicago: International City Management Association.

Rossi, David A. 2010. "Jumping the Gun: Iowa's Swift Adoption of Minority Impact Statement Legislation Points to Other Problems Within the State's Criminal Justice System." *Drake Law Review* 58 (3): 857–78.

Schedler, Andreas, Larry Diamond, and Mark F. Plattner, eds. 1999. *The Self-Restraining State: Power and Accountability in New Democracies*. Boulder, CO: Lynne Rienner.

Skrla, Linda, James Joseph Scheurich, Juanita Garcia, and Glenn Nolly. 2004. "Equity Audits: A Practical Leadership Tool for Developing Equitable and Excellent Schools." *Educational Administration Quarterly* 40 (1): 133–61.

State of Iowa. 2008. §2.56, Correctional Impact Statements, April 17. http://coolice.legis.iowa.gov/Cool-ICE/default.asp?category=billinfo&service=IowaCode&input=2.56.

University of California Regents v. Bakke. 438 U.S. 265. 1978. Retrieved from http://scholar.google.com/scholar_case?case=4987623155291151023&hl=en&as_sdt=6&as_vis=1&oi=scholarr.

Wholey, Joseph S. 1983. *Evaluation and Effective Performance Measurement*. Boston: Little, Brown.

9 BEYOND THE DIVERSITY PLAN: OVERCOMING RACIAL NERVOUSNESS WITHIN MPA PROGRAMS

In the end, arguing about affirmative action in selective colleges is like arguing about the size of a spigot while ignoring the pool and the pipeline that feeds it.

—Eric Liu (2012)

This chapter examines racial nervousness as it relates to diversity goals in Master's of Public Administration (MPA) programs. The Network of Schools of Public Policy, Affairs, and Administration[1] (NASPAA) is the accrediting body for professional education in public service. According to new 2009 NASPAA standards, programs seeking accreditation for their master's degree must demonstrate that their programs promote a climate of inclusiveness for faculty and students. MPA program faculty can do a lot internally to implement a plan to achieve such a climate for minority faculty and students. Examining internal climate issues within public higher education institutions, particularly in terms of race, is also a nervous area of government, largely because such conversations border on a direct or indirect discussion of affirmative action, an area of "race talk" that is preferably avoided in many university settings (see chapter 3 for a fuller discussion of race talk). Assessing a program's climate of inclusiveness may be uncomfortable for university faculty and administrators because, as detailed in chapter 4, it necessitates a critical analysis of organizational history, operations, norms, and policies.

However, "in many respects professional accreditation is a powerful force to motivate change" (Rubaii and Calarusse 2012, 222).

> This regulatory process can be a lever to move a professional field toward the aspirations of those designing the accreditation standards, in part due to the scale of the operation and the widespread level of participation. Programs generally consider the standards legitimate guidelines developed by professional peers whom they respect. (Rubaii and Calarusse 2012, 222)

NASPAA's 2009 accreditation standards relating to a climate of inclusiveness have significant implications in terms of race

Diversity remains an important value for MPA programs seeking accreditation or reaccreditation. Standards 3.2 and 4.4 articulate specific programmatic requirements relative to faculty and student diversity respectively (NASPAA 2009). Over time, this has largely evolved into MPA programs' developing a written diversity plan identifying broad diversity goals and specific strategies employed toward the pursuit of such goals. Traditionally, these plans include target goals related to faculty and student recruitment and retention. In addition to addressing the essential areas of faculty and student diversity, as well as diversity within the MPA curriculum, the NASPAA standards require programs to provide a climate of inclusiveness, which includes assessing a program's climate in regard to race.

NASPAA Standards

According to the 2009 NASPAA standards, public affairs and public administration programs seeking accreditation or reaccreditation for their master's degree must demonstrate their programs are in compliance in seven programmatic areas: (1) managing the program strategically; (2) matching governance with the mission; (3) matching operations with the mission: faculty performance; (4) matching operations with the mission: serving students; (5) matching operations with the mission: student learning; (6) matching resources with the mission; and (7) matching communications with the mission. Two of these standards specifically mention the requirement that programs promote a climate of inclusiveness. In terms of faculty diversity, Standard 3.2 states, "The program will promote diversity *and a climate of inclusiveness* through its recruitment and retention of faculty members" (NASPAA 2009, 5, emphasis added). Standard 4.4 focuses on student diversity, stating, "The program will promote diversity *and a climate of inclusiveness* through its recruitment, admissions practices, and student support services" (NASPAA 2009, 6, emphasis added).

Although there are multiple important aspects of diversity extending far beyond race, NASPAA Self Study guidelines require MPA programs seeking accreditation or reaccreditation to collect and present data in terms of race, ethnicity, and gender (Standards 3.2 and 4.4). Diversity plans across programs throughout many universities often give considerable focus to numerical counts of faculty and students by gender, race, and ethnicity, with particular emphasis on recruiting and retaining women faculty and faculty of color. Such a focus is essential in order to successfully advance a program's promotion of diversity. However, there also is often a true lack of innovation and expansion in terms of the methods employed to advance diversity. Over time, this has resulted in the implementation of common strategies, as well as common reasoning as to why such strategies have failed.

During my past sixteen years in the academy, I have been directly and continuously involved in many aspects of programmatic diversity related to race. Examples of these activities include service on diversity committees at the program, college, and university levels; active service in the diversity committee of NASPAA; service as a site visitor for NASPAA program reaccreditation; service on NASPAA's National Council; founder of the Minority Serving Institutions (MSI) initiative; membership on several faculty search committees at my home university, as well as service on faculty search committees at external universities; responding to formal and informal requests from colleagues in the academy to assist in identifying minority candidates for faculty positions; responding to informal requests from faculty colleagues throughout the profession in how they might attract more minority faculty and graduate students; and comparing conversational notes with other faculty members of color who have responded to similar requests from their colleagues.

These rich experiences and anecdotal conversations have led to some clear, thematic patterns. For example, many programs assert that they have tried to promote diversity through the appropriate posting of job ads and having minority faculty members "in the pool." Other programs cite geographic disadvantages, asserting minority faculty members "don't want to come here," with the "here" including a wide variety of locations in the United States. Many programs also cite the inability to hire new faculty due to economic conditions, lack of faculty retirements, and/or the inability to effectively compete in the academic labor market. While these anecdotal themes are not generalizable to all MPA programs, they do constitute a common area of concern that faculty in some MPA programs verbalize. These factors are often cited to connect the gap between a program's reported desire to hire more faculty of color and/or attract more minority students, and the lack of success in achieving this goal.

Fortunately, faculty have much more direct control and influence over the climate of their MPA program. As Pitts and Wise contend, "A question for the public affairs community is whether the increased importance and relevance of diversity is reflected in the organizational culture of public affairs programs, or whether academic institutions, like many other organizations, ignore potential consequences related to diversity" (2004, 125). Programmatic norms and practices related to diversity may comply with legal or university guidelines but actively do little to advance diversity from a cultural standpoint. Riccucci (1997) found that relative to diversity, organizational responses often fall short in terms of both conceptualization and implementation. The NASPAA Diversity Report also contends that effective diversity initiatives are linked to organizational culture (2000). Antonio (2003) and Rivera and Ward (2008) indicate that faculty and staff diversity efforts work in tandem to promote a climate of inclusiveness. Programs that do not offer such a climate may be in danger of promoting institutional racism or sexism, regardless of intentionality, because existing practices, along with the distribution of power and resources, serve to reinforce majority advantages (Halstead 1988; Price 1997).

Culture vs. Climate

NASPAA standards require programs to promote a climate of inclusiveness. The organizational culture and climate of an organization have many similarities. The terms are similar and often used interchangeably. Both are focused on the "internal social psychological environment of organizations and the relationship of that environment to individual meaning and organizational adaption" (Denison 1996, 625). Both terms are used to describe the collective social context of an organization. However, there are also important distinctions.

Culture refers to the deep structure of organizations and can be divided into five components: values, beliefs, myths, traditions, and norms. Values are the ways individuals assess certain activities as productive or wasteful. Myths are organizational folklore—important stories that often translate into warnings against change. Beliefs reflect individuals' understanding of the way the organization works and the probable consequences of the actions they take. Traditions are repetitive significant events, such as celebrations and awards. Norms are the informal "rules of conduct" regarding such activities as communication processes, work habits, and dress (Kennedy Group, n.d.).

Climate is typically the label used to describe specific dimensions of the work environment that can be measured more easily. Climate is often situational and linked to thoughts, feelings, and behaviors of organizational members. Leadership is the single most important determinant of organizational climate, with day-to-day decision-making wielding power and influenc (Denison 1996; Kennedy Group, n.d.). Significant changes in organizational climate can be directly influenced by an organization's leadership. Aspects of organizational climate include organizational structure (how the organization organizes itself and its operations), standards of accountability and behavior (ways in which individuals are held accountable for their performance and their behaviors); communication (direct and open language about lack of acceptable behaviors); and perhaps most important, vision and structure (Kennedy Group, n.d.). If an organization has a vision with clearly aligned

Figure 9.1 **Culture Modification Process**

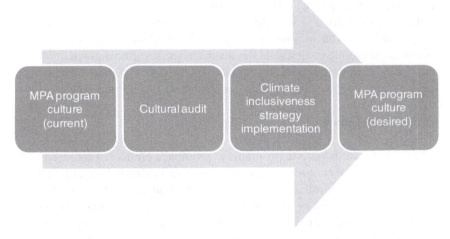

Source: Created by author.

proactive diversity strategies, then the organizational climate as well as the organizational culture will reflect the same vision over time

In essence, organizational climate is more malleable and situational than organizational culture, which is more entrenched and takes longer to change. In examining the formation of organizational climates, Schneider (1987), Schneider and Reichers (1983), and Reichers (1987) discuss the "attraction-selection-retention" process, which links climate formation to membership changes and socialization processes. There are multiple strategies that MPA program faculty, particularly MPA program directors, can use to promote a climate of inclusiveness for faculty and students as required under the NASPAA standards. Promoting a *climate* of inclusiveness is an essential step toward MPA programs' ultimately achieving a *culture* of inclusiveness. Figure 9.1 offers a conceptual depiction of the culture-modification process described in this book. This conceptualization is most appropriately viewed as a strategically driven process undertaken to improve policies and behaviors related to ultimately promoting a more positive organizational culture of diversity.

Performing a Cultural Audit

In establishing a climate of inclusiveness, an important first step is for the MPA program to examine its current organizational culture. Before any organization can implement significant change, it is important to first examine and understand its cultural status quo (see Table 9.1). Schein (2004) identifies three levels of

Table 9.1

Cultural Audit Summary Sheet Example

Culture Category	What to Look For	Gaps
1. Physical characteristics and general environment • What do the physical components of the department say about the culture? • Are diverse faculty and students included?	• Wall hangings • Symbols and logos • Program website • Brochures • Annual reports	
Specific climate actions to be taken (specify time frame; e.g., next month, six months, year)		
2. Policies and procedures • What do the MPA program's policies and procedures say about the importance of diversity?	• Mission statement • MPA program guide • Faculty search policies • Faculty promotion and tenure policies • Student application review policies	
Specific climate actions to be taken (specify time frame)		
3. Customs and norms • What regular behaviors and expectations are in place and affect the culture relative to diversity? • What impact do these have on diversity and inclusion? • Is consideration of diverse faculty and student interests a norm or priority?	• MPA program director-to-faculty interaction • Faculty-to-faculty interactions • MPA program chair-to-student interaction • Faculty-to-student interactions • Unspoken rules and norms	
Specific climate actions to be taken (specify time frame)		

(continued)

Table 9.1 *(continued)*

Culture Category	What to Look For	Gaps
4. Curriculum • How is diversity included within the curriculum? *Actions to be taken (specify time frame)*	• Diversity inclusion in core, required courses • Diversity inclusion in elective, stand-alone courses	
5. Research • How is diversity valued in faculty research and scholarship? *Actions to be taken (specify time frame)*	• Acceptance of diversity-related scholarship as a respected and tenable area of research • Support/advisement for diversity-related thesis or dissertations	
6. MPA program director leadership behavior • What priority does the department chair give to diversity? • How does this impact culture? • Are senior administrators who value diversity respected? *Actions to be taken (specify time frame)*	• How MPA program director communicates value of diversity to faculty, staff, and students • Perception of program chair's commitment to diversity by faculty, staff, and students • Routine dissemination and analysis of MPA program diversity data • Articulation of diversity goals to entire unit	
7. Rewards and recognition • How are departmental diversity accomplishments rewarded? • How does this impact culture? • Are diversity champions recognized and respected? *Actions to be taken (specify time frame)*	• Faculty and staff performance reviews • Types and quantity of diversity rewards offered • Faculty, staff, and student perception of reward value • Types of formal and informal recognition	

8. Communication
- How are messages regarding diversity both formally and informally communicated?
- How is the program's diversity history communicated?
- Do faculty members speak up on the importance of diversity?

  - How faculty, staff, and students learn about the MPA program's diversity priorities
  - Reporting of program's diversity history on website and in printed materials
  - Statements related to diversity during faculty search process
  - Statements related to diversity during student recruitment and application review

Actions to be taken (specify time frame)

9. Measurement and accountability
- What is the program's reputation in terms of diversity?
- How is the MPA program chair's diversity performance reported and evaluated?
- How are MPA faculty members' diversity performances reported and evaluated?
- What are the faculty demographics?
- What are the student demographics?

  - MPA program chair performance review
  - Faculty and staff performance reviews
  - Routine climate survey of faculty, staff, and students
  - Collection, dissemination, and analysis of MPA program demographic data
  - Budgetary support for diversity-related activities

Actions to be taken (specify time frame)

Source: Modified from Testa and Sipe 2011.
Note: Tables 9.2 and 9.3 provide examples of specific actions to be taken

culture: artifacts, values, and assumptions. Artifacts refer to things one may see, hear, or feel in the organizational environment. They include the physical layout and observable cultural signals. The next level describes beliefs or values. "Over time, these beliefs can be motivational in the sense that they can drive behavior, and restrictive because they may prevent a greater range of choices or options in solving problems" (Testa and Sipe 2011, 5). Schein's deepest level, assumptions, includes unconscious beliefs, perceptions, and feelings. This level may be casually described as "the way we do things around here." As Rice explains, organizational cultures can be modified (2004)

Performing a cultural audit of the public administration program can offer an important assessment of the unit's core assumptions and current cultural state. As the unit leader, the MPA program director is in the best position to make the cultural audit a clear priority. Claver et al. (1999) include the following eight factors in providing this diagnosis: (1) making a diagnosis of the present culture; (2) explaining the need for modifications; (3) defining the values desired; (4) involving management; (5) making collaborators aware of this new need; (6) changing the symbols; (7) changing training programs to incorporate the new values; and (8) periodically revising the values. The primary goals of a cultural audit are to examine cultural artifacts and determine their consistency with espoused values and assumptions; to identify conflicts in espoused and actual beliefs and values; to reexamine deeply held assumptions and identify their validity; and to develop an action plan for addressing inconsistencies in any of the cultural levels (Testa and Sipe 2011, 6).

As discussed in chapter 4, performing a cultural audit requires an organization to identify its vision, mission, values, and strategic goals; provide a description of the desired culture; select an audit team; collect data; interpret and report the findings. A cultural audit is most appropriately viewed as a tool to provide a gap analysis between the desired organizational culture and the actual organizational culture. The results of a cultural audit should lead to specific modifications in standards, principles or values, and observable behaviors. In other words, the cultural audit operates as a means for periodically monitoring and improving an MPA program's diversity outcomes and overall climate. Ultimately, this will lead to significant improvement in diversity within the MPA program.

The emphasis on values in this diagnostic is particularly germane to NASPAA MPA programs. NASPAA's new accreditation guidelines are squarely focused on public service values. As the preconditions for accreditation review stipulate, "The mission, governance, and curriculum of eligible programs shall demonstrably emphasize public service values. Public service values are important and enduring beliefs, ideals, and principles shared by members of the community about what is good and what is not" (NASPAA 2009, 2).

These new guidelines can motivate MPA program faculty to delineate the program's public service values as related to racial diversity and how the program itself demonstrates and models such values within the curriculum, to current and potential faculty, to current and potential students, and for the program at large.

Focusing on Program Specifics

Although there are multiple ways in which MPA programs can promote a climate of inclusiveness within each of these areas, a few illustrative examples include knowing the diversity history of the program; promoting the value of diversity within the curriculum; promoting diversity-related scholarship; and promoting the value of diversity within the program at large.

Knowing the MPA Program's Diversity History

Each MPA program has its own unique diversity history, but how well is it known, documented, and communicated to faculty and students? Developing an accurate historical narrative of diversity can serve as an important recruitment tool for potential faculty and students and foster a climate of inclusiveness. This sends a clear message that the program knows and values its own diversity history. Table 9.2 contains some sample items to include in such a narrative. Elements of the MPA program's diversity history can be placed on the program's website and in print materials. Many MPA programs produce electronic or print newsletters on a regular basis. A diversity-related article or brief factoid can be a standard component of such materials.

Demonstrating the Value of Diversity Within the Curriculum

The NASPAA 2000 diversity report suggested MPA faculty needed additional resources to infuse diversity into the MPA curriculum. Many scholars heeded the call, and more guidance is available to faculty who want to develop or enhance diversity within their courses. Much of this scholarship was published in the *Journal of Public Affairs Education (JPAE)* and was a hallmark of former editor-in-chief Mario Rivera's legacy (Rivera 2010). In recent years, *JPAE* has published at least three symposia on diversity-related topics. These articles provide directly applicable scholarship as MPA programs work to promote the value of diversity in multiple ways.

Susan White (2004) examined the extent to which courses in MPA programs covered cultural competency. Rice (2004) examined the teaching of diversity/diversity management in public administration education and its

Table 9.2

Examples of MPA Program Diversity History

Students	• Name and graduation year of first female MPA student
	• Name and graduation year of first minority MPA student
	• Recent enrollment patterns of female and minority MPA students (past five years)
	• Program's diversity history: Diversity today vs. thirty years ago; twenty years ago; ten years ago
	• Profiles of distinguished female and minority MPA program alumni
Faculty	• Name and hiring year of first female faculty member
	• Name and hiring year of first minority faculty member
	• Faculty scholarly contributions in diversity and diversity-related areas
	• Faculty service contributions in diversity and diversity-related areas
	• Faculty teaching in diversity and diversity-related areas
MPA program	• Historical development of diversity-related required courses and electives
	• Diversity excellence awards received by the university, professional associations, or the community

relationship to social equity. Rubaii-Barrett (2006) provided practical and normative justifications for the use of learning contracts in diversity courses. Wyatt-Nichol and Antwi-Boasiako (2008) examined the "diversity across the curriculum" standard, its implementation in required and stand-alone courses, as well as MPA/MPP program directors' perceptions of the standard. Tschirhart and Wise (2002) treated the academic course as an organization to assist public affairs faculty with diversity management. Mills and Newman (2002) examined the coverage of gender issues across multiple MPA programs. Hewins-Maroney and Williams (2007) examined the curricula of fifty NASPAA accredited schools to assess the extent to which programs are teaching diversity in the public administration curriculum. Pitts and Wise (2004) compared organizational responses to diversity across a school of public affairs and a school of law. Brintnall (2008) examined public administration education and training for minorities in Europe. Gooden and Wooldridge (2007) and Johnson and Rivera (2007) provided strategies to promote social equity and diversity into human resource management courses. Rivera and Ward (2008) outlined new directions for diversity-related research and diversity commitments for public administration departments. Twenty years ago, there may have been a reasonable claim that curriculum resource tools for integrating diversity into the MPA program curriculum were few. This is certainly not the case today.

Promoting Diversity-Related Scholarship

In promoting a climate of inclusiveness, it is important for MPA programs to examine the extent to which their faculty promote or devalue diversity-related research.[2] Faculty in MPA programs send messages to doctoral students and tenure-track faculty about the value of diversity in scholarship. Of course, women and minority faculty members may elect not to pursue scholarship that intersects with their communities, and white male faculty members may pursue diversity-related scholarship. However, particular concerns related to women and minority faculty members pursuing scholarship within their communities warrant consideration in promoting a faculty climate of inclusiveness. Publishing diversity-related scholarship also carries certain risks, especially for women and minority faculty.

Turner, Viernes, and Myers (1999) suggest that minority faculty are often criticized for pursuing research topics that relate to their own communities and face scrutiny for doing so. As Rivera and Ward (2008) explain, the result is that minority faculty members working in these environments face four problematic options: "1) attempt to assimilate by suppressing their cultural identity in trying to 'mainstream' their research, or other devices; conversely 2) fight back and become 'problem' faculty members; 3) make an effort to move on to more congenial and supportive institutions, and 4) simply give up" (15).

How might an MPA program promote a climate of inclusiveness for minority faculty who pursue diversity-related scholarship? Table 9.3 offers some suggestions. The MPA program director has the responsibility to ensure that the faculty member's research is evaluated by individuals who are qualified to offer an assessment of diversity-related scholarship. Additionally, the MPA program director can be helpful in identifying a senior faculty mentor who has built a successful academic career based substantially on diversity-related research. Practically speaking, this may require identifying someone outside of the MPA program, including senior faculty within the same university but in a related field, such as public policy, urban planning, management, or social work. Or it may involve identifying a senior faculty mentor in public administration at another university. Senior faculty can also promote a culture of inclusiveness by verbally articulating the value of diversity-related research in their professional associations, journal affiliations, and discussions with other senior faculty. Peer-to-peer discussion on the value of diversity can provide huge returns on investments.

For public administration programs with doctoral programs, what messages are conveyed from faculty to students, especially women and minority students, who propose writing a diversity-related thesis or dissertation? Some

Table 9.3

Promoting a Climate of Inclusiveness

Example: Supporting diversity as a valued area of tenure-track faculty scholarship

What the MPA program director can do	• Articulate the value of diversity-related research to the dean. • Appoint peer-review committees with faculty qualified to assess diversity-related research. • Review the vita of potential peer-review committee members for evidence of expertise in the tenure-track faculty member's area of scholarship. • Assign the tenure-track faculty member a senior faculty mentor who has earned tenure engaging substantially in diversity-related research. • Provide seed funding for diversity-related scholarship. • Include diversity activity reporting as an item on annual faculty performance evaluation reports.
What tenured senior faculty can do	• Recommend to faculty potential publication avenues for their work. • Pursue opportunities to co-author with tenure-track faculty member. • Verbally articulate the value of diversity-related research among journal editors and in editorial board meetings. • Ask for data regarding the inclusion of articles related to diversity-related research among journals in which they serve as reviewers or board members. • Propose diversity as a topic for future journal symposia, especially for public administration journals with sparse diversity-related publication records.

faculty may suggest that students "steer clear" of these topics so they (and their scholarship) are not marginalized, to increase their marketability in the field, and to delay writing on such topics until they are tenured. While such advice may be well intended, it also conceals the real racial message: As a person of color, your acceptance into the academy will be difficult due to bias and discrimination that exists in our hiring and selection processes. Choosing to write a dissertation in this area further disadvantages you because you are a person of color who is writing about a diversity-related topic, which is viewed as second-tier research and may not be respected by your promotion and tenure review committee. In essence, this acknowledges that widely held discrimination exists in university hiring and promotion processes.

Rather than continuing to passively support this discrimination and bias, a more effective approach is for senior faculty members to overtly support and promote diversity-related research as a first-tier area of research. With linkages to well-established domains of public administration, including personnel, representative bureaucracy, and public service, senior faculty should support related research topics and help educate their colleagues, members of promotion and tenure committees, and journal editors rather than passively upholding the status quo. It is most inappropriate for doctoral students and tenure-track faculty members to continue to carry this yoke.

In addition to individual costs, there are broader costs in discouraging diversity-related research to the field of public administration. If fewer scholars, especially minority scholars, are writing on these topics because they are largely counseled out early in their careers, it will suppress the overall advancement of diversity-related scholarship in the field of public administration. Just as professors want to continue to motivate and support the advancement of research by young scholars in budgeting, public administration theory, and policy evaluation, we should likewise continue to support the advancement of research on topics such as diversity, racial equity, and cultural competency in public administration. All of these behavioral challenges serve to actively promote a climate of inclusiveness for faculty and students.

Promoting the Value of Diversity Within the MPA Program At Large

There are many opportunities to promote the value of diversity and to foster inclusiveness outside of the classroom. MPA programs routinely communicate messages about the value of diversity in their personnel and budgetary decisions. How does an MPA program's budget reflect the value of diversity? Routinely tracking these allocations (and reviewing diversity-related budgetary items from previous years' budgets) will provide the program and those involved with reaccreditation a financial sense of how diversity values manifest themselves in budgetary allocations and expenditures. Individuals and organizations may articulate support for many values, but the budgetary expenditures provide an important indication of actual program priorities. How does the MPA program budget promote a climate of inclusion? Potential areas of examination include conference and travel support; analysis of departmental support to bring diverse speakers to campus; and departmental support or sponsorship for diversity-related events within the public administration profession, such as the Social Equity Leadership Conference, the Conference of Minority Public Administrators, the Section of Women and Public Administration, and the Gloria Hobson Norton luncheon. Budgetary goals should be routinely included and monitored in the MPA program's diversity plan.

For students, what messages about inclusiveness does the MPA program convey in the distribution of important student assistantships, such as the opportunity to work with faculty members on sponsored research or to serve as a co-author with a member of the faculty? If the program has an affiliated journal that hires student assistants, how are students selected? What does a review of current and recent student assignments reveal in terms of promoting diversity and a climate of inclusiveness? What is the extent of minority student inclusion?

Do faculty members (with an "s") routinely speak up regarding the importance of diversity in department faculty meetings and on search committees, or is this largely a one-person activity? If the MPA program as a whole values diversity and is promoting a culture of inclusiveness, it should be apparent in diversity-related discussions that constitute a nervous area of government. These actions serve as an indicator of congruence between values espoused in the unit's diversity plan and diversity-related conversations, situations, and opportunities that routinely occur. As Rivera and Ward explain, "One remarkable rationalization is offered, for instance, by academic departments that assert that minority applicants would not be happy with them because they have no other minority faculty, or because surrounding communities lack kindred minority populations" (2008, 14–15). Conversations of this nature do not align with a climate of inclusiveness.

Additionally, MPA programs should consider what messages regarding inclusiveness are conveyed through departmental pictures, hangings, and artifacts. Just as images on websites and program-related brochures and newsletters express diversity messages, so do the images located in the physical space of the building in which the program is located. Pictures and images in conference rooms and common spaces afford an important way to promote a climate of inclusion.

An excellent example is the 5 ft. × 50 ft. mural titled *Service* that appears on the first floor of the University of North Carolina–Chapel Hill's Institute of Government. Colin q uashie's creative interpretation of the Greensboro lunch counter sit-in of 1960 is the first in a series of murals that will commemorate the contributions of African Americans and Native Americans to the state. The importance of the location of this mural is clearly tied to public service:

> The life-sized depictions displayed at ground level will bring them face to face with 200 years of North Carolina history and invite them to contemplate the past and what role they will play in the future. After all, many of the students attending classes at the SOG are public officials who occupy similar positions in society showcased in the mural. (q uashie 2009)

Conclusion

The NASPAA accreditation standards require MPA programs to promote a climate of inclusiveness for their faculty and students. MPA program directors and senior faculty can do a lot internally to promote such a climate, and much of this promotion can be done without an influx of new budgetary resources. It does, however, require a serious assessment of current MPA program culture related to diversity, such as programmatic norms and messages, existing faculty actions and behaviors, and leadership dedicated to real change and success. Critically examining a program's climate of inclusiveness requires a willingness to operate within the nervous area of government. Performing a cultural audit is an important step in understanding the program's existing culture. Upon completion of the cultural audit, the program can identify specific actions to promote a climate of inclusiveness. The MPA program can then achieve long-term improvements in culture relative to diversity. Implementing a climate of inclusiveness is not rocket science, but neither is it a naturally occurring state. It requires the MPA program chair and program faculty to promote an active, inclusive diversity practice with clear, documented measures of performance along the way.

Notes

1. Formerly the National Association of Schools of Public Affairs and Administration. The organization was officially renamed in March 2013

2. For purposes of this discussion, diversity-related scholarship includes such topics as diversity, diversity management, social equity, race, gender, and cultural competency.

References

Antonio, Anthony L. 2003. "Diverse Student Bodies, Diverse Faculties: The Success or Failure of Ambitions to Diversify Faculty Can Depend on the Diversity of Student Bodies." *Academe* 89 (6): 14–17.

Brintnall, Michael. 2008. "Preparing the Public Service for Working in Multiethnic Democracies: An Assessment and Ideas for Action." *Journal of Public Affairs Education* 14 (1): 39–50.

Claver, Enrique, Juan Llopis, José Gascó, Hipólito Molina, and Francisco Conca. 1999. "Public Administration: From Bureaucratic Culture to Citizen-Oriented Culture." *International Journal of Public Sector Management* 12 (5): 455–64.

Denison, Daniel R. 1996. "What Is the Difference Between Organizational Culture and Organizational Climate? A Native's Point of View on a Decade of Paradigm Wars." *Academy of Management Review* 21 (3): 619–54.

Gooden, Susan T., and Blue Wooldridge. 2007. "Integrating Social Equity into the Core Human Resource Management Course." *Journal of Public Affairs Education* 13 (1): 59–77.

Halstead, Mark. 1988. *Education, Justice and Cultural Diversity: An Examination of the Honey Affair, 1984–85.* London: Falmer Press.

Hewins-Maroney, Barbara, and Ethel Williams. 2007. "Teaching Diversity in Public Administration: A Missing Component?" *Journal of Public Affairs Education* 13 (1): 29–40.

Johnson III, Richard Greggory, and Mario A. Rivera. 2007. "Refocusing Graduate Public Affairs Education: A Need for Diversity Competencies in Human Resource Management." *Journal of Public Affairs Education* 13 (1): 15–27.

Kennedy Group Executive Strategies. n.d. *Culture vs. Climate.* Chicago. http://thekennedygroup.com/_pdfs/culture_vs_climate.pdf (accessed June 28, 2011).

Liu, Eric. 2012. "What Asian Americans Reveal About Affirmative Action." *Time,* March 6. http://ideas.time.com/2012/03/06/what-asian-americans-reveal-about-affirmative-action/

Mills, Janet, and Meredith A. Newman. 2002. "What Are We Teaching About Gender Issues in Public Affairs Courses?" *Journal of Public Affairs Education* 8 (1): 25–43.

National Association of Schools of Public Affairs and Administration (NASPAA). 2000. NASPAA Diversity Report: An Agenda for Action. Paper presented at the NASPAA Annual Conference, Richmond, Virginia, October 18–21.

———. 2009. Accreditation Standards for Master's Degree Programs. Adopted October 16. www.naspaa.org/accreditation/ns/naspaastandards.asp (accessed June 25, 2011).

Pitts, David W., and Lois Recascino Wise. 2004. "Diversity in Professional Schools: A Case Study of Public Affairs and Law." *Journal of Public Affairs Education* 10 (2): 125–42.

Price, Alan J. 1997. *Human Resource Management in a Business Context.* London: International Thomson Business Press.

quashie, Colin. 2009. *Service.* Oil painting, 5 ft. × 50 ft. University of North Carolina at Chapel Hill School of Government.

Reichers, Arnon E. 1987. "An Interactionist Perspective on Newcomer Socialization Rates." *Academy of Management Review* 12 (2): 278–87.

Riccucci, Norma M. 1997. "Cultural Diversity Programs to Prepare for Work Force 2000: What's Gone Wrong." *Public Personnel Management* 26 (1): 35–41.

Rice, Mitchell F. 2004. "Organizational Culture, Social Equity and Diversity: Teaching Public Administration Education in the Postmodern Era." *Journal of Public Affairs Education* 10 (2): 143–54.

Rivera, Mario A. 2010. "Diversity, Continuity, and the *Journal of Public Affairs Education.*" *Journal of Public Affairs Education* 16 (4): 513–16.

Rivera, Mario A., and James D. Ward. 2008. "Employment Equity and Institutional Commitments to Diversity: Disciplinary Perspectives from Public Administration and Public Affairs Education." *Journal of Public Affairs Education* 14 (1): 9–20.

Rubaii, Nadia, and Crystal Calarusse. 2012. "Cultural Competency as a Standard for Accreditation." In *Cultural Competency for Public Administrators,* ed. Kristen A. Norman and Susan T. Gooden, Armonk, NY: M.E. Sharpe.

Rubaii-Barrett, Nadia. 2006. "Teaching Courses on Managing Diversity: Using Learning Contracts to Address Challenges and Model Behavior." *Journal of Public Affairs Education* 12 (3): 361–83.

Schein, Edgar. 2004. *Organizational Culture and Leadership.* 3d ed. San Francisco: Jossey-Bass.

Schneider, Benjamin. 1987. "The People Make the Place." *Personnel Psychology* 40 (3): 437–53.

Schneider, Benjamin, and Arnon E. Reichers. 1983. "On the Etiology of Climates." *Personnel Psychology* 36 (1): 19–39.

Testa, Mark R., and Lori J. Sipe. 2011. "The Organizational Culture Audit: A Model for Hospitality Executives." Paper presented at the International Council on Hotel Restaurant and Institutional Education Conference, Denver, CO, July 29, 2011, 1–16.

Tschirhart, Mary, and Lois R. Wise. 2002. "Responding to a Diverse Class: Insights from Seeing a Course as an Organization." *Journal of Public Affairs Education* 8 (3): 165–77.

Turner, Caroline, Sotello Viernes, and Samuel L. Myers Jr. 1999. *Faculty of Color in Academe: Bittersweet Success.* Boston: Allyn & Bacon.

White, Susan. 2004. "Multicultural MPA Curriculum: Are We Preparing Culturally Competent Public Administrators?" *Journal of Public Affairs Education* 10 (2): 111–23.

Wyatt-Nichol, Heather, and Kwame Badu Antwi-Boasiako. 2008. "Diversity Across the Curriculum: Perceptions and Practices." *Journal of Public Affairs Education* 14 (1): 79–90.

10 NERVOUSNESS IN A COMPARATIVE CONTEXT

We should never forget that everything Adolph Hitler did in Germany was "legal."

—Martin Luther King Jr. (1963)

The nervous area of government is a global phenomenon. Governments around the world encounter the challenge of espousing democratic principles but practicing inequity in their administration. "Governments in many countries have committed deliberated discriminatory acts against minorities, ranging from unfair taxes to slavery to mass murder" (Blatz, Schumann, and Ross 2009, 219). These injustices have long-term effects that are emotional and reinforcing. The historical inequities result in enduring structural inequities. These structural inequities are manifested in contemporary laws, policies, and practices. In essence, inequities cast a long shadow. While many of the blatantly discriminatory actions, once legally passed by government officials, upheld by courts, and implemented by public administrators, have been replaced by more just decisions by each of these groups, their shadow of influence remains. Contemporary inequities are strongly associated with previously intentional outcomes from legal discrimination.

Examining racial equity in a comparative context is instructive. The United States is one of many democratic nations that have historical records of legal discrimination. It is important to consider how governments try to reconcile this record. One direct remedy is to offer a formal apology from government that acknowledges the past injustice and an intention to correct past wrongs. First, this chapter provides comparative data on formal government apologies for human injustices. Then, it profiles racial inequities in the context of three democratic nations: Australia, Canada, and South Africa. It concludes by analyzing the International Convention on the Elimination of All Forms of Racial Discrimination, a fundamental instrument of the United Nations Charter designed to offer a global framework on eliminating racial discrimination.

Government Apologies

Formal apologies from governments for human injustices offer an important but largely underutilized remedy. Although apologies alone are not exhaustive, they are an important component that, when accompanied by reparations, can be a powerful healing package (Myers 2000).

> In short, nongovernmental antiracism organizations around the world as well as at home have embraced the view that remedies must go beyond laws prohibiting discrimination or even providing for affirmative action. Governments, in contrast, have adopted a less direct route: acknowledgment of the legacy of slavery and oppression as the cause of current racial discrimination, but reluctance to affirm direct apologies or reparations as remedies. (Myers, Lange, and Corrie, 2003, 333).

There is no universal standard for how governments should address previous human injustices. As Blatz, Schumann, and Ross (2009) write, in some cases governments downplay the harm or deny that the events occurred. For example, the Turkish government denies that Armenian genocide ever happened (Wohl, Branscombe, and Klar 2006). "Sometimes governments acknowledge the earlier injustice, but argue that it is too late, too difficult or too expensive to do anything about it" (Blatz, Schumann, and Ross 2009, 220).

As Brooks (1999) contends, for many years such positions had been used to substantiate the United States' historical refusal to apologize or provide compensation for legal slavery. In fact, it was not until 2008 and 2009 that the United States House of Representatives and the United States Senate respectively passed resolutions (HR 194 and SR26) apologizing to "African-Americans on behalf of the people of the United States, for the wrongs committed against them and their ancestors who suffered under slavery and Jim Crow laws." Similarly, in 2009, Congress issued an apology "on behalf of the people of the United States to all Native Peoples for the many instances of violence, maltreatment, and neglect inflicted on Native Peoples by citizens of the United States." Neither of these actions authorized legal compensation. Conversely, the Senate resolution explicitly states, "Nothing in this resolution (A) authorizes or supports any claim against the United States; or (B) serves as a settlement of any claim against the United States."

In other cases, governments indicate they have become enlightened, have largely corrected previous injustices, and need to focus on contemporary concerns (Brooks 1999). While these approaches (or a combination thereof) tend to characterize the dominant pattern, a more direct and responsible way for governments to address historical injustices is to provide a formal apology (Barkan 2000; Brooks 1999; Minow 2002).

An apology is an act of speech designed to promote reconciliation between two or more parties (Tavuchis 1991). Government apologies are public and represent "a formal attempt to redress a severe and long-standing harm against an innocent group" (Blatz, Schumann, and Ross 2009, 221). A comprehensive apology typically contains six complementary but distinctive elements:

> These elements include: (1) remorse (e.g., "I'm sorry"), (2) acceptance of responsibility (e.g., "It's my fault"), (3) admission of injustice or wrong doing (e.g., "What I did was wrong"), (4) acknowledgement of harm and/or victim suffering (e.g., "I know you are upset"), (5) forbearance, or promises to behave better in the future (e.g., "I will never do it again"), and (6) offers of repair (e.g., "I will pay for the damages"). (Blatz, Schumann, and Ross 2009, 221)

Additionally, government apologies explicitly assign responsibility for the injustice and help counter the tendency to blame victims for their circumstances (Lerner 1980). They assure the victimized group that the current government upholds the moral principles that were violated (Lazare 2004) and is committed to upholding a legitimate and just social system (Jost and Banaji 1994). Government apologies can be an important step in restoring trust between groups (Lazare 2004) and include a sincere offer of financial compensation (Minow 2002). A government's apologies offer an explicit recognition of the disconnect between its espoused values and its previous actions that directly contradicted such values. They operate as an important component in constructing a bridge reconnecting the two.

Blatz, Schumann, and Ross performed an analysis of governmental apologies. Table 10.1 provides a summary of their findings. After examining the issuance of apologies worldwide across two decades, these authors found a total of thirteen government apologies—for events that were intentional (rather than accidental); for historical injustices committed by governments against aggrieved groups (rather than single individuals such as an individual wrongly convicted of a crime); and that were formally issued by a governmental institution or its head of state (Blatz, Schumann, and Ross 2009).

Their analysis revealed that an assignment of blame to governments or its actors was included in 85 percent of the apologies. Similarly, a promise of forbearance was included in 85 percent of the apologies. An offer of repair or some form of restitution was included in 77 percent of the apologies. Sixty-two percent specifically disassociated the present system from the one

Table 10.1

Analysis of Apologies

Injustice	Apologizer	Description of Injustice
Internment of Japanese Americans	Congress (1988) George H.W. Bush (1991) Bill Clinton (1993)	In 1942, 110,000 ethnic Japanese (62% American-born citizens) were interned in relocation centers with inadequate housing, clothing, and food. Most experienced significant property losses.
Internment of Japanese Canadians	Brian Mulroney (1988)	In 1942, 22,000 Japanese Canadians (59% Canadian-born citizens) were expelled from homes in British Columbia (BC) and interned under poor conditions. Their property was sold off by the government to pay for internment. After the war, internees were forced to leave BC.
Overthrow of Kingdom of Hawaii	Congress (1993)	In 1893, U.S. naval forces invaded the sovereign Hawaiian nation, took over government buildings, disarmed the Royal Guard, and declared a provisional government. In 1898, the U.S. Congress approved a joint resolution of annexation creating the U.S. Territory of Hawaii.
World War II Comfort Women	Tomiichi Murayama (1995)	During World War II, an estimated 200,000 girls and women were taken from their homes in Korea, China, and other Japanese-occupied regions and placed in brothels to be used as sex slaves for the Japanese army.
Japanese World War II Crimes	Tomiichi Murayama (1995)	In the 1930s and 1940s, the Japanese military murdered between 6 million and 10 million East Asian civilians.
Seizure of Maori Land	Queen Elizabeth II (1995)	Under the New Zealand Settlement Act of 1863, over a million acres of Waikato land was confiscated. The Maori resisted the confiscation, and many died in the fighting that followed.
Apartheid	F. W. de Klerk (1997)	In 1948, the National Party implemented racial segregation in South Africa. Blacks were forced to move to "homelands" and lost their South African citizenship. In 1953, the Separate Amenities Act led to separate beaches, buses, hospitals, and schools. Blacks and "coloreds" were denied voting rights and obliged to carry identify documents to prevent migration and visitation to "white" areas.

(continued)

184

Table 10.1 (continued)

Injustice	Apologizer	Description of Injustice
Tuskegee Syphilis Study	Bill Clinton (1997)	In 1932, the U.S. Public Health Service began a forty-year study of the progression of syphilis with 600 (399 with syphilis) black men. They were never told they had syphilis, nor treated for it. By 1947 penicillin was the standard treatment for syphilis, but the participants were left untreated.
Australian Aboriginal Stolen Generations	John Howard (1999)	Between 1915 and 1969, approximately 100,000 Australian Aboriginal children were removed from their families by the government and church and placed in internment camps, orphanages, and other institutions. Some were adopted or placed in foster homes. The children in institutions were forbidden to speak their language, received little education, and lived under poor conditions. Physical and sexual abuse was common.
Chinese Canadian Head Tax and Exclusion Act	Stephen Harper (2006)	In 1885, the Canadian government levied a head tax on all Chinese immigrants to restrict the number of Chinese entering Canada. The $50 tax was eventually increased to $500, the equivalent of two years' wages. The Chinese Exclusion Act barred all Chinese from entering Canada from 1923 to 1947.
British Role in Slave Trade	Tony Blair (2006)	Between 1660 and 1807, over 3 million Africans were sent to the Americas in British ships. Many died during capture and transportation.

Source: Blatz, Schumann, and Ross 2009.

in which the injustice occurred; 46 percent praised the majority group (e.g., "Canadians are a good and just people, acting when we've committed a wrong" (see Harper's Speech 2006). Likewise, 46 percent offered explicit praise of the current government and laws. "Surprisingly, only five (38 percent) of the apologies included praise for the targeted minority groups" (Blatz, Schumann, and Ross 2009, 229).

> In his apology for Britain's role in trans-Atlantic slavery, Prime Minister Blair referred to the "enormous contribution today of Black African and Caribbean communities to our nation." (Blatz, Schumann, and Ross 2009, 229)

In light of the fact that governments offer apologies only for severe harms, what does the absence of a government apology for a severe harm convey? While this question is not specifically addressed by Blatz et al., it is a worthy consideration. Applying the six apology elements noted above, the lack of a formal apology conveys (1) a lack of formal remorse; (2) no formal acceptance of responsibility; (3) no formal admission of injustice or wrongdoing; (4) no formal acknowledgement of harm and/or victim suffering; (5) no formal forbearance or promise to behave better in the future; and (6) no formal offer of repair. Additionally, the absence of a government apology leaves a continuing void between its espoused values and its actions that directly contradicted such values. There is no formal bridge connecting the two.

Comparative Nervousness

Examining race and social equity, a nervous area of government, necessitates looking at discrimination (regardless of intentionality) and social exclusion. As Collins explains,

> The group of the socially excluded is defined rather as people who are effectively prevented from participating in the benefits of citizenship or membership of society, owing to a combination of barriers, of which poverty is merely one. Other barriers include poor educational opportunities, membership of a disfavoured racial minority, an inaccessible location, responsibility for family dependents, or, more commonly, a combination of such factors. (2003, 22)

Social inclusion can operate as the antidote to social exclusion by establishing a principle of justice that recognizes and acknowledges structural differences in the treatment of particular groups.

The notion of structural disadvantage combines two elements: first, an appreciation that there are patterns of disadvantage or that there are groups that seem to be disproportionately and persistently in worse positions; and second, that there are certain permanent arrangements, practices, institutions, and social structures that produce this outcome. The way in which we define the nature and sources of structural disadvantage provides a framework for the ambit of antidiscrimination laws. To understand this framework, it is helpful to disentangle three elements of the problem of structural disadvantage—the composition of disadvantaged groups, the nature of the disadvantage, and the nature of the structures that tend to produce that disadvantage. (Collins 2003, 26)

An earlier chapter detailed the saturation of intergenerational racial inequities across multiple policy contexts, including education, health, criminal justice, economics, environment, and housing (see chapter 2). These inequities are not randomly distributed but rather largely follow patterns constructed by once-legal discriminatory laws and practices. This saturation also exists in a global context operating as an embedded structure of racial discrimination and inequity against black and other nonwhite persons (Meron 1985). The resulting outcome is an exponential factor of white privilege in a global context. Whites are legally privileged not only by historical policies in the United States, but also through historical policies in other democratic nations as well.

Australia

Aborigines have endured extensive racial discrimination and inequities in Australia. As De Brennan explains, few people in Australia "can hold their heads high when it comes to the plight of Aboriginals and Torres Strait Islanders in this country" (2006, 35). At the core of the governmental discrimination and inequity toward the Aborigines are historical Eurocentric policies toward landownership based on the *terra nullius* doctrine of property ownership.

The *terra nullius* (meaning land of no one) doctrine is grounded in John Locke's seventeenth-century philosophy of landownership. "When a European discovered land that was inhabited by 'uncivilized natives,' the British adopted Lockean ownership principles to discount the moral claims of the indigenous inhabitants" (Short 2003, 492).

In an attempt "legitimately" to gain land, the Crown would ordinarily enter into treaties with the indigenous inhabitants. To be sure, in many cases such treaties merely reflected the unequal bargaining position facing the indigenous peoples and were often violated in practice. Nevertheless, in the USA and Canada, for example, the British recognized and treated with the natives. In Australia, however, the *terra nullius* doctrine prevailed. (Short 2003, 492)

Policies and practices dictating landownership were constructed against a racial hierarchy. Europeans were eligible to own or claim property. Aboriginal natives were not.

The right to participate in the political process was also historically denied to Aboriginal populations—a direct result of "white Australia" policies. As McAllister and Makkai explain, this shapes "levels of political participation and ultimately determines the ability of ordinary citizens to influence government policy" (1992, 269). Although voting rights for some Aboriginals date back to the mid-nineteenth century, these were not widely established until the Commonwealth Election Act of 1962. It was not until 1983 that the right to vote was fully extended to Aborigines through the Commonwealth Electoral Legislation Amendment, which removed optional voting for indigenous populations.

These structural inequities undergird a contemporary nervous area of government in Australia as it relates to Aboriginal citizens. For example, there are significant racial disparities in health outcomes, with indigenous people having poorer health and much lower life expectancy (Durey and Thompson 2012). The disparities between indigenous and nonindigenous Australians are stark. As Hollingsworth summarizes,

> The most well-known statistic is the gap in life-expectancy of seventeen years between Indigenous and non-Indigenous Australians. Recent government figures have adjusted that gap to eleven years but it remains a graphic indicator of the poverty and marginalization experienced by many Indigenous families and also of their difficulties in accessing health services. Other critical gaps in social indicators include the following: only 47 per cent of Indigenous students complete high school compared to the national average of 87 per cent; Indigenous juveniles are imprisoned at a rate seventeen times the national average; and the Indigenous unemployment rate is four times as high as the national figure. (Hollingsworth 2010, para 3

Canada

Compared to other democracies such as Britain, the United States, and Australia, Canada is far less racially discriminatory. There is significant policy evidence to support this claim, as Canada offers a dramatic contrast to the United States. The U.S. history of slavery and de jure segregation does not have a parallel in Canada (Rietz 1988). Similarly, although far from perfect, Canada operated in treaties with its indigenous population rather than ascribing to the philosophy of *terra nullius* (Short 2003). Across multiple important dimensions, Canada consistently demonstrates more racial tolerance than either Britain, the United States, or Australia. Canada simply does not have the same historical or policy record of direct and open hostilities toward racial minorities (Rietz 1988).

Yet, important racial disparities exist in Canada. For example, Pendakur and Pendakur found that "Aboriginal men and women face very substantial earnings disparity relative to British-origin persons with similar characteristics such as age and education" (2011, 62). For other minority groups, referenced as "visible minorities," significant earnings disparities exist among racial groups.

> After allowing for the effects of accumulated human capital, current labour market activity, immigration, language, location, aboriginal status, marital status, self-employment status, and occupational level, we find that Black men receive about 19 percent less than men who are not members of a visible minority, Indo-Pakistani men receive about 13 percent less, Chinese men receive about 12 percent less. (Hum and Simpson 1999, 390)

A more recent study found fewer racial earnings disparities among visible minorities compared to whites; however, the visible minorities included in this research were primarily Arab/West Asian, Caribbean, Chinese, and South Asian. Among these groups, women overall earn about 2 percent less than their white counterparts. This increases to a 6 percent difference among males (Pendakur and Pendakur 2007).

Although Canada has far less of a discriminatory history than the United States, there is also comparatively less *data reporting* of racial outcomes. As chapter 8 shows, performance measures with a direct focus on racial equity are important tools to assess equity implications. For example, in their analysis of racial disparities in police treatment in urban areas in the United States and Canada, Charbonneau et al. (2009) found Canadian cities are less likely to measure such disparities. Agocs and Osbourne reached a similar conclusion in examining Canada's Employment Equity Act, noting "employers face insufficient government and public scrutiny and few consequences for their failures to comply with the legislated requirements" (2009, 246). Importantly, Reitz suggests that while there is less racial conflict in Canada, there is also less awareness of racial disparities. "As a general distinguishing feature of Canadian social institutions, more has been said about lack of conflict than about lack of inequality" (1988, 431).

This suggests the magnitude of racial disparities in Canada is largely an open question. Relative to the United States, there is far less data and research analysis that address racial outcomes in Canada. Providing a racial equity analysis of Canada comparative to other democratic nations that have a stronger history of racial discrimination would be very instructive. However, the lack of such data is a significant concern and makes comparing racial outcomes difficult. An important challenge for public administrators in Canada is to more routinely collect and report outcomes by race.

South Africa

To say that race and social equity is a nervous area of government in South Africa is a gross understatement. Government consideration of the concept of racial equity in South Africa is comparatively new. The black majority in South Africa voted for the first time in April 1994. "It was the culmination of a struggle which the oppressed majority had waged in order to win acceptance of their claim to be recognised as human beings, of equal value to, and with the same rights as their oppressors" (Callinicos 1994, 2355). As journalist Mondliwaka Makhanya explained,

> This was not just a vote. It was a spiritual experience. Like the octogenarians who had cast their votes the day before, I felt my humanity had been restored. I made my cross next to the picture of Nelson Mandela, a man who a few years ago I could only sing about and whose photographs I used to hide at the bottom of the family deep-freeze. As I put my ballots in the boxes I almost suffocated with emotion as I realised the sanctity of the act I was performing. Together with millions of my black countrymen I was completing a journey that began more than three hundred years ago when the white man landed in the Cape and proceeded to strip away my humanity. (Callinicos 1994, 2355)

Yet, black enslavement and decades upon decades of legal discrimination and disenfranchisement in South Africa parallel historical government practices of the United States. The fundamental question for South Africa is whether its "new constitutional order will be able to assure basic rights for all citizens while reversing a legacy of privilege for the white population that rested on the dispossession of the black population" (Shank 1991, ii).

Stark racial disparities remain in South Africa. For example, poverty rates for Africans and coloreds are 61 percent and 38 percent respectively, compared with 5 percent of Indians and 1 percent of whites (May 1998). Similarly, although an equal right to education was explicitly stated in South

Africa's constitution, Fiske and Ladd (2005) found that important racial inequities remain:

> In sum, white students still attend schools with disproportionate shares of white students, and most black students still attend virtually all black schools. The movement from race-based to race-blind policies with respect to admissions, while symbolically important for all students and practically important for many middle class black students, has had little effect on the schooling opportunities for the large majority of African students in South Africa. (Fiske and Ladd 2005, 7)

Ironically, the racial equity challenges confronting one of the world's newest democracies is a challenge shared by far older democracies as well. There is a persistent pattern of governments, even democratic governments, developing and sustaining systems of structural advantages for whites and structural disadvantages for persons of color. Globally, many countries established legal structures whereby whites were structurally advantaged by historical design. The result was a global, exponential advantage for whites, compared to their minority counterparts. These advantages were specifically codified by policies and laws, which were reinforced by behavior and practices at the agency and individual level. Public administrators were direct agents of implementation. Even after countries change their policies making racial discrimination illegal, the ingrained patterns of structural inequities persist. Therefore, addressing racial discrimination is not only the responsibility of specific governments at the national and local levels, it is also an international concern.

Racial Discrimination and the United Nations

Described as "the international community's tool for combating racial discrimination which is at one and the same time universal in reach, comprehensive and scope, legally binding in character, and equipped with built-in measures of implementation" (UNESCO 1978), the International Convention on the Elimination of All Forms of Racial Discrimination (the Convention) is a fundamental instrument of the United Nations Charter). "The Convention drew its primary impetus from the desire of the United Nations to put an immediate end to discrimination against black and other nonwhite persons" (Meron 1985, 284). Article 1(1) defines racial discrimination a

> any distinction, exclusion, restriction or preference based on race, colour, descent, or national or ethnic origin which has the purpose or effect of

nullifying or impairing the recognition, enjoyment, or exercise, on an equal footing, of human rights and fundamental freedoms in the political, economic, social, cultural, and any of field of public life (UNESCO, as cited by Meron 1985, 286).

The Convention offers an important international framework. Four of its principles particularly apply to race and social equity: (1) the elimination of racial discrimination is the core goal; (2) a government's previous historical record relative to discrimination matters; (3) public organizations are responsible for ending racial discrimination; and (4) remedies to racial discrimination may be race conscious, rather than race blind.

A dominate goal of the Convention is to end racial discrimination, not minimize or reduce it. "Parties condemn racial discrimination and undertake to pursue by all appropriate means and without delay a policy of eliminating racial discrimination in all its forms and promoting understanding among all races" (Meron 1985, 292). This suggests the importance of governments' analyzing not only their legal policies, but their practices as well to consider several fundamental questions. For example, what practices do governments have in place to routinely monitor, report, and correct policies that have a discriminatory effect (whether intentional or not)? What criteria are governments using to gauge their progress in ending racial discrimination? What additional actions will governments employ to accelerate progress to comply with the immediacy provision of the Convention? The answers to each of these questions directly involve public administrators.

Article 2(1)c of the convention requires "each state to take effective measures to review governmental, national and local policies, and to amend, rescind or nullify any laws and regulations which have the effect of creating or perpetuating racial discrimination wherever it exists" (UNESCO 1978). The perpetuation of racial discrimination is directly linked to a nation's historical record. Often, current structural racial inequities were preceded by a legal discriminatory past. As Meron explains,

> Past acts of discrimination have created systemic patterns of discrimination in many societies. The present effects of past discrimination may be continued or even exacerbated by facially neutral policies or practices that, though not purposely discriminatory, perpetuate the consequences of prior, often intentional discrimination. (Meron 1985, 289)

Historical records provide significant guidance in terms of how governments should prioritize their racial equity work. Addressing contemporary structural inequities should not only involve the elimination of discriminatory policies, but also involve the establishment of new structures to promote racial equity among specifically historically disadvantaged groups

The provisions of the Convention have particular relevance for public administrators, as noted in the specific mention of "public life." Governmental entities are responsible agents in eliminating racial discrimination. Addressing racial discrimination is not a matter of choice or preference, but rather a public interest: "There is a compelling state interest in eliminating discrimination and assuring access for all to publically available goods and services, which includes not only tangible ones, but also privileges and advantages" (Meron 1985, 294). Structural inequities that result in a pattern of white privilege and advantages are in direct contradiction to the larger state interest of eliminating discrimination relative to public services. Public administrators, through their respective agency missions, can examine and develop aggressive policies to address such structural advantages.

Additionally, the Convention is clear that remedies are not required to be race-neutral. As Meron states, "Thus bona fide affirmative action programs cannot be challenged under the Convention, as they could be if the Convention mandated color blind policies" (1985, 305). Rather, Article 2(2) *obligates* states to operate in a race-conscious manner:

> Parties shall, when the circumstances so warrant, take, in the social, economic, cultural and other fields, special and concrete measures to ensure the adequate development and protection of certain racial groups or individuals belonging to them, for the purpose of guaranteeing them the full and equal enjoyment of human rights and fundamental freedoms. These measures shall in no case entail as a consequence the maintenance of unequal or separate rights for different racial groups after the objectives for which they were taken have been achieved. UNESCO 1978)

The very important discretionary language of Article 2(2) is the phrasing "when the circumstances so warrant," as it does not provide specific guidance in terms of when such measures are warranted. Meron suggests that a government's obligation to utilize affirmative action "should be determined by the group's degree of access to political and economic resources" (1985, 308). Applying Meron's criterion, data that report access to political and economic resources by racial groups can provide useful guidance in developing and targeting specific affirmative action policies. "The test is whether the group in question requires the protection and aid of the state to attain a full and equal enjoyment of human rights" (Meron 1985, 308).

Conclusion

Confronting a nervous area of government is a challenge for public administrators internationally. Racial inequities commonly exist with democratic governments, largely shaped by a disconnect between their democratic philosophies, their historical record of discrimination, and their contemporary structural inequities. Bridging this connection requires careful consideration and explicit linking across each of these three factors. There are many tools that governments can use to promote racial equity, including direct acknowledgment of historical discrimination through the issuance of a formal apology to harmed groups. While a formal apology does not constitute the completion of racial equity work, it is an important step. Similarly, the absence of an apology, particularly when considered against the context of governmental apologies issued to other similarly situated racial groups, is difficult to rationally or credibly reconcile. While a nation's historical record is expectedly unique, there are common themes and parallels that are instructive and can be used to create an international race and social equity agenda, guided by the framework of UNESCO's International Convention on the Elimination of All Forms of Racial Discrimination.

References

Agocs, Carol, and Bob Osborne. 2009. "Comparing Equity Policies in Canada and Northern Ireland: Policy Learning in Two Directions?" *Canadian Public Policy / Analyse de Politiques* 25 (2): 237–62.

Barkan, Elazar. 2000. *The Guilt of Nations: Restitution and Negotiating Historical Injustices.* New York: W. W. Norton.

Blatz, Craig W., Karina Schumann, and Michael Ross. 2009. "Government Apologies for Historical Injustices. *Political Psychology* 30 (2): 219–41.

Brooks, Roy L., ed. 1999. *When Sorry Isn't Enough: The Controversy Over Apologies and Reparations for Human Injustice.* New York: New York University Press.

Callinicos, Alex. 1994. "South Africa: End of Apartheid and After." *Economic and Political Weekly* 29 (36): 2355–63.

Charbonneau, Etienne, Norma Riccucci, Gregg Van Ryzin, and Marc Holzer. 2009. "The Self-Reported Use of Social Equity Indicators in Urban Police Departments in the United States and Canada." *State and Local Government Review* 41 (2): 95–107.

Collins, Hugh. 2003. "Discrimination, Equality, and Social Inclusion." *Modern Law Review* 66 (1): 16–43.

De Brennan, Sebastian. 2006. "Multicultural Australia: The Way Forward Post-Cronulla." *Australian Quarterly* 78 (4): 34–36.

Durey, Angela, and Sandra Thompson. 2012. "Reducing the Health Disparities of Indigenous Australians: Time to Change Focus." *BMC Health Services Research* 12: 151.

Fiske, Edward B., and Helen F. Ladd. 2005. *Racial Equity in Education: How Far Has South Africa Come?* Working Paper Series SAN 05–03. Durham, NC: Terry Sanford Institute of Public Policy, Duke University.

Harper's Speech. 2006. June 22. Text of Harper's Speech. *The Globe and Mail.* http://www.pm.gc.ca/eng/news/2006/06/22/address-prime-minister-chinese-head-tax-redress.

Hollingsworth, David. 2010. "Racism and Indigenous People in Australia." *Global Dialogue* 12 (2). www.worlddialogue.org/print.php?id=484.

Hum, Derek, and Wayne Simpson. 1999. "Wage Opportunities for Visible Minorities in Canada." *Canadian Public Policy* 25 (3): 379–94.

Jost, John T., and Mahzarin R. Banaji. 1994. "The Role of Stereotyping in a System-Justification and the Production of False Consciousness." *British Journal of Social Psychology* 33(1): 1–27.

King, Martin Luther, Jr. 1963. "Letter from a Birmingham Jail." April 16. http://mlk-kpp01.stanford.edu/index.php/resources/article/annotated_letter_from_birmingham/.

Lazare, Aaron. 2004. *On Apology.* New York: Oxford University Press.

Lerner, Melvin J. 1980. *The Belief in a Just World: A Fundamental Decision.* New York: Plenum.

May, Julian. 1998. "Poverty and Inequality in South Africa." Paper presented to the Office of the Executive Deputy President and the Inter-Ministerial Committee for Poverty and Inequality, May 13. Centre for Social and Development Studies, University of Natal.

McAllister, Ian, and Toni Makkai. 1992. "Resource and Social Learning Theories of Political Participation: Ethnic patterns in Australia." *Canadian Journal of Political Science* 25 (2): 269–93.

Meron, Theodor. 1985. "The Meaning and Reach of the International Convention on the Elimination of All Forms of Racial Discrimination." *American Journal of International Law* 79 (2): 283–318.

Minow, Martha. 2002. *Breaking the Cycles of Hatred.* Princeton, NJ: Princeton University Press.

Myers, Samuel L., Jr. 2000. "If Not Reconciliation, Then What?" *Review of Social Economy* 57 (3): 361–80.

Myers, Samuel L., Jr., LaJune Thomas Lange, and Bruce Corrie. 2003. "The Political Economy of Antiracism Initiatives in the Post-Durban Round." *American Economic Review* 93 (2): 330–33.

Pendakur, Krishna, and Ravi Pendakur. 2007. "Minority Earnings Disparity Across the Distribution." *Canadian Public Policy* 33 (1): 41–61.

———. 2011. "Aboriginal Income Disparity in Canada." *Canadian Public Policy* 37 (1): 61–83.

Reitz, Jeffrey G. 1988. "Less Racial Discrimination in Canada or Simply Less Racial Conflict? Implications of Comparisons with Britain." *Canadian Public Policy* 14 (4): 424–41.

Shank, Gregory. 1991. Introduction: "South Africa in Transition." *Social Justice* 18 (1–2): i–xxiv.

Short, Damien. 2003. "Reconciliation, Assimilation, and the Indigenous Peoples of Australia." *International Political Science Review* 24 (4): 491–513.

Tavuchis, Nicholas. 1991. *Mea Culpa: A Sociology of Apology and Reconciliation.* Stanford, CA: Stanford University Press.

United Nations Educational, Scientific, and Cultural Organization (UNESCO). 1978. Committee on the Elimination of Racial Discrimination. "33 UN GAOR Supp. (No. 18) at 108, 109, UN Doc. A/33/18." Statement presented at the World Conference Against Racism, Geneva, Switzerland, August. www.unesco.org/webworld/peace_library/UNESCO/SAD/MD2P3I2.HTM

Wohl, Michael J.A., Nyla R. Branscombe, and Yechiel Klar. 2006. "Collective Guilt: Emotional Reactions When One's Group Has Done Wrong or Been Wronged." *European Review of Social Psychology* 17: 1–37.

11 PRINCIPLES FOR CONQUERING NERVOUSNESS IN GOVERNMENT

It always seems impossible until it's done.

—Nelson Mandela

Race and social equity is a nervous area of government. It has a pervading emotional and historical context that can make avoidance and minimization appear attractive options. However, such behaviors are damaging, particularly for public administrators who are tasked with providing public services to all. Perhaps ignoring racial inequities can best be understood by the analogy of the cumulative effect of ignoring a dental cavity. While it may seem initially preferable to the option of an extended visit to the dentist's office, the condition, left untreated, only worsens. Similarly, addressing a nervous area of government requires active and sustained attention. Achieving race and social equity will not happen serendipitously. It requires intentional action. These actions can be emotionally and administratively difficult and, at times, even unpleasant and hurtful, but they remain necessary. Ultimately, addressing race and social equity in government is directly related to promoting societal health.

Conquering nervousness in government can be guided by ten fundamental principles in this important work.

Principle 1.
Public administrators have a responsibility to operate in the nervous area of government.

As discussed in chapter 1, the nervous area of government is how an organization considers, examines, promotes, distributes, and evaluates the provision of public justice in areas such as race, ethnicity, gender, religion, sexual orientation, and ability status. This area is "nervous" because examination of such areas has an emotional context. It is "of government" because public administrations are responsible for providing services to the public at large and because governmental agencies have an equity record, shaped by history, as well as current policies and practices. Measures of equity in government involve dimensions of procedural fairness, access, quality, and outcomes.

Racial equity is one such nervous area of government. Examining issues of racial equity in the provision of government services is fundamental to understanding how public sector institutions systematically provide services in structural ways that influence important outcomes. Operating with a color-blind approach can inhibit the engagement of entrenched societal challenges. The degree to which the American Dream is a reasonable expectation depends largely upon the equity work of public sector institutions in key areas, such as race.

Principle 2.
The legal history of racial discrimination is an important context that cannot be minimized, but rather offers instructive guidance.

Contemporary saturations of racial inequities are not randomly distributed, but rather are largely shaped by their historical context. In the United States this history exists across multiple policy areas, including education, housing, criminal justice, employment, and economics. The legacy of legal racial discrimination patterns directly parallels many racial inequities that exist today (see chapter 2). These differences compound exponentially to generate a cycle of racial saturation that continues across generations. Similar patterns exist as well in a global context among other democratic states. The legal history of racial discrimination is an empirical fact, with significant long-term implications. While it is understandably a source of embarrassment, particularly for democratic nations, its implications cannot be ignored by contemporary public agencies and public servants. Importantly, this history offers instructive guidance in identifying policies and practices that may appear race neutral but have important implications.

Principle 3.
Initial motivators to begin navigation of nervousness typically include some combination of political, moral, legal, and/or economic triggers.

Motivators for public agencies to actively operate within the nervous area of government are often external. In the political arena, racial-equity motivation is provided largely by elected officials. Much of the Seattle Race and Social Justice Initiative work was initially the result of political motivation. Motivators in the legal area include laws, regulations, court decisions, and/or litigation. Legal decisions are important advancers of social equity principles (Frederickson 2010). a n important trigger for examining racial disparities in the sanctioning of welfare clients in Wisconsin was based in legal motivation. e conomic triggers advance racial equity issues based in monetary terms, such as cost-benefit analysis or improved organizational dimensions. Moral motivators are largely the result of shifts in societal pressures that wield organizational pressure. t hese motivators are not mutually exclusive. For example, an examination of the environmental justice work of the e nvironmental protection a gency suggests motivators across several of these dimensions.

Principle 4.
Senior leadership is a critically important factor in realizing sustained progress.

a s chapter 4 discusses, leaders within organizations, by virtue of their position, formal authority, perceived and real power, and influence, routinely articulate strong messages to organizational members about what is important, what is unimportant, and what resides in the zone of indifference. Larger values of an agency, such as a commitment to racial equity, are largely affirmed or moderated by leadership action and behavior. Sustained racial equity commitment from senior leaders can lead to significant organizational change and progress. While front-line workers exercise important discretionary actions each day that affect the overall life changes of any particular client served, it is the racial-equity commitment of senior leadership that shapes and defines overall organizational culture, provides socialization to employees across the agency, and establishes clear norms and expectations of racial equity performance and accountability. practically speaking, actions of senior leadership largely influence the parameters of operations within the nervous area of government.

Principle 5.
At the individual level, public servants must recognize and eliminate behaviors that impede racial equity progress.

r ace talk at work is largely shaped by individual communication strategies. a s chapter 3 discusses, it influences the degree to which an individual public administrator is likely to raise, promote, engage, assess, and/or evaluate racial equity in the administration of public services within the agency. a bsent other motivators, such as compliance-related reporting or specifi legal requirements, the individual baseline level of nervousness provides an indicator of how likely or unlikely a public administrator is to independently promote racial equity in the provision of government services at work. It also provides some indication of an individual's predisposition to ignore or actively address racial inequities in providing public services. Some race-talk strategies at the individual level include avoidance, strategic colorblindness, melting pot, conversational variability, personal experience, cultural pluralism, and cultural mosaic. Conversations, dialogues, and meetings about race, racism, and the administration of public services offer individuals an opportunity to have an increased understanding of the role that social identity and group membership play in the provision, administration, and delivery of public services.

Principle 6.
At the organizational level, government agencies should
evaluate their socialization boundaries and extend them to
accommodate a wider range of racial-equity work.

Through the socialization process, organizations provide boundaries on racial equity activities that are required, permitted, discouraged, or prohibited. These boundaries include two key dimensions: public boundaries and real boundaries. The public boundaries are generally agreed-upon work activities. But they do not represent an employee's real boundaries, which are much broader. Although an employee will do more than is represented in the public zone, she will typically not operate beyond the real boundaries unless she is willing to risk venturing into the "nervous area" by acting beyond the compliance boundaries of the organizational socialization contract. Often, in order to perform racial-equity work, the externalities of the "real" boundaries need expansion in order to include activities that reside in the nervous area. This results in a cultural redefinition of the acceptable boundaries and more easily accommodates racial-equity work through a reduction of fear.

Principle 7.
There are no perfect solutions; however, solutions that embody
a race-conscious approach most directly facilitate structural
equity solutions.

Like all aspects of public administration and public policy, perfection is impossible. There will be challenging aspects, ineffective approaches, expenditure of political capital, important trade-offs, and difficult moments. Navigating a nervous area of government may involve uncomfortable turbulence. Beginning racial-equity work can be particularly difficult, and nervousness may peak here. Normalizing discussions about race and institutional racism is an early indicator of progress because it can facilitate direct racial-equity impact analysis of public sector policies and practices and the provision of public services. h owever, the engagement of solutions designed to facilitate racial equity must directly confront issues of race. a s powell suggests, "In our effort to get beyond race, we have paid too little attention to how it is constructed and to the work that structures and the unconscious do in creating racial conditions and meaning. r ace is not just an idea that we can choose to engage or not" (2012, 233). t he lack of a perfect policy approach should not lead to the rejection of a better, more racially equitable one.

Principle 8.
Racial equity needs to operate in a context of accountability.

performance goals should be developed, routinely assessed, evaluated, and updated. Such goals should be directly linked to the mission, organizational structure, and strategic planning of the agency. Government agencies should be invested in analyzing the racial-equity dimensions of their services from an intrinsic goal to demonstrate high performance and accountability. t his will facilitate routine racial-equity assessment in the public sector across the four equity dimensions of procedural fairness, access, quality, and outcomes; it will also lead to the identification of best practices. t his applies not only to examining the performance of governmental agencies, but also to examining how our Mpa programs, which are training public servants, provide a culture of inclusiveness in their educational environment.

Principle 9.
If legal barriers to racial discrimination have been largely eliminated, agency leadership, policies, practices, and innovations form the foundation of essential frontline racial-equity work.

t he elimination of racial discrimination is not a given. r acial discrimination still exists, and the UN's International Convention on the e limination of a ll Forms of r acial Discrimination offers an important international framework for eradication (see chapter 10). t he formal end of racial discrimination worldwide is a necessary but insufficient criterion in achieving racial equity. It also requires that individual public administrators and public sector organizations actively engage the nervous area of government. e xamining the structural inequities in public agency systems and making improvements is critical.

Principle 10.
Significant racial equity progress in government can be achieved.

A core contribution of this book is concrete examples of substantial racial-equity work at the federal, state, and local levels. The examination of local government action in Seattle, state government action in Wisconsin, and federal government action at the Environmental Protection Agency offers useful models for other government agencies to consider. While they do not constitute a "one size fits all" approach, these examples underscore how such racial-equity work may occur. Like other democratic nations, the United States is an imperfect democracy, but through the important work of public administrators, it can also be a less nervous and more racially equitable one. It may not be easy, but it is also not impossible. As Nelson Mandala reminds us, "It always seems impossible until it's done."

References

Frederickson, H. George. 2010. *Social Equity and Public Administration: Origins, Developments, and Applications*. Armonk, NY: M.E. Sharpe.
powell, john a. 2012. *Racing to Justice: Transforming Our Conceptions of Self and Other to Build an Inclusive Society*. Bloomington: Indiana University Press.

INDEX

Comparative context of nervousness
in Australia, 186–187
in Canada, 187–189
function of, 180
global phenomenon of, 180
government apologies and, 181–182,
183–184, 185
overview of, 180, 193
social exclusion and, 185
social inclusion and, 185–186
in South Africa, 189–190
in United Nations, 190–192
Correctness and justice, 62
Cultural audit, 166, *167–169*,
170–171
Cultural pluralism, 54
Culture modification process, 166,
166
Culture, organizational, 60–62, 75
Culture versus climate, 165–166, *166*

Darling-Hammond, Linda, 30
Davis, Dona Lee, 46
Deal, Terrence E., 60
Deepwater Horizon oil spill, 139
Defensive behaviors, 46, 72–73
Democracy, 3, 13–17
Denver study on homelessness, 7
Department of Workforce Development
(DWD) (Wisconsin), 105, 107
Discrimination. *See also* Racial
inequity
in contact, 11–12
in contract, 11
cumulative effects of, 149
defining racial, 190–19
illegal, 148
legal, 148–149
legal history of racial, as important
context, 197
Distributional equity, 14–15
Diversity in Master's of Public
Administration programs
history of, 171, *172*
peer-to-peer discussions on, 173
scholarship related to, promoting,
173–175, *174*

Diversity in Master's of Public
Administration programs
(continued)
value of
at-large, 175–176
within curriculum and, 171–172
Diversity Report (NASPAA), 165
Division of Workforce Solutions
(DWS) (Wisconsin), 103,
105–107
DOT, *35*
Downs, Anthony, 5
Du Bois, W. E. B., 10, 147
Dysfunctions of bureaucracies, 4

Economic triggers, *6, 7*, 197–198
Education public policy issues, 21, *23*,
28–33, *30*
Educational attainment and race,
28–29, *30*, 31
Emotional labor, 45–47
Employee training on race and racism,
86–89
Environment public policy issues, 21,
23, 33–34, *35, 36, 37–38*,
38–39
Environmental Equity Workgroup,
125–126, *127*
Environmental justice, 34, *35*,
132, 133. *See also* Office of
Environmental Justice (OEJ)
Environmental Justice and Service
Equity Division (SPU), 90, *91*
Environmental Justice Collaborative
Problem-Solving Cooperative
Agreement Program, 139
Environmental Justice Cooperative
Agreements in Support of
Communities Directly Affected by
the Deepwater Horizon Oil Spill,
139
Environmental justice grants and
programs, 137, *138*, 139–140
Environmental Justice Showcase
Communities Project, 139
Environmental Justice Small Grants
Program, 137, *138–139*, 139

ABOUT THE AUTHOR

Susan Tinsley Gooden is a professor of public administration and public policy in the L. Douglas Wilder School of Government and Public Affairs and executive director of the Grace E. Harris Leadership Institute at Virginia Commonwealth University. She is a fellow of the National Academy of Public Administration and has published widely in the areas of social equity and social policy. A native of Martinsville, Virginia, she received an AS in natural science from Patrick Henry Community College, a BA in English from Virginia Tech, and an MA in political science from Virginia Tech. She received her PhD from the Maxwell School of Citizenship and Public Affairs at Syracuse University.